W9-BRP-114

5

F

J4

C. DAVID CHASE

Mugged on Wall Street

An Insider Shows You How to Protect Yourself and Your Money from the Financial Pros

A Fireside Book
Published by Simon & Schuster Inc.
New York London Toronto Sydney Tokyo

Fireside
Simon & Schuster Building
Rockefeller Center
1230 Avenue of the Americas
New York, New York 10020

Copyright © 1987 by C. David Chase

All rights reserved
including the right of reproduction
in whole or in part in any form

First Fireside Edition, 1989

FIRESIDE and colophon are registered trademarks
of Simon & Schuster Inc.

Designed by Irving Perkins Associates
Manufactured in the United States of America
10 9 8 7 6 5 4 3 2 1
10 9 8 7 6 5 4 3 2 1 Pbk.

Library of Congress Cataloging in Publication Data
Chase, C. David.
    Mugged on Wall Street.

    "A Fireside Book"
    1. Investments—United States. 2. Finance, Personal—United States. I. Title.
HG4910.C52 1988   332.6'78   88–24309
ISBN 0–671– 62706–6
ISBN 0–671– 67163–4 Pbk.

This book is not intended as an investment guide, nor does it contain specific investment advice. The content of this book should not form the basis for specific investments without first obtaining independent professional advice.

Author's Note:
The following data are intended as an introduction to historical investment performance results.

If you would like more detailed information, consult the *Chase Global Investment Almanac,* which covers over 100 subjects from 1962–1988.

Chase Global Data Research
289 Great Road
Action, MA 01720
508-263-0404

Data are available through an annual almanac, a monthly update, and on diskette.

To Barbara, Danny, and Paul.

All anecdotes in this book are true; however, places and names have been changed to protect the innocent and not-so-innocent.

CONTENTS

Even if you're on the right track,
you'll get run over if you stand still.
—WILL ROGERS

Foreword

"Now I know why I lost money." That's the comment I've heard most frequently from readers since *Mugged on Wall Street* has been released. Most surprising to. me is that by and large brokers and financial planners have accepted it well, and were actually happy someone had finally leveled with the public about how to weed out the System's weaknesses. "Somebody finally told it like it is," seems to sum up their comments. My primary goal for investors was to have them *learn* the "inside" truth. Such truth is not always pretty, especially regarding investments. *Mugged on Wall Street* represented a change that hit Wall Street, and financial advisers in general. It no doubt hurt some sales. It explained to investors what not to do, and what to consider as an alternative. However, it is not a compendium of negatives but of potential investor pitfalls and ways around them. I'm pleased investors have learned about the realities of investing. Until *Mugged* came along, nobody was willing to lay it bare.

October 19, 1987 was another story indeed. The Crash has well emphasized the negatives inherent in investing. The public quickly learned in vivid detail how investors can see good results turn into bad, what risk truly means, and how badly professionals on Wall Street handled their own money, let alone others'. And the entire lesson took one day. The Crash of 1987 revealed weaknesses in the "System" like no government-sponsored warning campaign could ever do. It was a shame to see people lose money, but it was nice to see reality hit home, too. Risk, after all, implies that your money can be lost, and high fees paid to investment professionals hurt investors' returns . . . eventually. Every time. For about half a decade investors and professionals were forgetting about both these points.

Despite the crash and its negative effects, investors must realize what successful investors already know—no matter what is happening around you, good or bad, you must do your homework and allocate your assets intelligently. And when times are bad you shouldn't hide in a cave—for there *are* opportunities, many even in the most basic and safe investments. By no means is the answer the high-priced "sophisticated" deal. History has consistently proven that.

Investing for the 1990s will require an investor to have good advisers, brokers, and some basic, solid investments to attain the best returns possible. That doesn't mean one needs a lot of investments, just *some* good ones. Fees paid for these investments and services must be fair . . . and completely understood at the outset. Otherwise the investor will lose. Maybe not the first year. Maybe not even the second. But eventually the investor in programs which are less than solid, non-competitive, or simply fee-laden is *assured* of disappointment sooner, or later. Guaranteed.

Having analyzed many strategies along with selling many "sophisticated" programs over the years, I'm now convinced the best plan is the well-researched, conservative program with the low fee. A solid, low-risk strategy will rarely disappoint a client over the long haul (3–10 years or more). The investor may be bored with his portfolio, but he will be serene and his investments profitable. But finding advisers to present that fair and reasonable program for your investment dollar cannot be taken as a given. You *must* read on. You *must* learn to differentiate the good adviser from the bad, the fair product from the unfair, and a conservative low-risk alternative from a sweet-smelling, well-packaged lookalike. The latter could easily end up costing you money, and a lost opportunity. And aggravation to boot.

Yes, investors *can* attain financial success. That's a primary reason investors should read this book. But let me emphasize another. A simple, consistent, and minimal improvement in investment return can mean a *great* deal later. How? Let's take an example. If you invest $10,000 today and $2,000 more annually thereafter for 30 years, and if you managed to gain either just 1%, 2% or 3% more per year than your neighbor, you would have the following additional dollars in your portfolio:

> 1% annual improvement = $67,050
> 2% annual improvement = $151,559
> 3% annual improvement = $258,112

Considering the total amount invested was but $70,000 (spread over 30 years) gaining 1%–3% more each year has its rewards. In fact at 3% your total is almost double.

Through fee savings, error avoidance, and basic selectivity, investors can attain the above additional gains. Frankly, it's easy. The bottom line is—don't be taken, and don't make quick and trusting moves with your money. Protect yourself. Upon retirement you'll be multiples more wealthy than your neighbor!

*   *   *

It's difficult to advise today's reader what is the most important aspect of *Mugged on Wall Street*. Many reviewers loved the questions in each chapter which *must* be asked about investment products, and of financial advisers of all types. Others found the appendix of tables and charts, which clearly present the reality versus the myth of investment performance, a key aspect. Remember to consult it in years ahead, and you'll surely sidestep some hot sales pitches which sound so tantalizing—until the platitudes are compared to proven past performance . . . and reality.

Each chapter is important and unique. Yet their importance depends most on an individual's needs. As an investor, study most what appeals to you. And remember the questions. For mutual funds have many advantages . . . but also pitfalls. Tax shelters have too many weaknesses . . . but also a few obvious benefits. These days financial planners, insurance agents, bankers, and brokers are more alike than not. When in doubt, remember that. And remember that thought before you decide one area is more sedate or sophisticated than another. Never rush into an investment. When you are thinking of investing, to hesitate before buying is not to miss an opportunity, but merely to guarantee that you will have capital available for the next opportunity. Rest assured that as long as there are financial advisers and salesmen, there'll always be another idea.

Introduction

SURVIVAL IN MATHEMAGICLAND

> There are only two ways for a broker to get into trouble:
> Doing the business and not doing the business.
>
> —WILLY DARTBOARD

I was destined to be a broker ever since the age of seven, when I began reading the *Wall Street Journal* in addition to Donald Duck comics. By nine I was charting stocks. At eleven I was figuring out weekly batting averages and the pitchers' strikeout stats for all our neighborhood whiffleball games. At twelve I made my first investment—a profitable one.

At fourteen, I felt ready for the Street. I put on my only suit, a blue-striped seersucker, took the train from Jersey to Wall Street, and applied for my first job. The manager kept a straight face as he told me to "come back later." That summer I ended up walking racehorses at a nearby racetrack. By fifteen I had witnessed my first stock bankruptcy—Penn Central. Pop owned $2,000 worth, and I lived the stock's slide through his disgusted phone calls to his brother, rich Uncle Froyd, who had passed along that tip. "Penn owns tons of real estate," Uncle Froyd had said. "The book value is $100 per share." The stock was $36 when Pop bought it. He sold at $2.

I hit college with high math scores and a devotion to the *Wall Street Journal,* which I kept in my varsity baseball locker and read front to back before every game—much to the bewilderment of my teammates. Right after college, I joined my first brokerage firm.

As a rookie I put in long hours, studied hard, and learned everything I could from the experts. They were making tons of money, so I thought they must be doing something right—like making brilliant investments for their clients as well as themselves. Wrong. The

13

"experts" make money from commissions, not from the soundness of their investments.

I didn't learn what I know in the first month—or year. As a result, I sold more than I care to remember of the "hot deals" hyped by these experts. I still have nightmares about my first one. It was an oil deal "thoroughly checked out" by my firm, one of the top brokerage houses in the country. My relatives, several of my best accounts, and I lost every dime we put into the program.

The same thing happened the next year—with the same outfit. Why again? you should be asking. Because when you buy a turkey in one of these deals, it takes so long for the reports and returns to come in that you don't know the truth for years. By the time you do, you've probably made the same mistake at least twice. I still have clients who, like me, are haunted by the reports sent to us (required by law) from these dead investments. One seventy-five-year-old Boston blue blood told me, "I turn the reports over to their blank side, and they end up as the most expensive notepads I've ever had."

Another nightmare: One fall I and everyone else in my office sold the "Investment Package of the Month" (the Hot Deal), blessed by the VPs of my firm. Clients subsequently lost a lot of money—fast. My desk partner (we didn't rate a secretary yet) leaned over to commiserate with me, "That's the breaks. There are more clients where they came from." The branch manager also had a few comforting words: "Just keep on dialing for dollars. It wasn't your fault."

But it was my fault, and I knew it.

If I want to play for "breaks," I should go to the races. And flights to Vegas are free if you really like to gamble. My clients came to me for expert advice, daily research reports, and sales brochures and prospectuses, but they lost money. So just how expert were we? At that point I began to evaluate everything—and I was frequently shocked and disappointed at what I found: biased research, distortions, huge profits, fees most lawyers couldn't understand, and track records that would shame any horse off the track and into the glue factory.

So what had I learned? I learned that the ability to sell matters more than an intense interest in numbers, and how much you sell matters more than how well the products perform. Wall Street is a salesmen's business, and the buyer had better beware.

I had come to the proverbial fork in the road, and I had a decision to make: either learn everything there is to know for myself—without depending on the facts and bad guesses of "experts"—or get out of the business. Compromising was kidding myself.

Obviously, I stayed. But I stayed to win, and I was determined that my clients would win too. Now I do things my way, and I do enough business that my firm lets me alone.

Over the past twelve years, I have logged over three hundred thousand phone calls, consumed a thousand business lunches, run up expenses of $125,000 plus in credit card billings, attended hundreds of sales meetings, made uncounted mistakes and lived through more than a few disasters, hit a few major home runs (emotionally as well as financially), received more than my share of large paychecks, and have even acquired a streak of humility to temper my arrogance. I've won some awards and gotten a lot of recognition. But most important, after so many years I feel I've come to understand Wall Street.

Much of what happens on Wall Street reminds me of the exploits of my favorite childhood character, Donald Duck. One of Donald's many adventures was his discovery of Mathemagicland, a forest full of trees with square roots. Walt Disney may have named it, but Wall Street found it first. The Street, through its marketing ability, is extremely good at making magic out of math. And although its math may be "correct," it can also make either unrealistic or downright misleading impressions for the investors. Nevertheless, you invest your money and end up playing The Game. But you're always on the outside. I want to change that. I'm going to tell you how the investor gets mugged on Wall Street and how he can protect himself.

During my years on the Street, I've come up with several ideas and methods that are workable, logical, and surprisingly simple to understand. They don't blow up in my face, as in the old days. Your broker can make money handling your account—and you can make money too. But first you need to know a lot more about how Wall Street works—and you need to meet the players on the inside of the Street.

How the System Can Hurt You

Chapter One

UNDERSTANDING THE STREET

> It is usually agreed that casinos should, in the public
> interest, be inaccessible and expensive. And perhaps the
> same is true of stock exchanges.
> —JOHN MAYNARD KEYNES

Through the years I have learned an amazing fact: Investors know practically nothing about Wall Street. But I've also learned it's not their fault. The Street likes it that way—and takes advantage of it with complicated deals, confusing prospectuses, and hidden fees.

As a result, most investors mistrust Wall Street—from experience and intuition. They've either heard war stories or been there. They also know that Wall Street rakes in billions of dollars every year, that brokers top the list of big spenders, and that banks and insurance companies own most of the marble buildings in town. But investors don't know why their own investment profits are disappointing at best, or disastrous in too many cases—they just know it's so. And they don't know why the following situations can be allowed to occur over and over again:

A seventy-year-old woman lost 90 percent of her $500,000 portfolio through excessive and speculative trading by her broker, whose commissions totaled over $150,000.

Cash bonuses totaling $1.3 million were to be "awarded'" to twelve top executives for outstanding performance managing a tax shelter that is expected to pay investors a disgraceful settlement of ten cents for every dollar invested.

A hot real estate partnership was recently marketed by a small brokerage firm. It paid $428 million for the real estate, then immediately sold units in a partnership holding the same real estate for $757 million.

Was the deal fairly priced after such an enormous price jump of $329 million, or 77 percent? *Forbes's* headline read: HOW TO TURN $430 MILLION INTO $760 MILLION.

In a recent study of 116 glamorous public oil programs, only 11 were expected to break even or make a profit for their investors. Many would return their shareholders nothing.

A Florida broker toted up $5 million in commissions trading his great-uncle's account. Relying on his own elaborate computers, the broker gave his uncle false information that his $17 million account had grown to $55 million. In fact, it had been halved to $8.2 million.

Of course, it is only the worst horror stories that make the headlines—the proverbial tip of the iceberg. So where does that leave you, the investor? Well, if you've been doing business on the Street, chances are you've also been mugged there—like a million other people. Or worse, you may think you haven't been mugged and later find out you have. On Wall Street you don't have a chance of becoming Street wise. The same thing keeps happening again and again because Wall Street is an insider's game. You have to live and breathe it as a broker to know what is really going on. Everything else is "outside" information, or a "little bit of knowledge," which is a dangerous thing—to your wallet.

Even the scandals of Wall Street, like the insider trading case of Dennis B. Levine, are merely a peek behind the doors. Levine was a key member of Drexel Burnham and Lambert's mergers and acquisition department. After a bidding war for his services between the likes of Morgan Stanley, Kidder Peabody, and First Boston, Levine took a position in 1985 at a guaranteed salary of $1 million a year. He had worked previously at Citibank, Smith Barney, and Shearson Lehman—climbing the ladder within the mergers-and-acquisition league. A former colleague said Levine "spent his day working for information and looking for ways to use it to make a fee." Over and above his salary, he illegally made $12.6 million (and sent it to foreign banks) trading on inside information he either had access to or was given by friends. Levine pleaded guilty to four criminal counts. Levine's revelations to the SEC led to the Ivan Boesky scandal. Boesky pleaded guilty to one criminal count, paid $100 million in fines, and was sentenced to three years in jail.

Levine's and Boesky's stories are dramatic and newsworthy but ultimately hardly as significant for the average investor as the day-to-day problems inherent in the structure of the system itself. The money they made as insiders was indirectly siphoned from the investors who use Wall Street. But those dollars are nothing compared to the amount of money Wall Street loses for its investors through well-hidden fees, incompetence, and greed. That is the real scandal. A *Newsweek* article titled "Beware of Your Broker" said that there had been 15,915 complaints about brokers filed with the SEC in 1986, up 128 percent in four years. After Black Monday, October 19, 1987, complaints to the SEC mushroomed dramatically. To a large degree, Wall Street will always be an insider's game, but the sides can be a little more equal if you, the investor, know more about the game's strategies and rules. The Street can still make a profit even if we make the game fairer.

To do that, you must understand the players in the game. Many of them are brokers—and a lot of them are good ones. But you better know how to find them, because brokers are made, not born. And how they are made matters to your wallet. Consequently, we'll follow a broker's career from his first nervous cold telephone call as a rookie to the day when he has a fat Black Book of clients, a spacious corner office, and a private secretary—all marks of the Big Producer. His goal is always the same: to profit from sales as much and as often as possible. Unfortunately, transactions can often be made against your best interests. Although many good investments carry little or no fee, there is no guarantee your broker will mention them, because he doesn't make money that way. Even good investments are diluted into bad investments after they have made a run through the doors of Wall Street's "production" houses. And brokers are not alone. The same thing is happening with the competition from banks and insurance companies, and on Main Street, U.S.A., too—but worse.

Everything I've said so far is negative, but my real message is: Don't lose hope! Wall Street is still the best place for your money. The Street still offers the best alternatives to banks, insurance products, and Main Street's investments. However, this isn't a book with a lot of investment advice. I'm not going to tell you how to get rich quick or preach about windfall profits. My goal is to save you money. Before you can begin to make money on the Street, you have to know how to save it—and yourself. You have to know the system, the game, and how Mathemagicland works.

Mathemagicland begins on Wall Street, at the tip of Manhattan, but its boundaries extend to every state of the Union. So whether you are in Bangor, Maine, or Boise, Idaho, or Santa Barbara, California, you need to learn to recognize the players, the rules, and the moves. And I'm here to help.

In Section I, I give you a tour of Wall Street and introduce you to the Street's major players. I also discuss the commission structure that brokers operate under and point out things you must know:

— how the education of a broker creates a climate for abuse and dramatically affects your potential profits
— why a commission has a lot of names—and not one of them puts money in your pocket
— how fees and costs undercut the profits of your investments
— how an office manager can be your ally on the Street
— why the oracles—researchers, economists, gurus, newsletters, and headlines—can be oracles of error

In Section II, I take you down the block to meet Wall Street's competition—the banks, the insurance companies, and the lawyers, accountants, and developers operating on Main Street. Government deregulation has put everything—including your money—up for grabs. For your protection, here is what you need to know:

— how overrated Wall Street's competition—the banks, insurance companies, and Main Street—is
— how a financial plan can spell financial ruin or long-term financial security, and who should have one
— how a money manager can be the best thing that ever happened to you, or the worst
— how a money manager affects you and your pension funds, even though you've never met him

Section III covers two of the most popular investment areas—mutual funds and tax shelters. The new tax reforms of 1986 seemed to eliminate the need for tax shelters. But beware. The Street has transformed the old tax shelters into new breeds of partnerships and syndications—but the old problems are still there. Before you invest you need to know:

— how mutual funds aren't all the same animal, and sometimes not what they appear

— how even in the record markets of the first half of 1986, the average mutual fund was up 19.5 percent while the Dow Jones rose 24.7 percent

— how tax shelters, partnerships, and syndications sometimes work, but often don't

— how prospectuses are designed to inform you (legally), but at the same time confuse you

— how to recognize and evaluate an assumption, then how to run the other way

In the final section, Section IV, I tell you how to get the best products and service for your money. I analyze over ten investment products. You'll learn how to deal advantageously with your broker and his or her manager when investing your money. And finally, I review several financial publications and suggest which to read for what type of news. You'll end up with the straight scoop, not a sales pitch. You'll learn:

— which investments will keep your money safe—and growing

— how to find, keep, and sometimes fire your broker

— how to evaluate his performance

— which financial publications are the best for you, and why

— the rules for being a successful investor

Last, but not least, I provide an appendix of tables and charts that profile the history of various investments. You'll see how these investments have performed in the past and what you should know before you invest in them today.

These charts alone are worth the price of this book. For years, I and others have wondered just how one investment compared to another, over the years and in various periods of time, but we've never had the data to be able to compare apples to apples—Swiss francs to U.S. dollars, gold or silver to stocks, and bonds to savings accounts. Something always got in the way of comparisons.

Now, with these charts, you will be able to ignore the salesman's self-serving historical quote on an investment's performance. He probably quoted from the most propitious time frame anyway. Now you can compare his figures to the facts of history, and his investment suggestions to alternatives he might not have mentioned. And you will be surprised. For example, many cautious investors think the Swiss franc is one of the best investments. Not true. It was the worst investment of the last twenty-five years and more volatile than you might have guessed.

I love being a broker. It's an exciting, high-energy job. And never boring, because the range of services and products is too great. I don't want only to manage portfolios of stocks. I want to keep doing all the things a good broker can do. The job is just plain fun, especially when you aren't losing people's money.

One of the nicest aspects of my job is getting to know a variety of talented people—in addition to several characters who frequent brokerage offices. Like the guy who recently visited my office and tried to get our cashier to accept his briefcase full of dry, brown leaves as collateral in a margin account. He wanted to buy fertilizer stock. One client, who has become a good friend, founded a successful New York Stock Exchange (NYSE) company. He's made me a lot of money, and I've helped him make a lot more. But I've also lost him some money too—primarily in one awful tax shelter. (I sold only one tax shelter after that, and now I even regret that one!) Yet he has remained loyal, perhaps because he always seems to birdie the eighteenth hole and clean me out on our standard wager. Yet Jim doesn't even know the information that is in this book, although we've worked together for ten years, on and off the golf course. It would have taken uncounted golf games and fishing trips for me to tell him half of it. But he deserves to know. And you do, too.

This book is for the investor with an IRA, for the investor with five thousand dollars or millions. I'm writing for anyone who has ever held stock or owned a $1,000 CD. I'm writing for the nervous investor, the angry investor, the mistrustful investor, the astute investor, the "shopper" (and even for the rookie broker who wants to do a good job and make money). They all know there are better deals somewhere. This book will give them and you a fighting chance. Getting mugged on Wall Street will be a thing of the past.

Chapter Two

THE EDUCATION OF A BROKER: LEARNING AS YOU GO

> A terrible thing happened. I realized I joined the wrong mob.
>
> —DEPORTED GANGSTER LUCKY LUCIANO
> AFTER HE HAD VISITED THE FLOOR
> OF THE NEW YORK STOCK EXCHANGE

A broker remembers his first day of cold calls for the rest of his life. I'll never forget mine. I was nervous, but my desk partner, Lenny Leftover, was more so. Yet Lenny made the first sale by calling someone cold about a stock offering. Amazingly, the new client said yes, he'd take a hundred shares, but he wanted to know the payment date for the stock's upcoming dividend. Lenny didn't have the foggiest idea where to look this up, so he put his new client on hold and nervously waited by the desk of an experienced broker who was taking a phone call. Every so often Lenny would look over to see if his phone was still blinking, hoping his new client hadn't hung up. Desperate, he turned to the guy's desk partner. "Jim," he said, "I got this guy who wants to buy one hundred shares of Con Ed. How do I find the dividend payment dates?" Jim, a big guy, looked up and then lumbered to his feet. "Look," he said, pointing a finger at Lenny. "I'll give you some advice. Get out of this business. You're not cut out for it." Then he sat down, turned around, and started dialing. His blunt message: You don't have to understand the stuff, just sell it.

HOW A BROKER'S EDUCATION AFFECTS YOU

Today major firms hire people under the age of thirty-five, train them, and turn them loose to prospect for clients. You the investor are the gold in this venture. The rookie is looking for you. That is why it is important to have the inside view of a broker's training program and his early years on the job, to know just what he has been taught to do. A broker is trained to sell first and advise second—if he knows how. And part of his education is funded by you, the investor, so let's see what your money buys.

Although I use the pronoun he exclusively, it is simply for ease (his/her, him or her, he or she would get cumbersome) and reflects nothing about my view of the Street; after all, many investors and brokers are female.

Who Gets Hired

The stockbroker is someone who sells, sells hard, and the first thing he sells is himself—to the branch office manager. The aspiring broker writes a persuasive résumé or makes persistent phone calls in order to get an appointment with the manager. He presses his suit, gets a haircut, practices his handshake, and for homework reads the company's annual report or, better yet, talks to another broker. During his half-hour interview, he must convince the manager of his ability to sell by the way he sells himself. This interview is more important than the applicant's résumé, college education, who his father is, or who his roommate was. Salesmanship. "Can he sell our products?" That's what the manager wants to know.

The usual background of a broker is sales—IBM, Xerox, or self-employed. Firms look for self-motivation, avarice, youth, self-assurance, and "has he been tested in the real world?" It costs major firms $40,000 to $50,000 to train a broker, so they don't like mistakes.

Once the applicant has the manager's support, he takes a psychological test with such questions as "What would you rather do on an afternoon off?: Sit in the park, go to the movies, play football, or read a book?" (Football indicates a more competitive personality.) The final step is an interview with the regional director, who gives his OK only about half the time.

The Rookie: New Kid on the Street

Once hired, the new broker begins a four-month training process tailored to each firm's specifications. The broker studies at home nights and reports to his office each day, where the manager oversees his work. He also takes weekly tests and fills in on odd jobs. (It is generally acknowledged that "Merrill Lynch trains the Street." Many brokers begin there and then leave for greener pastures. A few years ago a Boston alumni party was held for four hundred Merrill Lynch graduates who currently represent over forty different organizations!)

When he finishes the course and passes the major exam (given by the NYSE), each rookie spends one to three weeks at the home office in New York, where firm specialists in areas such as tax shelters, syndications, options, insurance, mutual funds, "prospecting," and "cold call strategy" explain their products and selling methods. Some rookies treat this like a vacation: One guy in our class folded his chair and rearranged the seating so he wouldn't be marked absent, skipped the remaining classes, slept with the hotel maid every morning, and found midnight poker games at which the guns were laid on top of the table. We who went to class also learned the firms' executives' behind-their-back nicknames and who the Big Producers were and why. We were treated to enough lavish dinners to whet our appetites for the grand style of life. After New York, rookies go home yearning for money, and ultimately it comes out of your pocket.

Cold Calling and the Numbers Game

Once back at the branch office, the rookie is given an empty desk in a room with twenty to thirty other brokers, a push-button telephone, a computer with unintelligible software, and worst of all, an empty Black Book. He arrives at the office around 8:30 (the market opens at 9:30) and begins to place cold calls to prospects from his daytime phone book or lead directory. In any given day a hustling rookie makes beween one hundred and two hundred calls and gets to speak in detail to about forty people. He might meet seven to twelve prospects each week for anything from a short office call to breakfast, lunch, or dinner.

One of the hardest things was making those first calls elbow to elbow, in public. "Hello, I'm David Chase of Merrill Lynch, and I'd like to tell you about an offering on. . . ." In any one day a rookie might call a list of doctors cold, a potential client who attended last week's office seminar, or, my favorite, the main telephone number of a major corporation and ask for the treasurer or vice-president of finance . . . or he might call you. If he sounds nervous, it may be his first week on the job. Be polite, but tell him your dinner is burning.

Success is selling a percentage of these connections. There is no right person to call. Early-rising brokers call fishermen, bakers, and

people in construction. If a broker's firm issues a stock recommendation on automotive companies, he might call fifty tire distributor-
ships, a hundred auto dealers, and a hundred related companies. I
know one broker who prospected only people in blue-collar towns.
They had saved a ton of money in their local banks. They were flat-
tered by his attention, and he showed them how uncompetitive their
bank rates were. He is now making $200,000 a year, and he's been in
the business only four years.

The Rookie's Sales Pitch

The usual topics of a rookie's sales pitch are: whatever product the
firm is introducing that month; the investment he thinks or hopes he
understands; plus the ones he found exciting in New York. By and
large, brokers sell dreams—complex investments reduced for them
into summary form and prominently positioned on their desks to be
pitched on the telephone. Often firms provide "scripts" for rookies
to call clients with—and they become the rookie's dog-eared bible.
A scripted sales pitch can be the only thing the newcomer knows
well. It is therefore something to avoid because the broker doesn't
really know if this investment is good for you.

At this stage a broker must be immune to people saying no. And
in spite of warnings, the first no is always a shock. So having a tough
hide is more important than buying a third blue suit. A glance at
other brokers around the office always reassured me that we were in
the same war. I've been hung up on only two times in thirteen years
because I soon discovered that people could be led into a brief con-
versation. I'd say we sent them information they had requested on
an investment. The firm *had* sent them information, but they were
on a list of people who hadn't responded. Maybe (doubtfully) they
had been interested. Anyway, no one else bothered to call them—
except me. Amazingly, about 30 percent listened—which is not bad
in a numbers game. Luckily I didn't know any better. I made call
after call because I didn't want to flop on my first cut in the real
world. In one year, I became a global champion of a giant brokerage
firm.

Fred, a broker who was hired with me, succeeded in spite of his
nervous personality, his inability to study for exams, and his introduction using the firm's entire name—"Hello, I'm Fred Babbler,
from Merrill Lynch, Pierce, Fenner and Smith." "Shorten it," we'd
yell to him, but he couldn't. He worked every night until 9:00
P.M.—I know because I was there till 11:00.

As a rookie, I had my goals: I was twenty-three years old, didn't have kids, and my best girl was in Paris for her junior year. My roommate and I were living in a sixty-dollar-a-month apartment with no heat and no doors on any rooms—we used sheets. I came home every night about eleven, cooked one of my three menus, and read research reports and the *Wall Street Journal*. I stayed in the kitchen to be near the heat from the oven and away from my roommate and his lady friends cavorting in the bedroom behind a "door" sheet. Once I made it, I was gone. I still have a phobia about tents.

Boardroom Games

The stress of the job is responsible for a lot of the rookie's fun and games in the boardroom—similar to the tasteless cadaver jokes medical students play on one another to get through the stress of internship and residency. Every day has new headaches, and it helps if rookies can laugh at something. Last month two new guys had their ties cut off at the neck—by other rookies who proclaimed the ties too wide and ugly. Yesterday one of the brokers in my office was moving and brought several plants into his office. It started looking like a greenhouse, so a broker put in an order at the local plant store (charging it to the office manager), and a half dozen more plants completed the greenhouse effect.

Sometimes the stress of making call after call reached hysteria levels—particularly when the 150th person to say no was especially rude. A Really Rude Prospect was apt to receive half a dozen calls for an hour after he gave a rookie a bad time—this time from someone selling used cars.

Then there were the games rookies played on each other during "dialing for dollars" days. I received many messages saying, "Mr. Fish called. Call back phone no. 673-3465" (the aquarium). There was also Mr. Beare with phone number (of the zoo) and Mr. Byrd with phone number (the Audubon Society).

I remember one rookie who returned from his New York home office trip, sat down at his desk, and a mean live turkey flew out from beneath his feet. Weighing in at twenty-five pounds, the bird flew around the boardroom, messing up desks, nipping at legs, and was not about to be caught. Fred Babbler (they had things in common) finally shooed it out the door, and it was last seen on Washington Street heading for Filene's basement. The broker's friends were not-too-subtly preparing him for a type of client he will eventually put in a specific Black Book—his turkey book. Every broker has one, consisting of the broker's worst clients. This book is always secretly marked—for example, with a triple *T*—so clients won't catch on when they visit the office. That filter system allows the broker to speed up the process of finding his best accounts.

Selling Your Wares

One of the rookie's first priorities is to learn his firm's investment products. Few senior brokers, let alone rookies, have time to study all the firm's offerings. Therefore brokers often specialize in several areas and ignore others. The firm knows that brokers can do ample business even if they are knowledgeable in only a few product areas.

Unfortunately, it is *you* the investor who loses in this situation; you can't learn from the average broker which investments are available and most appropriate for you. Even a knowledgeable broker often doesn't have the time to explain various ways you might invest your money. He merely explains his favorites. But exceptions are made for investors with a $100,000 liquid or more. When $500,000 clients appear, the cameras roll. The broker puts a hold on his calls, he serves coffee or Scotch depending on the hour of the day, and goes into his talk-show routine, sometimes bringing in several specialists to provide a more complete product choice. At this point the broker plays the part of Ed McMahon to "Heeeeeeeere's Johnny." This approach is used because any client is more apt to spend his money when he is given a choice of ways to do so.

Brokers often prospect for new clients by teaching a seminar, but sometimes the only people who show up are other brokers checking out the competition. Several years ago, three of my officemates went to a competitor's seminar and were astounded to be the only ones there. They had counted on free drinks and jumbo shrimp and had hoped to blend into the audience. Instead, the sales pitches were directed at them. But they had fun asking some tough questions— and ate well.

THE PRESSURE TO PRODUCE BIG BUCKS

A crass reality of the brokerage industry is that the broker needs to produce business on any given day—just like the magazine salesman, the car salesman, and the insurance agent—and the level of tension on the office floor reflects this.

Today the average gross sales by brokers with major firms is approximately $225,000 per year, which translates into an annual salary in excess of $75,000. In an office of twenty-five brokers, probably fifteen to twenty make over $50,000 a year. Senior brokers usually earn at least $125,000, and the most successful brokers make well over $250,000. The ceiling on salaries is set only by talent, hard work, and sanity. The Crash of 1987, however, affected both profits and brokers' pay. Many Big Producers are seeing their 1988 income fall to one third that of 1987 or 1986.

THE SCHOOL OF HARD KNOCKS

Given the lack of structured training during the broker's first two years, a rookie's primary education is the school of hard knocks. Ask any stockbroker about his nightmares. Much of my own education was a by-product of errors with investors' money.

It is a fact of life that rookies make mistakes. All brokers know that losses are inevitable, so they develop degrees of fatalism. The riskier the investment, like option trading and commodities, the more you become accustomed to not just losses but total annihilation. There is a saying that 90 percent of all commodity-trading clients lose everything they invest. Everything. It's a rough business, but if a rookie survives mistakes, bad markets, bad luck, and more mistakes, then he will convince himself and his firm that he'll be a long-term winner in a precarious industry. Firms expect mistakes, but they want to see the broker pick himself up, dust off his three-piece suit, and get on with the game.

On the other hand, clients do not expect mistakes or losses. Therefore a broker must convince them that such an event is infrequent—even if it happens at least once a week. As you might imagine, it is quite a juggling act for a rookie to blame the vagaries of the brokerage business while at the same time convincing his clients that it's a science. In fact, the market bears a far greater resemblance to Las Vegas than MIT.

Therefore the broker must take defeat, loss, and disaster in stride. Some days (like October 19, 1987) seem like replays of the Crash of 1929. But he (and you) should remember that over a period of years, the average stock/risk-investment decision is correct approximately half the time—the same percentage as flipping coins. The Coin-Toss Axiom is a fact of life most rookies appreciate early in their careers.

Over time, a rookie learns he can't look back. When he loses a client's money, he chalks it up to education. He accepts the failures and risks for the potential rewards and moves on to new trades as well as new clients. He learns to pick up the phone and say, "It appears at this juncture that what we wanted to happen with XYZ Corporation will not be occurring. I suggest we consider taking a short-term loss and buy ABC investment." Sound familiar? The sophisticated broker then softens the blow by saying how little has been lost after all tax considerations are accounted for, and how other investments did lousy too. He wants the client to think the market—not his broker—nailed him.

One broker I know never calls a client with bad news without another plan to offer as good news. His transitions are as graceful as anything Shakespeare ever wrote. And he's better paid. It is amazing how often this works. Another hardworking broker I've known for years finally divulged his "formula for success." It avoided his getting killed and losing all his clients in one fell swoop from bad advice and/or bad markets. He reluctantly admitted that he divides his clients into two groups. He tells the first group the market is going to hell and to sell, or sell short. He tells the other half the market will rise and buy, buy, buy. He's an old-timer of fifteen years making an annual salary over $100,000. He could be your broker.

Bookkeeping headaches create another hazard for the broker. In my rookie days, one client bought 100 shares of GM. Simple enough. But it was entered as a sell order in the wire room. The entry to neutralize the error was another error, and the pattern continued until the client had a twelve-page statement for one transaction. He even had to face paying extra taxes when some of the erroneous entries created dividends during their momentary stay in his account. By then, the firm had taken back the dividends, but they had already reported them to the IRS. Eventually Bookkeeping got it right.

THE PAYOFF

The solicitation process runs for one to two years before a broker has enough clients in his book—or has given up and left the business. At this point, the calling of established clients is relatively easy, requiring far less time than calling a new prospect. As one broker said, "Damn, it's great not to have to go through the secretary to the secretary to the secretary. Or be asked 'From what company?' "

Rookie brokers are hired for a minimal salary but promised larger rewards if they work hard. "The sky's the limit," they are told. And they believe it, or they wouldn't be in the business. Consequently, from Day One the pressure is on because the rookie's initial salary is slowly scaled down from a guaranteed minimum to a partial guarantee combined with a small percentage of his commissions.

This formula emphasizes the reality of the situation: His paycheck will soon reflect only his previous month's effort. But this doesn't intimidate the ambitious soul; he recognizes the opportunity to make a hell of lot of money and welcomes the control over his own destiny. The incentives are real enough: larger paychecks, expense accounts, private secretaries, and freedom to ignore management requests to sell products, like them or not. Luckily, my freedom to ignore "certain tidbits of garbage" was an immediate reward for early success. It is possible for a second-year broker to earn $50,000 to $70,000 or more if he is good. (It is also true that over half of all second-year brokers drop out, although this attrition rate has decreased because of better recruiting methods and a current healthy market.)

Alarmingly, masses of people are being subjected to mail-order house or correspondence course–educated brokers. In 1984 nearly five hundred thousand people took one basic exam alone. Potential salespeople are being thrown against the wall. A certain number stick. The regulators of brokers and insurers test and license a lot of aspiring brokers and agents, but it is up to you to weed out the turkeys. These days, feathers are flying everywhere.

WHEN DO YOU USE A ROOKIE?

A good rookie does have some strong points. He can be intelligent and hardworking because he's been carefully screened for these two attributes. He is probably a good choice for someone who is just beginning his or her own career and who, together with the rookie and this book, can make good solid first investment choices. If you find him trustworthy and attentive, a rookie may even prove more productive than a busy and inattentive Big Producer. And after all, Big Producers were rookies once.

FINALLY THE ROOKIE BECOMES AN EXPERT—IN GUESSING

At the end of about three years, many brokers have established a specialty in bonds, stocks, tax shelters/syndications, insurance, commodities, or options. Choices are growing—interest rate futures, annuities, managed money for retirement funds, municipal bonds, even money market accounts. But specialization doesn't always make the broker an expert. Often he just begins to build an above-average business in an area he enjoys. The firm, in recognition of his effort, encourages him toward further specialized education. The broker then portrays himself to his clients as a specialist; the clients are duly impressed, and business increases. *Voilà* the specialist! The firm has marketed a person as well as a product. And you are the buyer.

Nevertheless, the pressure to specialize continues, because remaining at the same sales level is a sign of failure. Just as the surgeon completing medical school sharpens his scalpel on someone, the branch product coordinator carves up your wallet while he's finishing his education. I seldom use the word *expert* anymore regarding Wall Street because I know how often people are guessing. And I seldom see experts put their own money where their mouths are. Therefore, the wise investor treats Wall Street "expertise" like the "hot tip" at the racetrack—an educated guess.

JUGGLING THE THREE *D*S: DIALING, DOLLARS, AND DEPENDENT CLIENTS

After the new broker has established a book, his next challenge is to service his active accounts at the same time he prospects for new ones. This is the point at which many brokers reach a plateau. They are either unable to juggle these two activities, or they are sufficiently happy with their income level and have decided not to buy a yacht. Or they are bored.

These years have their temptations. One that constantly plagues brokers is the temptation to trade their personal accounts each day while they trade for their clients. It is difficult for a broker not to lose his shirt in a market that he finds exciting enough to make brokering his career.

I remember a survey that was done in my Merrill Lynch office many years ago. After New Year's, one curious broker would sidle around to everyone's desk and ask: "Did you end the year ahead in your own personal account?" The answer was always the same: Out of the office's thirty brokers no one ended the year ahead in his personal account. No one. We all laughed—which seemed better than crying. The next year, the same results. (My excuse is that I was a rookie.) The third year our surveyor left to buy a laundromat, and his desk partner later departed to start a dating service. Obviously, a broker's compensation comes from commissions made from investing your money. Few brokers launch a yacht on their own trading profits.

One of my proudest achievements is that I am well ahead of the stock market in my own account. I've recognized the market for what it is—an emotional crap game. The less you respect it as rational, the better off you are. I once thought the so-called experts couldn't be wrong and followed their lead . . . like a lemming into the sea. Now I never trust the Street's experts with serious money. I make decisions on my own, and I make money. (But I own race-horses, not a yacht.)

THE BROKER PERSONALITY: A WOLF IN WOLF'S CLOTHING

I've seen enough brokers revolve through my office doors to know that successful ones have similar personality traits—not totally surprising when you consider that the manager and the psychological test were looking for these traits at the beginning.

A Broker Has a Telephone Personality

First, a broker can't survive in this business if he doesn't have a telephone personality. He needs a totally natural presence while talking. I "see" my clients on the other end of the phone. The successful broker makes his client feel that he is sitting on the other side of his desk when he is in fact miles away at the other end of an 800 number. Personal meetings can't replace telephone calls; they take too much time.

A Broker Can Sell

Second, product knowledge is not half as important as closing a transaction, though one helps the other. A rookie broker usually stays with basics. Later, he solicits business in more complex areas, such as tax shelters, annuities, and speculative stocks, but until then he may even use canned sales pitches. Finally, a broker's self-confident attitude, even a certain degree of cockiness, will help build a client's confidence. Unfortunately, confidence doesn't make profits; experience does.

A Broker Is Avaricious

This sounds crass, but avarice is essential in the broker's personality. Unless he has a continuous growing need—a second car, a growing art collection, twins, alimony, a second wife, a second husband, a pied-à-terre in London, triplets, a third wife or husband—he or she won't be driven to increase their income. Therefore, brokerage firms hire people who have expensive tastes for expensive acquisitions. The broker who is satisfied with a certain level of income soon reaches a sales plateau. Too many like him will hamper the firm's growth.

THE BIG PRODUCER: THE WINDOWS OF POWER

Obviously, the Big Producer is not a timid soul. He has all of the above traits plus a business style that requires self-confidence, self-motivation, and persistence. Over the years, the Big Producer has created a book of clients (usually from three hundred to one thousand), with his core business generated by about 20 percent. This produces commission business for him in the range of $300,000 to $1 million per year. His salary is about 35 percent to 40 percent of this. In addition to trading for these clients, he also opens about eight to ten new accounts a month—mostly through referrals. But as with all brokers, each month brings a new report card and a different paycheck. If transactions or enthusiasm falter, so does his ability to pay his mortgage—forget the yacht.

The Big Producer as Specialist

The Big Producer is a specialist in at least one or two areas, such as commodities, options, tax shelters, insurance/annuities, managed money, or bonds. If stock-oriented, he is usually a trader—a broker who persuades his clients to make transactions more quickly and more often than the common holding periods of six months to one year or more.

The normal arena for Big Producer/traders is commodities or options—volatile marketplaces in which losses (and gains) occur with very little notice. Thus his rationale is: When you either make a profit or start to take a loss, sell fast. This is self-serving because the broker receives a commission on sell as well as buy transactions. With few exceptions, large stock specialist producers churn business—they trust their "superior judgment" to justify frequent strategy changes. And they've long since convinced their clients of the legitimacy of frequent trading.

The Big Producer Demands Client Control

The Big Producer wants clients to rely on him rather than on the *Wall Street Journal* or *Barron's*. And he usually has above-average control over clients—either subtly or openly—because he's an expert in an area most clients don't understand, or because he's aggressive, overbearing, or charming. I've heard these brokers tell clients, "All my clients are doing this. You need to do this too." Clients are lulled into obedience, asking only, "Where do I sign?" Once this breed of broker controls your money he also controls the frequency of transactions. This practice, known as discretionary trading, is carried on by many large producers. It means that a broker can do what he deems prudent or "what he damn well pleases."

Discretionary Trading Is Not the Better Part of Profits

The rationale for a discretionary trade is that the broker has a "feel" for the marketplace and his important fast-breaking information becomes less valuable if he needs to phone for your approval before initiating the transaction. According to him, a few minutes' delay— let alone a two-hour delay—may lose you thousands of dollars because of bad market action. Brokers might broach the subject in this way: "Mr. Smith, I know that we should sell now. News may be out very soon that will kill us. If I can't reach you, is it OK to head for the exits?"

Most brokerage firms strongly discourage discretionary trading and keep it well monitored because it results in too much trading, too many questionable commission expenses, and finally, losses for the client. Unless specific paperwork has been signed allowing discretionary trading rights, it is difficult legally for a broker to justify excessive trading. In such cases, the firm normally loses the lawsuit or settles out of court. Typically, the overzealous broker is then charged his portion of the commission (or more) as a penalty for settlement, and the brokerage firm assumes the difference.

One problem is that Big Producers subtly tend to rule the roost even at large brokerage firms and therefore do quasi, if not outright, discretionary transactions as a norm. But few discretionary transactions benefit the investor long term, let alone in the short term, and the reason is simple: Frequent trading generates large commissions that slowly eat away at the client's principal.

As a rule, never sign discretionary papers unless you want entertainment. Consider the whole thing an electronic racetrack. Not surprisingly, *stock jockey* is a Wall Street term for a hard-riding, stock-trading (sometimes churning) broker.

Churning: Buying and Selling and Buying and Selling and Buying and . . .

Your account can be "churned" even though you haven't signed for discretionary trading. If you are paying annual commissions of more than 10 percent to 20 percent of your account's value, you're probably being churned—unless you are trading options or commodities, for which commissions are higher due to normal high levels of trading. If you're involved in excessive trading, interview several other brokers about your situation. Someone may be able to show you ways to continue doing what you want, but with less expense. Second opinions in this case are free, but get more than one because you may find your second consultant is just another jockey riding under different colors.

Life in the Fast Lane

One way to identify a Big Producer is to visit his office. Does he have a corner office with a view of the harbor or the sunset? Is there a personal secretary ready to serve coffee and put in a buy or sell order immediately? Does your broker have an assistant broker with a protégé's mien? Is he a vice-president? Look around your broker's office—is he on the way up or already there? How he lives at work is a direct reflection of his success.

Firms treat a Big Producer well because they know his life is hectic and tense. He deserves the view of the sunset because he is often there to see it happen. He is much more profitable to a firm than several brokers who together do the same amount of business. The overhead costs of phone bills, bookkeeping, supervision, mailings, and the potential for errors are far less with a Big Producer. He also has a greater level of expertise and knowledge of the firm's system, which can be tapped by fellow brokers. One manager said, shrugging his shoulders, "If my Big Producer wants two girls in harem outfits and a silk tent, he can have them."

Arrogance at the Top

The Big Producer, in turn, knows what he's worth and develops an ego to match. He avoids dealing with small clients with only $10,000 to invest, except on rare occasions, such as a visit from his mother. His average account is six figures or more. Time is money to a Big Producer, and larger transactions mean larger commissions. He simply doesn't have the hours or patience to share his expertise with small clients, or, at times, even his fellow brokers. So he may be the biggest guy in the office, but he isn't always popular. "I couldn't care less what the other guys think of me," one Big Producer said, "I busted my tail to get where I am, and I don't owe anybody the right time of day." Another Big Producer said, "I made four times what the manager makes, and I have ten times his freedom. I don't even pay taxes, I'm so smart. Clients should be happy I take their calls— if I feel like it."

Occasionally, that arrogance can get a broker into trouble. One physician client was so disgruntled over his broker's handling of his account that he disguised himself as a Santa Claus and abducted his broker from a Christmas party. For twelve days, he kept the broker chained and handcuffed to a bed in a do-it-yourself torture chamber. He broke some ribs and the broker's nose. I know about this incident because a client with a sense of humor (I hope) sent me a copy of the newspaper clipping. On it he'd scrawled a one-word message: "Beware."

THE LIFE SPAN OF A BROKER

The actuarial statistics for a broker are terrible. Many brokers succeed, but far more fail. The time frame is usually from one month to two years before the faltering broker clears out his desk, turns his book over to the manager, and slinks out of the office.

Even the seasoned broker has his troubles; he might find, for example, that losses from the upturns and downturns in the market have slowly eroded his client base. Or his mind. If he fails to find new clients, his base eventually disappears. When this happens, his income drops to a level at which he must rebuild his book (most brokers pray every night that they'll never have to do that again) or leave the business. Maybe that's why most brokerage offices have revolving-door entrances. In fact, my veteran broker friends and I rarely meet brokers who have been in the business longer than we have—over a dozen years. As one friend said, "You can't help wondering who's getting out of the business next. It doesn't get any easier, that's for sure." And the Crash of 1987 is only making things worse.

Firm-hopping

Then there is another sort of exit that is almost a game in the industry—changing from one brokerage firm to another. Brokers change
companies for various reasons: A firm has reduced its emphasis in his
specialty or reduced its payout rates, the broker's book was crippled
in the last market dive, or he needs the cash bonus offered to jump
ship to a new firm. Pay attention. If you're important to him, he'll
try to take your account with him.

I remember when Lenny and I made our last move. We of course
played by the rules, which are: Skulk around while talking terms
with your future employer; always quit on a Friday after 4:00 (when
the market closes) so you can call your clients over the weekend (before they are distributed among your old officemates) and persuade
them to change to your new firm; photocopy all your Black Books of
clients—in advance, but not at the office; and once you have told the
manager, be ready to leave in five minutes. He's going to toss you
out that quickly anyway. In our case, we left just after receiving
awards for being Big Producers. By the time of the awards party,
rumors had spread that at least two people were leaving. The office,
always looking for good wagers, started a betting pool. I was an
odds-on bet. But my friend wasn't. He actually had to place a five-
dollar bet on someone else, which helped keep his cover intact for
five days.

That week we smuggled our Black Books out of the office (the
firm keeps them when you leave), hid them in the trunk of my car,
and drove around Cambridge looking for a late-night photocopy
place—a rarity in 1977. Between us we had a dozen books filled with
client names and records. The copy man almost fainted when he
saw all the work. It took him until 1:00 A.M. while we nervously
stood guard in case some other broker might walk by, see the evidence, and blow our covers.

Finally Friday came. Normally the office is empty at 4:00, but on
this particular Friday we had full attendance, and silence. It was like
the TV show "What's My Line." I stood up—no surprise. Little
money would change hands in the betting pool. Then my friend,
Lenny Leftover, stood up (probably at four to one), and there were
some surprised faces. Then Roscoe, the number-one producer, a
senior "quiet man" nobody ever dreamed would leave, got up. He
won the Gasp Award and was no doubt a ninety-nine-to-one shot.

The manager was stunned. Between us about 25 percent of his office production was gone. Shortly thereafter he left too.

Late that day, we went to our new office, where everything was set up for us: forms already made out, temporary secretaries hired for the weekend, account numbers already assigned to transferring accounts, and all the coffee we would need for a year of prospecting. We started dialing, calling all our best customers first to tell them that we had moved to a new firm and still wanted their business. We left behind our turkey accounts. Leaving firms provides a polite way to abandon your gobblers, or the people your secretary hated to deal with but was too polite to let on.

We really worked hard. We knew that on Monday morning at 9:00 sharp our old office manager would divide up our clients from the Black Books we were forced to leave behind, passing out the names and numbers to the other brokers who would then start a blitz of telephoning, trying to recoup the deserting accounts. Managers hate to lose brokers because they hate to lose clients. It's not unusual for managers to offer prizes (TVs, booze, trips), and 5 percent bonuses to brokers who succeed in persuading clients to stay with the firm their broker has just left.

That weekend was one of the most exhausting times I've ever spent. By Sunday night we had consumed two cases of Coke and wolfed down twelve corned beef sandwiches, heavy on the mustard. We succeeded in keeping our best clients for our new Black Books. That's how it works in firm-hopping. I'd estimate over 75 percent of brokers change firms at least once.

TODAY'S REALITIES: THEY MAY CHANGE TOMORROW

It should be comforting to know that there are good products on the Street, and some good brokers who can help you find them. Alternatives are, in most cases, worse. In a later chapter I'll tell you how to qualify your broker and how to avoid the rookie who is a salesman first and an expert later.

At present, the optimum scenario from the Street's point of view is to train the rookie to build a client book, sustain it through the years, and bring in a large stream of commissions. The worst scenario is when the broker quits, but even then the firm still retains the broker's accounts and distributes them among senior brokers. Many clients (though usually not the broker's best ones) remain with their present firm. This inertia is why the brokerage industry is not severely hurt by the brevity of many brokers' careers. Brokerage firms are most interested in building and expanding their own client base and prefer to have as few brokers as possible generating that base. So when a broker gives up his number and hangs up his spikes, only his training costs are lost—the clients he's brought to the firm are still in the bleachers. The game goes on.

Chapter Three

COMMISSIONS: YOUR BROKER'S PAYCHECK; OR, NOBODY DOES THIS FOR FREE

> Business: the art of extracting money from another
> man's pockct without resorting to violence.
> —MAX AMSTERDAM

The most important envelope a broker receives contains his paycheck, which reflects commissions on investments both bought and sold by his clients. Some investments, on a dollar-for-dollar basis, pay brokers more than others. That is why a broker's paycheck is a mosaic of different percentage payouts. In order to be a more successful investor (if not a more defensive one), you should know if and how this commission mosaic affects your broker's advice, and understand the commissions you would be paying on the investments he recommends.

INVESTMENTS: FIFTY WAYS TO PAY YOUR BROKER

Agency business occurs when your brokerage firm acts as middleman in a transaction, such as entering and executing a trade on the NYSE. In such a transaction the firm does not handle all aspects. For example, the NYSE specialist is making the market in the stock (being the central trading mechanism through which buy and sell orders are traded), not your broker. Others profit in the transaction, but the charge levied by your broker is the commission. Conversely, in principal transactions the firm makes a greater profit by being the marketmaker. The marketmaker receives the order to buy or sell a security and matches the transaction with others seeking to trade their shares in the opposite manner. He finds the best buyers for sellers and vice versa. In addition, he carries an inventory every day in the security and stands ready to deal the security through his inventory. Carrying inventory is the marketmaker's risk, and he charges a fee on all transactions in order to profit and cushion himself from risk. Overall, in spite of the inherent risks, the role of marketmaker is usually a profitable one. Principal transactions normally offer a greater payout (the broker's percentage of the commission) to the broker; examples of principal transactions are trading in OTC stock, municipals, and government bonds—all from a firm's own inventory.

Historically, special products such as tax shelters, insurance products, annuities, mutual funds, and unit trusts offer a greater payout than normal agency business. They either emanate directly from the firm (thus requiring less or no profit sharing with outside sources), or they require less overhead expense, such as inventory risk and financing expense, or they simply do not generate much paperwork, such as monthly statements, confirmations of trades, and/or dividend checks. For these reasons they are more profitable, and their sale is encouraged through a greater payout to the broker.

THE ANATOMY OF A COMMISSION

Have you ever been sitting in your broker's office when there was an announcement made over the loudspeaker—an announcement you couldn't understand although you knew it was in English? "Fifty thousand shares of General Motors available at $80 per share with a point and a quarter." That "point and a quarter" represents $1.25 per share commission to the broker—a higher commission than usual, paid by the seller as an inducement to unload his unwieldy, large block of stock. If they had used the word *commission* it might have made you too nervous to buy. But you, as the buyer, will be paying no commission. The seller is taking care of it. So you may have a bargain—or a lemon.

P/C. Production credit. Markup. Markdown. Add-on. Production. Gross. Annual fee. Start-up fee. Referral fee. Withdrawal penalty. Wraparound fee. Levy. Sales charge. Deferred sales charge. Load. All of these terms mean the same thing: commission. Before deregulation of the commission structure in May 1975, there was no need to disguise commissions because they were the same for all players. Since then, as competition increased, Wall Street has begun to deemphasize the term *commission* by charging fees that are difficult to label, trace, and quantify. Now commissions are levied in diverse ways and with different terminology, depending on the firm and even the various departments within a firm. The game is one of semantics. Bottom line, the above terms translate into money in the bank for the broker.

A Commission Is a Commission Is a Commission . . .

Because fees are disguised and charged in a number of ways, you should know when "Recommendation A" pays your broker three times more than "Recommendation B," even though your cash outlay is the same. (He knows.) This can happen even when there is no sales charge, but instead a withering withdrawal penalty.

The withering withdrawal is an after-the-fact "back-end" sales charge. But it is a sales charge that is levied only when the client withdraws assets after purchase—voluntarily. The fee is imposed on a sliding-scale basis and usually drops a percent each year for about five years until it disappears altogether. The initial withdrawal fee is about 5 percent to 6 percent. Normally, all income may be taken from the investment each year without any penalties. Only principal withdrawal is affected by the charge. As long as the client is informed of the fee initially and acts accordingly to keep his principal intact, this fee will seldom be levied.

Determining commissions can be difficult, however, since each firm has its own style for charging fees. Because an analysis by firm would be both confusing and quickly outdated, I will instead give you a general picture of how fees are collected for certain investments under the following terms.

Commission. This is the most obvious fee, and it is clearly labeled on your transaction reports. The fee's percentage can be computed easily by comparing the fee to the overall value of the transaction. Typical areas using a commission fee are exchange listed (agency) securities, OTC agency (middleman) transactions, options, listed bonds, and tax shelters/syndications. The charge as a percentage varies from about .25 percent to as high as 8.5 percent and occasionally more.

Markup. In the past this was always a confusing and hidden fee. Recently, however, an SEC ruling required firms to openly disclose on their confirmation slips that they acted as marketmaker/principal in the transaction, and what the commission was on all OTC transactions. Unfortunately, many clients are still not aware of the full meaning of this term. A markup applies only to buy transactions by clients and to all principal transactions when the broker is dealing from his own inventory. There is no middleman, and the cost of all expenses is included in the price of the security, which has been marked up to include a commission. The broker adds his commission to the price by increasing the "ask" (best available price to buy the security). (The "bid" is the best available price at which the client can sell his security.) The difference between the bid and the ask is the "spread." Of note, brokerage firms must disclose the marked-up commission. But they still do not have to disclose their markup spread if they made the market in the security you are purchasing.

When the broker is a marketmaker, his profit/fee is routinely the spread, plus the marked-up price above the ask price. The broker justifies the spread charge as a fee for taking the legitimate risk of constantly carrying a security inventory in order to make an adequate market for buyers and sellers each trading day. The additional charge, or markup, is his commission. These markups are monitored by regulating agencies to avoid abuse. Examples of investments using these fees are: OTC principal (marketmaker) transactions (now more cleanly disclosed) and principal, nonexchange bond transactions—corporate, government, and municipal bonds, and Ginnie Maes.

Markups vary from small fractions of a percentage for large transactions in the bond markets to 1 percent to 3 percent plus for orders on the OTC and municipal and government bond orders of approximately $1,000 to $25,000. I have heard of unscrupulous penny stock (stocks priced under a dollar per share), and some OTC transactions in which markups are 40 percent or more. The investor must someday sell the same security at a markdown (see below), perhaps through the same greedy broker. When dealing in marked-up stocks or bonds, your charge should be about equal to an agency fee. But abuses do happen, so beware.

Markdown. This fee is the opposite of markup and applicable only to sell orders. Markdowns are frequently a smaller fee than a markup, by as much as 50 percent. Areas of such sales are the same as those noted above that use markups.

The gouging through markups and markdowns can be enormous. For example, when is a $32.50 stock worth $22.50? The answer: one second after you pay $32.50—if you bought it from the wrong guy. I recently met a broker who had worked two years for a well-known regional firm. He said he left because he couldn't take the heat from wives of clients crying about their family's losses, or the typical two or three daily conversations in which the client was screaming at him. All he sold were OTC stocks—stocks the firm made markets in and marked up and down on sells and buys. In two years he never sold a stock priced above $8 per share. He could remember only one stock that made a profit.

His company usually sold stocks at around $3 to $5 per share. They almost always marked the buy order up ¾ of a point, and the sell less so, about ¼. He told me about a $2.50 stock. If the stock was bidding $2.50, the ask was $3.25, or marked up ¾ point. Thus, to buy it the client paid $3.25. If the client was selling the same stock, he'd sell it at the bid price of $2.50, minus the markdown of ¼ point. If you did the trades instantaneously, you would buy at $3.25 and sell at $2.25. Not a very good deal. That's a full one-point of spread (profit) to the firm for a $2.50 security. "It's a 40 percent profit each time they find a sucker," he said. "They mark up 30 percent and mark down 10 percent."

I had never heard of such wild pricing—or greed. For a better perspective multiply the whole example by ten. You have a $25 (2.5 × 10) stock bought at $32.50 (2.5 + .75 = 3.25 × 10), and you sell at $22.50 (2.5 − .25 = 2.25 × 10). Not an easy way to make money. No wonder relatives called crying and the screamers screamed. He said his manager sold like crazy and managed less. In his old office about half a dozen brokers made $100,000. The rest got by, were fired, or exited quietly. That's called "churn 'em and burn 'em."

Sales charge. It should be designated in your transaction by percentage and/or an actual dollar amount. Examples of investments having sales charges are: mutual funds, unit trusts, and bond income funds. Sales charges vary from as little as 1 percent to as high as 8.5 percent. Higher fees rarely mean a better investment or service, so shop around for lower fees. But beware of the no commission charge on no-loads (items that have no initial sales charge), for many have significant and varied "additional" charges.

Wraparound fee. This annual fee is charged to managed portfolios. It provides that all commission transactions will be performed for a set annual fee. Sometimes it includes a management fee as well. After the "wrap" fee, no further fees are charged for custodial services or commissions.

This is a good arrangement if you prefer to have your money managed, yet you want to keep commission costs set and under control, prior to all trading. The normal competitive maximum wrap fee is 3 percent of the portfolio value per year. For smaller accounts, management fees may be extra at .5 percent to 2 percent, depending on your money manager. These fees may be reduced to as little as about 1 percent total for larger accounts in the multimillion-dollar range.

Not all firms offer the full wrap fee arrangement, and fees vary. For best results, use a firm committed to the concept of the wrap fee. In addition, some firms allow selected individual trading brokers to charge a flat annual percentage (about 5 percent) of the client's account value in lieu of the normal commission charges for a year's trading. The fee is computed at the outset of each year (billed quarterly) and can be readily quantified, whereas normally total commissions are an unknown until the year has elapsed.

Withdrawal penalty. This fee is collected by the firm that paid your broker a fee at the outset of the transaction, though no fee was charged to you. In such investments, "internal" commission fees to account executives vary from 1 percent to 4 percent of the amount invested, with payouts usually based on the broker's total production at the firm. In some cases, the firm pays the broker a small annual renewal fee (about .33 percent) for keeping you in the investment, the result of which allows the firm to collect its annual management fee.

The withdrawal penalty is usually a diminishing one. Also, the penalty normally allows for some amount (about 10 percent) to be withdrawn annually without penalty. Investments commonly using this penalty are annuities and several no-load funds, in-house brokerage firm mutual funds (not money market funds), and some forms of lump-sum contribution insurance contracts.

A word of caution: Be suspicious if you are strongly encouraged to invest in areas that generate high commissions. However, the fact that a broker receives more compensation for one investment than another *does not* make the investment a poor one. Other factors, in addition to your broker's motivation, should influence your choice: your investment needs, your tolerance for risk, your liquidity requirements, and your investment experience.

HOW MUCH DOES YOUR STOCKBROKER MAKE?

Just about everyone believes that stockbrokers make a lot of money. Statistics for 1987 show that the average account executive, or AE, produced about $250,000 in revenues, depending upon which brokerage house you examine. In a comprehensive 1984 study on this subject, results showed that brokers make significant incomes, but their potential to continue at such a pace would be affected by dramatic changes, such as lower payouts in the future.

According to the Securities Industry Association (SIA), which represents approximately 95 percent of all securities firms, the average payout to brokers in 1983 was 41.9 percent of the commission dollar. In 1978 the statistic was 37.6 percent. Today, because of increased costs and many firms' lower profits, payouts are moving toward 1978 levels. And all levels of producers are now being affected. Even though we are dealing with means and averages, a $250,000 middle-tier producer averaging a 37 percent payout makes a salary of $92,500 per year. Now that same producer receives about 35 percent, or about $5,000 less per year. With today's trends the lower-end producer will be affected most. He receives approximately a 25 percent payout and is in many instances quickly fired or weeded out over twelve to eighteen months. The Big Producers will likely receive few or no cuts, despite general reductions, and in many cases will receive what amounts to a raise. These brokers bring in revenues of $1 million or more and take home about 40 percent plus of the commission dollars they raise.

As in other professions, brokers often change firms to improve their incomes. In the past, firms attracted successful brokers by offering up-front money (sometimes as high as 40 percent of the past year's production in cash), perks such as expense accounts, higher payouts (for a short period), and various noncash items such as elegant offices, fancy equipment, and extra secretaries. The crash of 1987 slowed down AE perks and pay, however. Yet revenues per AE increased from the 1982 average of $164,000 to today's $250,000.

BEHIND THE BIG WALL STREET DOORS

As a result of rising expenses, most of the major firms (which account for about two thirds of employed brokers) have revised their payout schedules so that the broker receives a smaller percentage of the commissions he generates. Broker compensation now accounts for approximately 20 percent of the industry's overall expenses, second only to interest costs. Certainly brokers aren't starving, nor are they likely to become unionized. But more turbulent times could see a further erosion of profits and payouts. As long as the Street feels its profits are under pressure, trimming broker payouts will continue to be considered a solution.

THE QUINTILE SYSTEM

Brokers have to create commissions; managers have to encourage and oversee them. The math is everywhere, starting with the Quintile System.

Just about all the major houses use the Quintile System to evaluate broker performance. Here's how it works. All of a firm's brokers are divided into groups by seniority: one year in the business, two years, under five years, five to ten years, and over ten years. Those categories are then divided by production levels into fifths, or quintiles. First-quintile producers, from the top 20 percent of their peers, are the firm's best. Fifth-quintile producers are the firm's worst.

Brokers usually remain fifth-quintile for only a few quarters, and beyond that time frame they either quit or get fired. Fourth-quintile producers don't last long either. Middle-quintile producers may be subtly harassed and pressured to improve, depending on the style of management in each office, region, or firm. Managers are ranked by how many first- and fifth-quintilers they have in their branch.

Needless to say, it isn't fun or profitable to be a low-quintile broker. And he can be dangerous for investors. If your broker is a fifth-quintiler, he probably is intimidated by his job, is being forced to sell you something, anything, and doesn't understand a variety of investments or your needs as an investor. Or he has started to tune out you and investments altogether because he is looking for a job as a computer salesman and won't be talking to you next month. You may want to avoid putting $20,000 into his latest real estate syndication just before he exits.

WHEN COMMISSIONS ARE LIKE DRUGS TO YOUR BROKER

High commissions can be addictive; a broker constantly needs more and larger commissions in order to succeed. Management considers a plateau—even at high levels of production—a sign of weakness. Now, as a result of changes, whether in the form of minimum production targets or smaller payout to the smaller producers, brokers at all levels of production are under new pressure to produce even more commissions. There are always some brokers who have learned that even a small account can create a lot of business if it is traded frequently or charged too great a markup on its transactions.

Sometimes the broker's own firm sets the stage for another form of abuse with the structure of its payout schedule. It is telling the broker through differentials in payout that not all dollars are created equal. One transaction will pay the broker more than another. So the broker has a vested interest in selling you the product with the highest commissions. A higher payout is icing on his cake.

On the other hand, as the broker advises more frequently in a few areas, he genuinely understands those forms of investments better. Also, the firms involved in those areas may offer better pricing to the investor because they sell those products in such size and frequency. They have good inventory and management, and they may even mark up the investment less because their costs are lower. Obviously, the "conflicts" equation is a complex one.

An obvious way to address this problem is to ask your broker to tell you his areas of specialization. And test his knowledge. If his products, such as municipal bonds, are not identical in pricing/benefits with all competitors (as a share of AT&T would be from any broker), consider a price comparison of his quote with a competitor's. And when you do, interview more than one broker. In addition, recognize that prospectus item products require a review with a magnifying glass focused on the fine print. Few brokers or clients do that. Also determine if annual fees will be charged, because these can sometimes be high if the initial fees are low. Sometimes both are high. Finally, remember the simple question: How much of what I invest actually goes into the investment after one day?

SMALLER BROKERAGE FIRMS: THE WINDFALL

For the most part, small firms are reaping the benefits of changes at larger firms. Because they have not markedly reduced their payout, their efforts at recruiting Big Producers have been more successful. In some instances the recruiting is unnecessary, for many smaller firms are now being approached by brokers. A major attraction of the smaller firms is their employee stock and asset accumulation programs. In these programs, brokers are able to put away substantial sums of money with excellent returns. Some of the money they put away will be yours. Make sure you are getting a fair deal for spending it.

WHY ARE THE PROFIT LEVELS SO HIGH?

After reading about 35 percent and 45 percent broker payouts, some of you might be asking why brokers are paid such a big piece of the action. Many brokers deserve every dollar they make. The brokers whose paychecks keep rising are the survivors, the best of the breed. I regularly worked seventy-plus-hour weeks. Many projects end up in smoke because of politics, changes in interest rates, and bad markets. Clients move away, go broke (without my help), die, or lose interest in their investments. And stock crashes make matters worse, for years at a time. Yet those lost clients need to be replaced. That's called prospecting, hard work, and more stress. So being a broker has to have its rewards—and the biggest reward is money.

Chapter Four

MANAGEMENT: POWER AND PROFITS

> At any given moment 30 percent of the revenues of this
> office may get up and leave for XYZ brokerage firm.
> This place is full of hypertensive Type As. They can't
> pay me enough to manage this menagerie.
>
> —FORMER BRANCH MANAGER

Late one evening in my second year as a broker, I was alone in the
office boardroom, tired and taking stock of my life. I looked around
at the sea of desks—six rows with five brokers in each row—and the
broker's lot in life became clear. I was the only nondivorcé in my
row, and there was only one like me per row. (I was single at the
time and worried how I would manage as a family man.) About 80
percent of my colleagues were divorced—some more than once. The
office's Big Producer made a fortune but was constantly broke from
mailing out three alimony checks each month. Tempers were often
short, and the noise level was like an airport's. It was my first sense of
how much stress the job puts on everyone, especially a broker's family.

Suddenly I realized what a complex juggling act the manager
had. His job was to oversee all these brokers who weren't Prince
Charmings at home or in the office. In fact, most brokers don't really
care if the other brokers or their manager likes them, or vice versa. If
a broker's paycheck is high, no one is likely to tamper with his position. This attitude of benign neglect/respect probably won't change.
I remember once when I needed help (much like my friend Lenny)
from a more experienced broker. Stan's ear was usually glued to the
phone, so catching him was tough. But I was desperate. I had a new
client on hold with a question about a bond I was selling him. When
Stan hung up his phone, I stepped forward. "Stan," I said, "I need
to ask you a question about a bond." Actually, I needed to ask five

questions—I hated bonds. Then Big Producer Stan pulled his charm routine on me. He picked up his phone and dialed, never breaking stride. Then he looked at me and said, "Talk to me after the market closes." That was six hours away. (Beware of rookie brokers who need to ask questions before they answer yours.)

During one brief period, I managed (part-time) a small branch office. I hated the job. Clients had their bad moments, but the brokers' were worse. I remained a broker, but with a new respect for managers and a vow to never manage again.

WHY SHOULD YOU CARE WHO THE MANAGER IS?

A manager can be an important person for an investor to know, and there are many ways to use his service. Introduce yourself, shake his hand, and consider him for some of the following situations:

— for an interview and a referral to a broker
— for a referral to other financial people in the community, such as accountants, laywers, bankers, and financial organizations
— for help in initiating a large transaction through a brokerage firm, such as venture capital financing or investment banking
— for a fair opinion about his competitors' services and alternatives to using him; he is capable of discussing strengths and weaknesses
— for an overview of investing and the economy as held by his firm's investment and research department
— to receive all complaints about substandard service from your broker or firm (when they have been ignored or not rectified)

Remember, your commissions are helping to pay the manager's salary, so consider him an element in your broker's performance and responsiveness to your account.

WHO'S MINDING THE STORE?

The number of stockbrokers has increased dramatically. According to the Securities Industry Association (SIA), there were 58,662 full-service brokers in 1981, and by 1987 they numbered approximately 75,000—an increase of 28 percent in six years. That number of aggressive people requires a lot of management.

Most firms have divided the country into regions. Typically, a major firm with five thousand brokers will have ten or more regions, each responsible for the profits of its branch offices. Each region has a regional vice-president, who is frequently an executive vice-president and among the top twenty-five individuals in a fifteen-thousand-plus-employee firm. The best regional people are promoted to the home office in New York City. Here the firm has several divisions (for example, institutional sales, retail sales). When a regional officer moves to New York it usually indicates that someday he'd like to be president or chairman of the firm.

At this level, profits matter less because executives are put into long-term creative roles where immediate profits are impossible, or they are placed in problem areas that need to be turned around. Here the environment is truly political; for the first time in an executive's career, who he knows is as important as what he knows. Welcome to the rest of corporate America, Mr./Ms. Manager.

One noted exception to this path up the executive ladder was a branch manager who succeeded by way of the beach, where he spent his time with bikinied women (even though he insisted his brokers remain in coat and tie all day). His car had an elaborate phone system with a direct trunk line to his office. When he received a call from upper management, his secretary would place it on hold while she alerted her boss on his beeper. He'd then answer the car phone as if he'd just come in from his office's boardroom. As a rule, however, managers aren't working on their tans; they're working on their production numbers.

Each firm has a different breakdown of divisions, and many firms have wholly owned subsidiaries, which may include consumer credit, insurance, mortgage companies, etc. Symptomatic of the times, brokerage firms are themselves becoming subsidiaries of larger companies, such as Prudential-Bache, Dean Witter/Sears, Shearson Lehman/American Express, and GE/Kidder Peabody. However, as competition intensifies and giants merge, weaknesses are surfacing. For example, it is now evident that Wall Street's ability to sell outweighs its management expertise. This makes the entire industry more prone to boom/bust cycles and to "crisis management."

WHERE DO MANAGERS COME FROM?

Scratch the typical branch office manager and you'll find a former successful account executive (AE) underneath the management facade. AEs rose to positions of authority by making big salaries and showing the boss that they had staying power. They got to know a product well and often became branch office product coordinators (the branch office AE considered expert in a particular area), a position that forced them to interact more with colleagues, under management's scrutiny. Finally, when the aspiring AE proved he could weather market fluctuations and a changing clientele and work well with others, he rode the wave of success straight into a manager's office. At least this was true in the past—recently things have changed.

Now the prerequisite of above-average salesmanship is being deemphasized, although not totally ignored. As Wall Street's expanded programs create a demand for more and more managers, firms are analyzing the responsibilities of the manager and redefining his role. They realize that some account executives, who might be weak in direct sales, may have strengths as managers. Because much of a manager's time is spent handling problems, settling disputes among brokers, and responding to client questions and complaints, it is more important that he is patient and a good listener rather than a hotshot AE. Many managers see themselves as shrinks and are at least as well paid.

THE BOTTOM LINE

Once promoted, the new manager doesn't expect the pressure to go away. Major Wall Street firms are multibillion-dollar outfits swimming in a sea of money, and they want to keep it that way. It is an aggressive, sales-oriented industry run by aggressive, sales-oriented individuals. If an office doesn't live up to that description, something usually gives.

Even though a manager isn't a hotshot Big Producer himself, he still is responsible for the performances of his brokers—and several of them better be Big Producers. "Scorekeeping is easy because profits are in hard, cold dollars," one top executive said, pointing to a computer printout. "When you pull up production numbers you quickly find out who's doing the job and who's not."

This may sound coldhearted, but it's true. Most evaluation methods are based on profits. Therefore, most rungs of the management ladder are evaluated via mathematics (preferably addition rather than subtraction), the everyday, immediate scorekeeping of business. In each branch, New York computers daily report each broker's past day's commissions, even by special product totals. Offices' statistics and monthly production numbers are analyzed along with the region's results. When the daily wires go out everybody at all levels knows how much business he and others did. And who they are beating, and who is beating them. But often, given the pressures of the business, it is the investor who is taking the beating. Although the pressure of the bottom line never goes away, this standard does eliminate much of the politics of management evaluation common to other industries.

THE BRANCH OFFICE MANAGER: PSYCHOLOGIST/MOTHER GOOSE/PINCUSHION

In orchestrating success, he is the most important person in brokerage management—the second lieutenant. The success of your broker's office reflects his manager's aggressiveness, organizational skills, and experience. He carries out the day-to-day duties with clients and brokers; he educates and motivates the troops to sell; he is responsible for office morale and firm loyalty; he knows the range of products, which ones will work best for all involved, and then he emphasizes these in sales meetings; he opens all mail for his office; he handles customer complaints; and he directs the firm's business within the community. Last, but not least, he hires the brokers who will work for him. If he has managed the office for a number of years, he has probably hired most of the employees, and he knows them well. He knows their strengths and weaknesses and can refer you to the strongest person for your investment needs. To an extent the office reflects the ambitions and personality of the manager. Over the years I've worked with seven office managers in six different offices. I recall an Irish Catholic who wanted to hire O'Learys and Sullivans, a jock manager who worried about the office softball team winning big, and an ex-marine who was looking for a "few good men."

JUST HOW MUCH MONEY DOES A MANAGER MAKE?

Most firms tie their managers' compensation to a formula—a percentage of total profits (about 10 percent) from the branch office, a salary, and some commissions from old accounts. A few firms rely on an assessment of the manager's performance to determine a "bonus." The largest portion of his compensation, however, comes from the profit percentage; if a manager's office does well, he does well. If a broker sells you something, the manager gets a small piece of it.

Most firms have the following positions and relative levels of estimated annual compensation. (Actual salaries/bonuses of the following positions are among the best-kept secrets in the business.) A branch office product coordinator earns a $10,000 to $30,000 bonus (over and above normal commission business); a branch office manager, $80,000 to $200,000 salary, with an average of $125,000; a regional sales manager (number-two executive in the region), $175,000 to $250,000; a regional vice-president (number-one executive in the region), $200,000 to $400,000 or more; and top-echelon management in New York earns $200,000 to $1 million or more. A lucky half-dozen or so earn at least $500,000, and a couple earn over $800,000, especially in high-profit years. Several years ago, during a weak earnings period on Wall Street, Dean Witter's top executive drew mention in a trade publication. Since Dean Witter's acquisition by giant Sears Roebuck, profits had been poor. Nonetheless, Dean Witter's head was paid $1 million. Ironically, Sears Roebuck's chief executive, who manages a corporation multiples larger, made only slightly more than his Dean Witter subordinate. As I said, running a brokerage firm is a tough job, but it pays well.

There are numerous perks to being a manager: He chooses his own employees and can also fire them. Expenses are left to his discretion and seldom reviewed. At most firms, the manager eats well, drinks well, attends all the right political functions (usually Republican), and always has tickets to symphony concerts or a box at world championship games. And he makes a lot of money. Want playoff tickets? Now you know who to call.

THE PRODUCER VERSUS THE NONPRODUCER

Depending on the firm, the manager is either a producing or nonproducing manager. A producing manager is one who still maintains his own Black Book of accounts, and his salary reflects this activity. A nonproducer does production merely to keep accounts from his AE days happy and to avoid getting rusty. It helps him to know how it feels to be selling in a particular market. Most nonproducing managers derive 75 percent of their income from office profits and salary, not commission income.

From a client's perspective, dealing with a nonproducer manager is preferable. He's not distracted by trading stocks for his clients or upset by the gyrations of the market. His compensation comes from the profitability and smooth management of his office, so he is more inclined to create a supportive atmosphere for his brokers—for your broker. Finally, and most important, when you are seeking a referral to a broker, the nonproducer will match you with the broker most knowledgeable in the investment areas you want. The producer manager is much more likely to put you in his own pocket. How can a client find out who is who? Ask.

IN THE TRENCHES: THE PROBLEMS OF A MANAGER

In spite of money and perks, the branch manager's life is not easy. As a result, few successful AEs want to become managers. AEs like their life: They create their own clientele, choose the products they sell, make lots of money, and ignore upper-level politics. Recently a friend was considering becoming a manager, then one day he told me, "I must be crazy. Lock me up if I ever mention it again."

Occasionally, I join some managers for drinks and listen as they moan and groan. "The job has changed for the worse." "Big Producers are arrogant SOBs." And sometimes brokers have harsh words for managers. Many years ago I heard about a manager from another firm, nicknamed the Czar, who was such a tyrant that several of his brokers took a baseball bat to his Rolls-Royce's windshield. Needless to say, the "climate" he created for his brokers both before and after that incident probably had adverse affects on his office's clientele as well.

Not only are new managers hard to find, but today's managers are quitting and returning to the "easy" life of the successful AE. Managers who are not seriously thinking of a switch now may do so as the business becomes more complex and their problems multiply. These problems affect you—because they affect your broker's manager, and ultimately the way you and your broker do business.

Wall Street's Dictum: "Increase Those Sales"

One of Wall Street's basic tenets is that firms are expected to increase their incomes each year. This puts a lot of pressure on the manager and isn't easy when market conditions discourage sales. A real estate partnership has less chance of being profitable when its mortgage rate is 15 percent than when it's 10 percent. Yet when mortgage rates are 15 percent, brokers still have to make a living, tax shelter/syndication departments are expected to grow, and managers want their own offices to sell more partnerships than other offices. It is up to management to create an environment competitive enough to survive tough periods, yet consistent enough not to lower the firm's standards. In bad times you learn how strong your management is.

When 1984 came and went, we breathed a sigh of relief that we had managed to limp through what turned out to be a terrible year for Wall Street profits. As insurance companies and banks further encroached on our turf, many firms decided that changes were called for—not only to increase profits, but also to run their companies more effectively. Most firms regularly analyze the numbers. And after the Crash of 1987, they're looking even harder for some answers.

Rising Costs

As firms became more cost-conscious, they discovered that expenses were growing faster than sales and this would continue despite strong cost containment. For example, at one firm the cost of merely keeping one broker "on location" rose 27 percent in 2½ years to $48,000 annually. Upon further analysis, many firms changed their payout schedules, reducing the percentage brokers make from each commission dollar. This trend is expected to continue into the late 1980s because the broker's paycheck still looks fat and vulnerable. And there are fewer obvious places to cut.

Perhaps a strong indication of how things have changed is the example of the 1984 Merrill Lynch acquisition of A. G. Becker. (Becker was one of several Wall Street firms consolidated within a larger firm.) Normally, the eight-hundred-person sales force would have been an integral part of the merger. Merrill, however, chose to allow these employees to fend for themselves in finding work, something that hasn't happened on the Street in years.

In addition, overhead expenses have skyrocketed. The combined cost of rent, telephones, stationery, salaries, and other necessary expenses, increased 31 percent in the same year (1984) that revenues decreased by about 28 percent. This actually resulted in a break-even status rather than a highly profitable one, but if these trends continue, it will be disastrous. Management needs to manage better. Even good products will not change that fact.

Complexity

Complexity is often a function of competition, and it tends to increase client misunderstandings and complaints. These complaints get parked on a manager's doorstep because he is the firm's voice to the public. Managers usually respond promptly and attempt to be fair to clients while keeping the firm's interests in mind. Managers do not automatically back the AEs' position, in part because they don't want complaints forwarded to the home office or to the Securities Exchange Commission (SEC). In the majority of cases, managers solve disputes to everyone's satisfaction. Many managers rate their good and bad days based on the daily tally of "screamers"—complaints by clients or brokers. Three makes a bad day.

Legal and Compliance Problems

Legal and compliance problems are growing as more attorneys specialize in suits against brokers and firms. Approximately one fourth of all brokers are finding themselves under some form of complaint during their careers. As a result, a few of even the best brokers are leaving the business. Sometimes just one unusually demanding client or an unfair but time-consuming lawsuit causes a broker to turn unproductive and conclude that the stress isn't worth it. Many suits have no validity, but they do create worry and work for the manager. And there was a surge of new suits after the 1987 Crash.

High Staff Turnover

Turnover in support staff (secretaries, wire room operators, etc.) is a major problem for the office manager. While most brokerage firms pay more than their bank cousins, they are usually not as generous as law firms or accounting firms. As a result turnover rates are high and employee complaints the norm. Managers are held accountable for these departures because they are expected to foster employee loyalty toward the firm. But nobody promised them it would be fair or easy.

Isolation

In addition to needing administrative and arbitration skills, the manager is a slave to violent swings of the marketplace and the accompanying euphoria or disappointment. Yet he must be upbeat in the face of adversity. "Some days I feel like a cheerleader," one manager said. "Only the pom-poms are missing." He knows that if he reveals his own fears when times are bad, that attitude can swiftly spread through an office like a plague. Thus, most managers stay somewhat aloof from office camaraderie. In this sense, management can be a lonely place.

The loneliness compounds because of the strong likelihood of no further advancement. Many managers are vying for the few executive positions. For those who want to leave office management via promotion, the frustration can mount, especially if the manager gave up clients as a requisite of entering management. Many feel (correctly) that they burned a major bridge—that to start over as an AE and rebuild a client list would be unthinkable. But some still quit to become successful AEs once again.

Audit Reviews

Another headache of being a manager is the constant audit review either by the NYSE or his own firm. Audits review the entire ongoing operation of an office and the manager's ability to maintain compliance with everyone's rules—state, federal, and those of the firm. A manager's typical audit report runs 70 to 100 pages, depending on the size of his office. It's the height of drudgery.

Drudgery Work

In addition to these duties, the manager is also responsible for his office's handling of checks, correspondence via mail and phone, local advertising and publicity (both authorized and—heaven forbid—unauthorized, as in the case of the broker VP who made headlines for running a high-class call-girl ring), and seminars, with their potential for erroneous comments made to a large audience.

BEING A MANAGER HAS ITS LIGHT SIDE

Few people know that every manager is required to open and review all mail sent to his office. This practice facilitates identifying complaints about brokers or transactions that otherwise might be deep-sixed by the broker to whom the letters were addressed. But instead of complaints, several office managers have become privy to the love lives and laundry lists of everyone from secretaries to Big Producers. All pink-scented, heavily engraved stationery, marked "Personal" in purple ink and carrying the message "Meet me at the Plaza at six," will be opened first by the manager. I know a broker who was sent indiscreet Polaroid photos by a woman who didn't know they would first be reviewed by the manager, rereviewed, and almost framed.

Brokers' pranks can cost a manager bucks too. I remember when a lifetime subscription to *Playboy* was awarded to twenty-five brokers—compliments of an unsuspecting manager. Or the enormous shipping bill one manager received for having a score of wild turkeys delivered to his branch office. (It was not Thanksgiving.)

MEET THE MANAGER

You are helping to pay part of your broker's manager's salary, so introduce yourself to him, get his card, and remember his name. Chances are, he is a competent professional with a good perspective on exactly what is going on in his office. That is reason enough to make him part of your team.

Chapter Five

ORACLES OF ERROR: WALL STREET'S RESEARCH ANALYSTS

> The information contained herein has been obtained from sources believed reliable, but is not necessarily complete and cannot be guaranteed. Any opinions expressed are subject to change without notice.
> —TYPICAL BROKERAGE FIRM DISCLAIMER

As a rookie I remember my trips to the men's room. Before computer terminals and squawk boxes, daily research reports were pinned to a cork bulletin board everybody had to pass on the way to the bathrooms. (That's called good management.) Everything on the board was a buy. Nearby, on the receptionist's desk, was the research report titled "Selections," which in one page covered the month's top ten picks in given areas—high-risk stocks, low-risk stocks, high-yielding common stocks, and "select" convertible issues. We called it the "tout sheet."

Most brokers avoided "Selections." In fact, a standard lunchtime debate concerned which half-dozen "selected" issues should be "shorted" (traded for profits derived from the stock's anticipated eventual decline). A short seller sells first at the higher (pre-fall) price and buys after the decline at the lower price to complete the transaction. Our reasoning was twofold: First, by the time the firm's research department recommended the stock and printed the select lists, about 85 percent of the buyers had already bought. Good institutional clients are telephoned by institutional brokers about buy recommendations and thereby advised long before the printed reports are circulated one to two weeks later. Meanwhile, the total of eventual sellers has grown larger.

Second, to create more commissions, brokers would advise clients to sell at the first sign of weakness, even if the profits were small, saying, "Take any profit you can get and run." Or "If it isn't working correctly, let's move on to something better" (often from the next select list). Frequent trading is commonplace for stocks placed on wire houses' select lists. Brokers can justify it and blame their company's analysts when the stock goes down.

Let's take another trip to the men's room. That board was an intellectual's dartboard, offering a dozen new recommendations a day. In four years I remember only two sell recommendations. I actually made money on the second sell because I'd learned to read the board not for advice but for information. So I eagerly looked for the next sell but never saw another one. Eventually I left the firm, but I did learn one thing: to second-guess the experts. In fact, now I automatically mistrust them all, whether they're on Wall Street or in courts and hospitals. Show me an expert, and I'm already looking for his victims.

RESEARCH ANALYSTS: FROM IVORY TOWERS TO THE STREET

Ten years ago analysts were heard and not seen. They led ivory-tower lives, learning an industry inside out, and then they wrote lengthy reports complete with title page and footnotes. The large commissions built into their firms' transactions supported their solitary work. May 1, 1975, changed all that with the death of fixed commissions. Suddenly investors were allowed to scramble around for the best deal, which forced brokers and analysts to promote their expertise as the reason to use their services. Now analysts' reports have become a selling tool as firms look to them to predict what will be hot tomorrow, next week, or next month. Analysts have a vested interest in issuing reports that say buy, not sell, even though they may lose you money. Why? One reason is that top corporate clients don't like "hired help" (the brokerage firm) issuing sells on the corporate client's stock. Analysts get away with buy reports because they all issue them. Therefore, their mediocre results seem acceptable. Everybody's doing about the same thing. This is another reason the investor needs a good memory and a built-in hesitation mechanism before acting on an analyst's advice.

Even when analysts are negative and might mean to say sell, only a sophisticated investor would be able to translate their opinions. For example, when a bank analyst for Morgan Stanley & Company realized that Continental Illinois would probably not pay its dividend, he said in his report, "We are extremely uncomfortable with the risk return trade-off presented by the stock because of the tremendously uncertain outlook for Continental's basic business." Is that clear? Other analysts rated Continental Illinois a "weak hold" or put it in a neutral category. Only a few told clients to sell, and only when clients asked.

THE ANALYST'S PERSONALITY

Ask a broker to describe an analyst in one word, and he'll say "arrogant." Recently, an analyst was having dinner with one of his firm's brokers and the president of a small company that the firm sought as a client. Unsolicited, the analyst told the company president, "Your company is too small. Following it would jeopardize my making the Analysts All-American team." When my associates and I telephone analysts and leave messages, they are not always returned. Some analysts never call back. Wall Street gossip has it that the only calls analysts regularly return are those from headhunters.

Ask a broker for another word to describe an analyst, and he'll say "wrong." I know of few brokers who really trust an analyst or their research department. For one thing, it is difficult to evaluate an analyst's record because there is no standardized way to rate analysts (other than the politicized choices on the All-American team of analysts). They often write vague reports, which confuse people who want to look back and point an accusing finger at them. In addition, analysts have been known to "modify" their track records. Some analysts have been accused of having a case of selective amnesia when it comes to explaining their record of previous calls.

Ironically, even though most brokers distrust their own firm's research, they often pay attention to the research of another firm. My partner Lenny summed it up. "You know, it's crazy. Brokers at ABC firm don't trust their own firm's research. But when a report from XYZ firm comes into their office, they photocopy the hell out of it and follow its recommendation without hesitation. Meanwhile, the brokers at XYZ firm have deep-sixed that same research report and want to read reports from ABC firm—reports ABC brokers would never follow because they know better. Talk about greener grass."

Many seasoned brokers learn to depend on their own research. In my experience, the good analysts are wrong at least a third of the time—the standard for average forecasting is slightly better than fifty/fifty. And supposedly they are the experts. Would you allow a doctor or lawyer that margin of error? Never. I am amazed at how long certain analysts hold their jobs. I remember one very popular analyst. We liked him because he was always wrong. We felt comfortable in our market maneuvers as long as he was going the opposite direction. We revered his consistency. Competition is slowly changing the Street, however, and it is now harder for the bad analysts to survive.

WHO BECOMES AN ANALYST?

You name it. Many analysts have been former taxi drivers, boxers, engineers, academicians, lawyers, and dentists, in addition to the usual graduates of MBA programs. It's a tough business, and it takes pull and chutzpah to get to the top. Today there are about fifteen thousand analysts. About four thousand work for Wall Street brokerage firms; the remaining eleven thousand either work for independent money managers, pension funds, or as independent researchers for research firms and think tanks.

THE ANALYST'S CAREER

The career of an analyst begins when he—or she—graduates from business school or leaves an industry related to one he plans to follow. He usually serves as an assistant to a more senior analyst for a few years, rarely following more than one industry. For example, an analyst might concentrate on electronics, banking, or industries such as automobiles, software, apparel, sports, medicine, or food.

The analyst learns everything about his industry. He reads trade publications and journals and government reports. He follows the *Wall Street Journal, Barron's,* and his firm's economic surveys and estimates. Next he puts himself on the mailing lists of the major companies in his industry. He reads their 10-Ks (financial reports required by the SEC), prospectuses, quarterly and annual reports, proxy statements, and his competitors' research reports. Then he travels—visiting plants and interviewing personnel and management of the company's various operating divisions. In a typical week he also meets with key clients of his firm, such as company presidents and selected money managers.

It's a difficult job, but analysts feel the salaries are worth it. Some analysts make over $250,000 per year, and many earn $100,000 or more. But it is no longer a scholar's life. Analysts are now selling something—and the buyer who should beware is you.

ANALYST: A MAN IN TOO MANY HATS

The most graphic representation of the analyst's lot was a drawing that accompanied an article in the *New York Times* business section by N. R. Kleinfield titled "The Many Faces of the Wall Street Analyst." It shows the back of an analyst adjusting his tie in front of a four-way mirror, each mirror reflecting him wearing a different hat. Kleinfield calls analysts "idea men," "financial detectives," "wizards of odds," and "noncommissioned salesmen." In my experience the last description is the most apt and at times leads to a conflict of interests. For example, brokers and money managers often complain that analysts are unrealistically positive when touting companies for whom their employer is presently investment banker. Also, analysts tend not to write up a sell on a favored client company even when their detective work warrants it. And it is difficult to be an analyst at a firm whose individual clients want immediate positive results from stock picks as opposed to institutional clients who can wait for longer-term results.

FROM AN ANALYST'S REPORT TO YOUR PORTFOLIO

Analysts' recommendations are passed along to you through your broker. Mornings in most brokerage houses begin with a meeting called Morning Call, Profit Line, Roundup, or Selections. At this time, analysts gather together and, one by one, pass down the word through a PA system or speaker phones (squawk boxes) as if they were Moses on the mount. Some firms encourage listening brokers to ask questions, which is a big plus because analysts are infamous for refusing to talk to anyone except their bosses or large institutional clients. This arrogance has created the assistant analyst, who is often just a recent business school or college graduate in a one- to two-year hands-on training program. Assistant analysts create most of the brief reports that you the investor read. Sometimes, when I can't get through to ask an analyst questions, I'm dismayed to think that both the synopsis report on my quote machine screen and the summary of my firm's latest news opinion were written by someone four months out of philosophy class.

These brief one-page reports are sent out every day by major brokerage houses' sales forces. They can be accessed on the broker's quote machine, printed out in hard copy, and given to clients—but only after the appropriate disclaimer is added. This disclaimer says in legal terms not to blame the brokerage firm if this opinion is a mile off and you lose your shirt. So much for confidence in research departments.

PROFILE OF AN ANALYST (NOW IN A STRAITJACKET)

As a rookie broker, I worked with Fred the Chartist who, although not yet a technical analyst, fancied himself one. Fred was eccentric. He maintained that all stocks moved up or down because of trading interrelationships, not because they reflected the company's operations or profitabilities. (Fred never knew or cared if XYZ Corporation made widgets, cars, or lingerie.) Strewn all over his desk were charts that he said bore out his "Walking Through the Woods Theory."

At least once a week he'd buttonhole some poor brokers and say, "Gentlemen, let me draw you a diagram." Then he'd grab one of Lenny's notepads—his own were always buried under all the charts—and make a quick sketch. "I'm lost in the woods and I see a stream," said Fred, poking his pencil at the woods. "I try to cross the stream several times but stop short. The final time I take a running leap over the stream, and I'm out of the woods. What happens in nature when you get lost out there is happening every day with stocks. Stocks go to a certain price, drop back several times, and then finally rise above the resistance point. We just have to see it and get back to basics. I tell you, men, this theory is revolutionary."

The trouble with Fred's theory was that too many clients got lost in the woods or drowned in the stream and also lost their shirts. Later, Fred left us to become a technical analyst for another major firm. He was also rumored to have started a newsletter on technical analysis and stock trading. The latest word has poor Fred operating out of a white padded cell.

BOTTOM LINE: THE ANALYSTS' TRACK RECORDS

Zack's Investment Research follows fifteen hundred analysts and three thousand companies. It believes that, overall, analysts' predictions are too high. Ben Zacks is quoted in *The New York Times* as saying, "They're constantly revising downward. They're in the game to sell stocks. They're too bullish." He has the facts to back this up.

The New York Times used his facts to list "Industry groups in which analysts' forecasts of 1984 growth in earnings per share showed the most error, and the error in the same forecast for the S & P 500":

WIDE OF THE TARGET

Industry	E.P.S. Growth Forecast	E.P.S. Growth Actual
Entertainment	1,377.3%	279.5%
Aluminum	1,683.3	744.8
Airlines	477.5	859.3
Miscellaneous Metals	83.6	0.3
Homebuilding	44.5	−39.1
Savings and Loans	77.1	−1.0
Coal	50.0	−9.7
Forest Products	125.9	67.5
Finance Companies	40.5	−17.7
Industrial Machinery	70.5	124.5
S & P 500	30.4	19.0

Copyright © 1985 by The New York Times Company. Reprinted by permission.

As you can see, in all but two cases analysts were way off the mark. In fact, history is strewn with the skeletons of analysts' major misses. Penn Central was considered gilt-edged and solid up to the day before it declared bankruptcy. Three Mile Island was not recognized for its risks either before or after the 1979 debacle. Bookkeeping frauds continue to evade reviews by analysts—remember the Equity Funding scandal! That financial calamity was a classic. The stock of this New York Stock Exchange insurance company rose dramatically because of its fast-paced earnings growth. Many analysts recommended buy—until word got out that the company was a fraud. Reported sales and insured individuals never existed. Company heads had fashioned a sophisticated lie that fooled analysts and investors for quite a long time. Shortly after the lie was discovered, the company was bankrupt.

Many people still wonder why analysts didn't figure out that home computer manufacturers were in trouble earlier. One look at the heavy discounting in stores, poor attendance at computer fairs, and slow software sales should have been enough. Texas Instruments lost $100 million in one quarter in 1983, and the stock dropped forty points in one day. I remember because I was short their stock that day and made a bundle. Where were the analysts with the sell beforehand?

THE ANALYSTS' PERSPECTIVE

Martin Zweig, a noted analyst often seen on "Wall Street Week," once immodestly commented in *Barron's* about his profession. "A rabbi, a Hindu, and a technical analyst ask a farmer to put them up for the night. The farmer says okay, but one of them will have to sleep in the barn. First, the Hindu goes. But five minutes later, there's a knock at the door. It's the Hindu. He says he's sorry but he can't sleep in the barn because there's a cow there. So the rabbi goes out. But five minutes later, there's a knock at the door and it's the rabbi. He says he's sorry but he can't sleep in the barn because there's a pig there. So the technical analyst goes out. Five minutes later, there's another knock at the door. It's the cow and the pig."

There are many reasons for the analysts' poor performances. As one major analyst remarked, "there's no relationship between business fundamentals and stock prices. Companies lose millions of dollars, and the stock price won't go down. Years later, these companies may make millions of dollars, and the stocks won't go up. A lot of things affect stock prices. So it's unfair to judge analysts on stock prices alone." Unfortunately, that is exactly what the investor owns after listening to analysts—the stocks, which he and his wallet judge by their fluctuations.

One former auto analyst said that she knew everything about "multiple-valve engines and discus couplings"—information relevant to the investment. But she said that analysts are not up on where interest rates may go, national crises, or the temper of the stock market. "Most analysts don't even have quote machines on their desks. They operate in a vacuum. Very often analysts would make recommendations while having no idea what the market will do. Very often analysts are as obtuse as anyone you can imagine."

Analysts can also be critical of one another, especially when they feel a highly paid analyst's reputation is undeserved. Said one analyst of another, "He's a guy who's 100 percent right 10 percent of the time." Another analyst admitted, "The pressure is on to maximize your income. So you don't want to be controversial, hopefully not get bagged on any stock, and make the lists as fast as possible."

The lists? There are two lists—compiled by Greenwich Research Associates and *Institutional Investor* magazine— which rate analysts in every category of analysis, such as computers, steels, utilities, and defense. The best ones are labeled "All-Americans." Sounds like football's Heisman Trophy, and it pays about the same. However, even analysts agree that making lists is not always a result of good stock picking or making John Doe Investor money. It can be who you know or who you know who wants-to-know-who-else-you-know, like a CEO of a big company. Many times investment bankers, analysts, and analyst-headhunters have told me how politically astute some analysts are in "politicking" their way to lists—despite their uneventful track records. One major plus from appearing on the lists is that your employer feels you are pulling in substantial commission revenue, or "soft" dollars—"soft" because, unlike broker-produced revenues, there is no precise way to estimate accurately how much in trades each analyst is responsible for generating.

RESEARCH ANALYSTS: HOW THE NYSE COMPANIES VIEW THEM

I have two clients who have worked with multibillion-dollar NYSE companies constantly researched by Wall Street analysts. Both held executive positions and were the chief spokespersons and liaisons with Wall Street for a combined total of over two decades.

Their general opinion is that analysts are bright people who do their homework in an aboveboard, honest way. But they both found it easy to "lead along" most analysts, to subtly feed them information that supports a buy recommendation rather than a sell or hold. For example, a smart liaison knows what's hot on the Street. Without lying, he will emphasize his company's business or expansion plans in areas that are hot and deemphasize what is cold (out of favor). Forget that half the company's revenues are from an area covered with icicles, or that those areas are losing a fortune. They make sure the analysts know their company is making money somewhere else (or will).

The skillful spokesperson also furthers his cause by confusing more than one unsuspecting analyst. The liaison gets several analysts to follow his lead about the hot (rather than the cold) direction in which his firm may be headed. These analysts write reports which are circulated, and this in turn leads to wider acceptance of the liaison's perspective of his company's operating status because analysts read one another's reports. It reminds me of a fox hunt, where the fox manages to confuse a few lead dogs, and soon there are thirty hounds going in the wrong direction. Good liaisons easily confuse poorer analysts, at least for a while, and by then the analysts are reviewing a new pile of data and "facts."

THE INFORMATION FLOW BETWEEN INDUSTRY AND THE STREET

"Garbage in, garbage out," says my seasoned executive liaison friend, Bart Salmon. According to him, a major problem is that about 90 percent of the people who represent public companies to Wall Street analysts are lower-level assistant treasurers, or worse. They aren't qualified to inform the Street's analysts, don't have authority to speak on certain happenings, and often don't fully know what is going on within their companies. Consequently, analysts' reports either reflect the "leads" offered by a seasoned, knowledgeable liaison, or they reflect inadequate information given by a low-level spokesperson. Having spoken to these executives about what they did over the years, I have a better appreciation of why my old officemates looked for stocks to short from the select list over lunch.

EARNINGS ESTIMATES: RECIPES FROM MATHEMAGICLAND

Most companies don't predict earnings; they simply tend to agree or disagree with forecasts made by the Street. After a while the moving numbers of estimates get narrowed down to the popular forecast estimates you and I read in the financial news. But it is what happens before forecasts are made that makes me nervous and amazes my liaison friends.

"If I don't know what my company's earnings are going to be next quarter, in two quarters, or in a year, how the hell can an analyst know?" That comment on Wall Street research is by a senior executive of a major NYSE company. He's not alone. It is well known that

Wall Street analysts constantly write reports based on mathematics from estimates that are fundamentally no more than guesses. While some industries and trends, such as utility usage and food consumption, are easier to estimate, other industries spawn estimates that are off the wall. Analysts create these numbers, and investors/brokers use them as if the entire equation of a research report were based on scientific axioms. My insiders say that revising just a few numbers on a corporate model estimate for a coming year completely blows up previous estimates; therefore, the whole thing is a flaming guess. One liaison said, laughing, "We'd be sitting around shaking our heads, beating our brains out to make a creditable estimate of our company's profitability for the coming year, and then the next day an analyst shows up. He'd want to assign an estimate to not just the coming year, but the next five years. And you know what: He'd walk off with numbers. He'd make his estimate, and six thousand reports would roll off the press." He shook his head, "That's why I stay in T-bills."

EXPERIENCE IS THE BEST TEACHER

My experienced liaison friends don't buy many stocks or pay much attention to reports that originate on the Street. When I asked one of them, Pendleton Powersaw, why, he said, "I don't gamble." When his own company's stock would gyrate up and down over the years, he would call his analyst friends, and together they would try to decipher the situation. "We rarely could," he said. "We hadn't a clue why things were going up or down." Pendleton laughingly recalled one bit of wisdom from a big-time analyst. "I guess there are more buyers than sellers," the analyst said. As Pendleton put it, "I need an analyst to tell me that?"

He feels that the "smarter" analysts spend time understanding the company rather than meeting the chairman and introducing the CEO to his boss. He also said there is a definite synergy between analyst and the topic company. It is important that the analyst's reports create enthusiasm for the company. Accurately forecasting earnings is much less important—besides, few analysts do that well. He went on to point out how "at the beginning analysts seem to group their forecasts close together. As the year progresses they become more bold and differentiated from one another." So much for long-term guesses. Although these liaisons never tell one group of analysts anything different from what they would another, they are surprised how few ask the right questions, probe deep enough to find weaknesses, or refuse to swallow the diversionary leads of the liaison.

As we've noted, there are a lot of analysts and the quality varies all over the lot. And they don't automatically stay long in one place. Pendleton said this of the situation, "Many good ones are gone to run money independently by the time they're in their mid-thirties. That's where the big money is. But then again, many poor analysts also leave to run money. Just look at some of those mediocre money-manager track records." Bart Salmon offered his opinion. "The very best analysts stay with brokerage firms and collect huge salaries as they are chauffeured to and fro in their company limousines."

So, does the investor win in this situation? No. But the head-hunters do. Headhunters prosper dealing in the analyst trade. And analysts almost always return their phone calls. There are few loyalties, big bonuses, and lots of files moving around the Street.

The Street's Competition: They're Experimenting with Your Money

Chapter Six

THE BATTLE FOR YOUR BUCKS

> If you bet on a horse, that's gambling. If you bet you
> can make three spades, that's entertainment. If you bet
> cotton will go up three points, that's business. See the
> difference?
>
> —BLACKIE SHERROD

There has been a dramatic change in Wall Street in the past few
years. Wall Street used to be laid out in sharp little blocks—brokerage firms, banks, and insurance companies all had defined areas
in which to operate. When I started in 1974 as a broker, I had no
competition for stock order taking, not even from discounters—they
didn't exist. I didn't sell CDs; banks did. Brokers rarely sold insurance; insurance agents did. Universal life insurance didn't exist. Tax
shelters were relatively new. We didn't know very much about them,
never mind other "special products."

Today your financial planner, banker, lawyer, insurance agent,
and CPA will tell you about their "private placements"—even
though, like brokers in the early days, many of these "newcomers"
are learning about them as they go. And as you spend. In fact, look
at all the new titles: "Investment Counselor," "Financial Consultant," "Investment Adviser," "Certified Financial Planner," and
"Account Representative." And these are just a few.

As a result there are too many salespeople with too-similar titles,
but too little knowledge about too many newly created products.
You, the investor, are being circled for the kill. Instead of one or two
guns pointed at you, there are ten. They can't all miss. You are the
most important part of the new Wall Street jungle—the quarry.

WHY ALL THE COMPETITION?

The Street has become an overgrown jungle of salespeople, products, and services for two reasons: There are more investors and more money (and therefore more profits to be made—if you can catch them), and recent government deregulation has eliminated many of the barriers previously erected to prevent the key players from competing with each other. The 1975 elimination of fixed commissions was the harbinger of discounting and further upheaval. It will take several more years for the dust to settle. Don't let your wallet get buried as it comes down.

As a result of deregulation, brokerage firms are at a distinct disadvantage. Historically, brokers have been involved in areas of greater risk, like a gyrating stock market. People associate brokers with risk and losses (perhaps because of some bad memories), as opposed to the traditional (and stabler) areas of banking and insurance. People are accustomed to doing business with banks and insurance companies because most people have checking accounts and insurance policies before they even think about investing. But investors seem to be dropping their guard as they use these more staid organizations to venture into inherently risky new areas—in effect, something like wearing a tuxedo into a swamp full of quicksand. But risk is risk, and fees are fees. You shouldn't assume just because a financial adviser was traditionally conservative that the same will hold true when he trades commodities for you. He is in that competitive arena to make a buck. Any benefit to you is secondary.

Another effect of deregulation is that competition is becoming synonymous with experimentation—and you are the guinea pig. The combatants are trying to determine what products to market, how to market them, and to whom. These experiments are frequently being conducted by inexperienced guessers providing services and selling products they don't fully understand. When they do a good job it may be by chance. In time, the players will get better, but meanwhile, consider yourself the equivalent of a hamster with a wallet in his pocket.

BANKS: THEIR SIN USED TO BE LOW RATES; NOW IT'S BAD INVESTMENTS

Banks have been the best examples of the principle that it's easier to steal a dollar from 10 million people than $10 million from one person. They've been nicking and sticking the consumer for years.

SIDNEY WOLINSKY, PUBLIC-INTEREST LAWYER
—(As quoted in the *Wall Street Journal*)

Banks are my least favorite competitor. And I've got some famous company. Thomas Jefferson once remarked, "Banking establishments are more dangerous than standing armies." Yet banks remain overrated by a lot of people who feel that they have two major strengths—massive size and stability. They are right about one—size. For example, according to a recent study by the Securities Industry Association (SIA), the two largest banks, Citibank and Bank of America, together have more capital base than all NYSE firms combined. (However, Bank of America is reducing its capital lately through massive losses.) Yet the SIA is more apprehensive about competition from diversified financial competitors like Sears/Dean Witter, Shearson/American Express, and Prudential-Bache than from the banks. Why? So far, banks have a dismal track record competing with brokers and insurance companies, and this doesn't seem likely to change.

A CLOSE-UP OF A "CONSERVATIVE" COMPETITOR

People have learned to be wary of brokers and insurance agents (for good reason), but they still trust bankers. Many of these investors have become competition casualties.

Casualty number one: Recently a sixty-five-year-old woman visited a broker in our office. She had $100,000 to her name, mostly in a CD at her bank, but she was unhappy with the shrinking interest rate. The broker suggested that she diversify and purchase a guaranteed annuity, U.S. government bonds, or a government money market fund. All are safe and provide ample liquidity. She politely listened, then returned to her bank where the CD was. The bank had an "investment" department of four people, one of whom suggested that she invest in a public real estate tax shelter, which had a minimum investment of $5,000. The bank employee advised her to put *all* her money into this shelter. She did. (The same bank is rumored to have persuaded an individual/trust to invest $1 million in this same program.) It was the only real estate program the bank sold, so therefore it was a strong recommendation, especially when she didn't want a CD. It also paid an 8 percent commission to the bank.

When our broker heard about it, he strongly urged her to stop the transaction. It was wrong for her because a large public real estate shelter program returns cash slowly, can be too optimistic in cash distribution projections, is not at all liquid, and often turns into a poor investment. The brokers in my firm know this because we've sold them for years. I don't touch them now because I haven't liked the results. But this program is all the bank had. And it could have been all that sixty-five-year-old woman had to her name, with some tragic consequences. Fortunately, the broker and his client had the trade "busted." But people like her continue to trust banks because they have a conservative image. Banks haven't lost any money for them—yet, just paid them mediocre rates. In a few years a lot of people will have lost a lot of money at banks in a variety of different ways because banks are experimenting with their customers' money.

Casualty number two: Last year I had a prospective client with $300,000 he'd saved in his bank over the years. He wanted me to quote a yield (interest rate) for a tax-exempt bond issued by our state, so as to avoid state and federal income tax. I gave him a quote for what he wanted—bonds maturing in five to eight years. He wasn't impressed (yields for those maturities are modest), so he called his bank and asked if they could help. They did, in a flash. They quoted a bond maturing in thirty years, not one for the five- to eight-year time frame (but they did at least get the state right). They beat my quote by quoting apples to grapefruit. A few months later my client told me that before he knew what happened the bank had bought him the bonds. He never expected the confirmation he got in the mail because he had never given the go-ahead for purchase. He did understand, however, that his CD account was debited to buy the bond. He said he was seventy-four years old and wanted to be around when the bonds matured—in thirty years. At 104? Not a good bet. I have forty years on him, and I may not be around when those bonds mature. He did get a higher yield, but also much more risk, the wrong maturity, and a lot of confusion. And no explanation. Like many, he had trusted his bank. The moral: Don't trust anybody anymore.

Casualty number three: Recently, a broker had a client who left him for a bank discount commission department but wound up dealing with the bank's investment department as well. Their suggestions ended up in his portfolio, sporting a discounted value by the time he left them in disgust. The overall market had gone up dramatically, but he lost about 20 percent. All in all, he figured his portfolio lost about 50 percent of its value considering that even a mediocre portfolio manager could have almost mirrored market results. The bank had periodically misquoted prices far higher than he expected (on markup items such as municipal bonds and OTC stocks) and butchered his trading confirmations and statements with bad bookkeeping and reporting.

MODERN BANKING: NEW RISKS

If you think it's OK to second-guess or distrust your broker and insurance agent, you're right. But you're only half right if you forget to include your banker. It's true that the government oversees the banks' operation and aids in their insuring themselves, but the government (federal and state) basically does the same for brokers and insurance companies, although in different ways.

First of all, banks have already lost the competition in several financial service areas. Their trust departments are notorious on Wall Street for poor performance; their index of managers almost always underperforms Wall Street's brokers and insurance companies. I've gained a number of clients from bank money managers, enough to draw up a profile of the "victim."

The client "victim" is often (1) someone who doesn't pay serious attention to his investments' performance more than twice a decade; (2) a conservative individual who inherited most of his or her money; and (3) a glutton for punishment. Amazingly, some of these bank referral clients remain with the bank, fully aware of their shortcomings, no matter what I say. They complain that the transfer of assets is too complicated (three or four signatures are required), and they privately fear grandfather might turn over in his grave. (Bottom line: They don't trust brokers.) Actually, grandfather might be spinning in his grave knowing how his assets are underperforming at the bank, because more often than not a bank's "conservative" performance is a lousy performance.

Ironically, trust departments are often either low-profit or unprofitable for banks. In most cases, however, they are retained to foster the bank's image of sophistication and full service. But image isn't service. It is well known that the better trust department employees use their employment as a training experience, then leave for more profitable pastures. In desperation, many banks now farm out the management of money to local money managers, hoping to improve their performance and gain referrals.

Banks aren't doing much better with other new services, such as their discount broker transaction departments. So far, many of these departments are losing money. In an attempt to avoid this, several large banks have bought discount brokerage firms, acquisitions that appear more viable than using a farm-out middleman discounter for clients' trades. But banks are now facing client dissatisfaction with muddled bookkeeping, poor executions, and unwise transactions that are causing losses (the kind usually associated with brokers). This is producing a new negative image, and many banks are sorry they ever got involved in discount operations. But that's competition. Major brokerage firms have known that the bulk of discount business is the small onetime trader. It's tough to make a profit on him, so they gladly surrendered him to the banks.

Another new service is complete portfolio and asset management. Banks are trying to upgrade their market for these services, looking for people with minimum incomes of $100,000 (people who have traditionally stayed as far away as possible from banks). "Private banking" is one of their new marketing techniques. It offers high credit lines, premium travel cards, bigger safe deposit boxes, separate banking facilities handled by executives, no waiting lines, the snob appeal of rubbing elbows with fellow rich folk . . . and some new ways to lose money through risk investments. Snob appeal isn't expertise.

Several major banks have spent a lot of time and money advertising financial planning for people with incomes of $30,000 or more. Again, results have been dismal. A few New York banks have tried marketing financial plans for under $100 and have been embarrassed by the results. They are in direct competition with brokers who are selling similar financial planning packages to the same market.

YESTERDAY'S GENTLEMAN BANKER IS TODAY'S SALESMAN

Once deregulation put banks in new service areas, they have had to undergo a major change in philosophy in terms of the salaried employee versus the commission employee. In the past brokers and insurance agents were primary culprits who could be accused of creating a "need" that thereby created a commission; they sold, supposedly, even when the client shouldn't buy. Because they were salesmen. Well, guess what competition has wrought. Salesman bankers. And they don't always advertise fairly, either.

A bank a hundred feet from the door of my branch office has advertised "No bank or brokerage firm can beat our smart money IRAs." The branch manager called state banking overseers to complain, but nothing was ever done. The sign remained. The manager said if he put out an ad like that the SEC would probably fine him and hang him from the rafters, and our lawyers would have coronaries. We'd have to pay penalties to any client proving otherwise. But it seems the Banking Commission is not as conscientious as the SEC in its scrutiny of fair practices and truth in advertising. After all, an IRA can use many forms of investment—nobody has the best of all in everything.

Banks are now peddling, and their employees are paid commissions in more and more instances. Today, in a boutiquelike atmosphere, you can buy your FDIC/FSLIC-insured CD, take three giant steps across the marble floors, and find yourself staring at a sometime commission salesman hawking stocks, take a few more steps to your right or left, and another salesman is pushing real estate or a financial plan. The problem is that you perceive the banker as an adviser and the broker as the salesman. That's old thinking. One consultant now working with a half-dozen Chicago banks said, "What we're doing now with financial-service centers is merchandising banks to the level of the Neiman-Marcuses, the Bonwit Tellers, and the Bergdorf Goodmans."

Another bank, Bank One, is considering installing the whirring machines that count coins and sort checks into a showcase two-story front-window display in its Columbus main branch to create visual excitement. Even the lighting matters. One bank "is experimenting with lighting that projects a gentle halo over its automated-teller machines." All this merchandising is being done under the flag of your friendly "conservative" bank—conservative until you buy a risky investment. Ever stop to think that "conservative" might be a polite way of saying "banks don't make you much money?" Their CDs may be insured, but their investment and trust departments aren't. "Conservative" today, in terms of investing on your bank's advice, could mean disaster.

Even the stodgy savings-and-loans (S&Ls)are changing. Their advertisements market everything—mutual funds, insurance, bonds—everything but the usual S&L products. In fact, their brochures are almost indistinguishable from a broker's or an insurance agent's. Some S&Ls have added to the competition fray by using INVEST, a joint effort created by S&Ls for S&Ls. It provides independent financial planners who service bank clients—for a piece of the action. There are now about 250 bank lobbies with an INVEST section/office/desk and the potential for 5,000 more. My local INVEST bank had the "perfect" IRA. A few years ago, employees suggesting investments in these bank lobbies were salaried, but now some are changing to a hybrid salary/commission compensation. So far, over 70,000 customers have signed up for INVEST products, which include stocks, bonds, mutual funds, portfolio management, financial planning, real estate partnerships, and life insurance. Make sure you recognize the fox in his three-piece suit, no matter what forest you are in.

KNOWING YOUR ABCs: ACCRUING AND BORROWING CORRECTLY

Two misunderstood areas of competition deal in the very basics of finance: earning interest on money and borrowing money from a lender. Banks have historically paid interest on CDs, on passbook savings accounts, sometimes on checking accounts, and recently on money market "checking accounts." FDIC/FSLIC deposits are insured by the government up to $100,000 per account (subject to the FDIC's definition of ownership capacity), but all banks do not offer the same rates. In addition, your bank charges a penalty on early withdrawals, but the bank also has the right to charge more than the accepted minimum. The minimum is about 1 percent if you violate the terms of your CD, but some banks charge 2 percent to 4 percent penalties. You have to read the fine print, for higher-yielding CDs usually have greater penalties. (The problem is you often can't find the fine print until you buy the CD, because it's on the back of the CD certificate itself.)

For years banks have refused to come up with decent rates for short-term loans. How do you feel paying 16 percent to 20 percent on short-term credit card balances when the prime rate is 7.5 percent? How much does 7.5 percent plus a 1.5 percent markup versus a 20 percent rate translate into profits? A lot. Granted, credit cards represent an important alternative to carrying money around—or borrowing it on the spot. But most brokerage house money market accounts act the same way—when you need money you merely write a check against an available limit. Your savings on interest charges could be enormous. Why? Because brokers typically charge a level roughly equal to the prime rate to borrow from them. And 7.5 percent is a lot better than 20 percent. Now that deregulation has allowed the competition to join the action, you should be seeing some fancy footwork by the banks as they try to make amends for their years of greed.

CHECKING ACCOUNTS/MONEY MARKET ACCOUNTS

Increasingly, banks have a new array of rules for their checking accounts: minimum required balances, limits on the number of checks that can be cashed, fees for breaking these rules, fees for using automated tellers, and even fees for making deposits. In fact, they have such a morass of new charges that sometimes the interest accrued on your account doesn't cover the expense of operating it. Only the banks' upscale checking account (with greater minimum required balance) has a rate of interest competitive with brokers. The same applies to passbook savings, although they are no longer restricted and some banks are raising their rates to become more competitive. Yet some banks have lowered interest on passbook savings accounts. Articles in various publications have long noted the potential for improved bank rates, but banks haven't fallen all over themselves to raise them.

Another area in which banks are not responsive to the consumer is in crediting deposits quickly for interest accrual. Your bank credits interest to your account only after your funds have been collected from the bank where the deposited check was drawn, subject to only recently imposed maximum periods of delay. Banks are even tinkering with the time of day a deposit must be made by to be credited as "today's" deposit. In the old days you had to deposit by 3:00 P.M. Then it changed to 2:00 P.M. My local bank recently went to 11:00 A.M. Such shortened deposit times—two hours out of the eight hours they are open for same-day crediting—will surely gain banks an extra day's float with your money. My local bank also reserves the right to credit my account after two business days on checks deposited from one of its own branches—even the same branch. Out-of-state checks can be delayed up to five business days. That is an improvement, but all that free float has helped build fancy buildings, pays for halo-lighting effects, and covers some bad foreign loans. But do *you* want to pay for that?

ARE BANKS SAFE? LOANS IN MATHEMAGICLAND

In the wake of recent deregulation and change, and with banks competing in new areas and operating so differently, the above question is certainly warranted. Yes, banks are insured, but just what does this mean if push comes to shove? The following are recent banner headlines from major newspapers.

WORRISOME BANK OBLIGATIONS—
$1 TRILLION OFF BALANCE SHEET
DEFERRED LOAN LOSSES AT THRIFTS AND BANKS
SNOWBALL ACROSS U.S.
AGENCIES THAT INSURE BANK, THRIFT DEPOSITS
FACE MAJOR PROBLEMS
U.S. REGULATORS WANT BANKS TO COVER RISKY LOANS BETTER
BANKS' CAPACITY TO HONOR DEPOSITS
COMING UNDER GROWING SCRUTINY
BIG BANKS' STOCKS FALL—
INVESTORS CHALLENGE WORTH OF FOREIGN DEBT

There is definitely something wrong here. The number of problem banks followed by the FDIC has increased over fivefold in the last four years, from two hundred in 1981 to eleven hundred in 1985. Big-bank stocks have fallen precipitously as rumors circulate as to the real worth of foreign debts—which may or may not be repaid someday. According to the *Wall Street Journal,* "Privately some bankers talk about freezing deposits, attaching assets, rushing to court and seeking U.S. Government aid in the event of repudiation." If the loans start to go upside down, "lawyers say that surprise and speed may be crucial in staking claim to what may amount to then scarce assets." Banks are much too complacent about the unthinkable ever becoming tomorrow's headline, yet foreign loans may be the trigger. Precedents are rare, but they exist, and the results were disastrous.

CAN WE LEARN FROM HISTORY?

In 1917 the Bolsheviks reneged on czarist debts. The United States then moved to freeze assets abroad as collateral for the loans. The Roosevelt administration settled claims with the USSR sixteen years later—yet the U.S. creditors didn't get paid until 1959, forty-two years after the fact. The payment: 10 cents on the dollar. There are a lot of American dollars lent out to foreigners right now, and a lot of bankers wish they had never made the loans. In 1987 the top ten U.S. banks were carrying on their books at 100 cents on the dollar about $55 billion in loans to Latin American nations and the Philippines, hardly stable economies. The loans represented 150 percent of their stockholders' equity. Experts believe that such loans are really worth only half that number—but what's $27.5 billion among friends? Another stat: Writing off just 10 percent of this debt would consume most of the combined annual profits of these banks. But our government, through the Secretary of the Treaury, wants banks to make more loans to these countries. Banks comply because they realize that if they approve more loans, regulators won't downgrade the loans they already have out, which would obviously be disastrous to them.

INVISIBLE LOANS: INVISIBLE DANGERS

Then there are other loans that are *not* on bank balance sheets at all. Nevertheless, they are legal and binding obligations made to borrowers by federally insured banks. They are called off-balance-sheet loans. They are off balance sheet because they are loans not made yet, but they have been formally committed to borrowers to be made on demand; for example, letters of credit that have not been exercised. Your line of credit, a "second mortgage equity loan," could be one of these loans. Recently the banks have been pushing these loans like crazy. The borrowers pay fees in advance for the commitment, and these fees show up in today's bank earnings. The banks are making money on these guarantees, and a lot of borrowers like the concept, too, because all the paperwork is done in advance. But it is happening at too great a pace now and needs to be given a lot of scrutiny. How much is off balance sheet? Too much!

These "guarantees" are now equal to a mere $1 trillion—$1,000,000,000,000!! Twelve zeros on the wrong side of the decimal point and equal to half of all of Unce Sam's ballooning debt. Uncle Sam would certainly be hard pressed to help with a number that large. Yet the numbers aren't even reported on bank balance sheets. At the nation's fifteen largest banks the commitments represent more than the combined total worth of the banks. "The raw numbers are a little scary," said a director of the Federal Deposit Insurnce Corporation (FDIC). That's an understatement. The FDIC (that's the government, and you and I are taxpayers) should worry, for in a recent ruling the courts stated that if a bank fails, standby letters of credit were *equivalent to deposits* and the FDIC must make good on these "deposits" along with the standard kind.

Also, there is our Farm Credit system with its $70 billion in trouble. Already $6 billion is past due on loans totaling $15 billion. One state S&L officer, recognizing the problem inherent in these massive debts, summed up the situation. "Nobody wants to pick up the dog because of all the fleas on it."

JUST HOW SICK ARE THESE "CONSERVATIVE" BANKS?

It's worse than you imagine. Continental Illinois, the bank that had a major run (a sudden withdrawal of assets by depositors who were losing faith) and was bailed out in 1984 by the FDIC, required $1.5 billion to keep afloat. The bailout has tied up 15 percent of the FDIC's annual cash flow indefinitely. Amazingly, the financial world didn't see it coming. Today, about 465 S&Ls are operating insolvently, hoping for a bailout. The total cost of the bailouts is estimated to be over $20 billion, far in excess of FSLIC's reserves of $4 billion. The losses would likely be Uncle Sam's. But he doesn't want to swallow too hard now.

An obvious question is: How solid is the banks' capital that justified lending out so many of these dollars? Swallow hard. Federal Home Loan Bank Board Chairman Edwin Gray in a *Wall Street Journal* article conceded that FSLIC accounting procedures cause a "vast overstatement" of the industry's capital. Statistics indicate that 89 percent of the S&Ls' net worth of $32 billion at the end of 1983 was the product of accounting gimmicks. Also, a former FSLIC director, Peter Stearns, commented on FSLIC "insurance" monies and their perceived growth in the *Wall Street Journal*. "The reason it [FSLIC] is growing is becaues the FSLIC isn't resolving any cases [of thrift insolvency], so it's a mirage." Even one Reagan administration official has said, "We have considerable doubts about the accuracy of [the FSLIC] numbers." Another official said, "There's a lot of concern that if we stress the lack of viability of FSLIC that we cause more trouble."

THE CURE THAT KILLS

Always inventive in ways to make profits, banks are "refining" their lending practices by selling their large wholesale business loans to other banks. Such banks lend money, collect fees on these loans, and then sell the loans at a markup to another lending institution. Once the marketed loans have left their books, they then make new ones. For example, in the fall of 1985 Manufacturers Hanover Trust Company lent $180 million to a major oil company. Weeks later, Manufacturers Hanover sold half of that loan to other financial institutions around the world. One senior vice-president from Bankers Trust Company said, "Loan selling is at the core of our strategy as a bank."

This practice is beginning to concern government regulators because the better loans are obviously more salable, which leaves the weaker loans in the banks' portfolios, slowly eroding the quality of the banks' entire retained loan portfolio. Another problem is that the purchasing bank may be less capable of judging the quality of what it is buying because it did not originate the loan. There's a famous example from recent history. This situation occurred in the loan syndication collapse of the now-infamous Penn Square Bank in July 1982. Banks bought energy loans from Penn Square Bank but didn't do their own credit analysis of the borrowing companies. They lost enormous amounts of money when the loans went belly-up. Continental Illinois was one of those purchasing banks.

As a result, loan-selling departments are being more cautious, sometimes requiring the buyer to do his own evaluation of the borrower. Even so, one Wall Street banking analyst predicted the market could quintuple in the next five years. He said recently, "I consider loan sales to be one of the most significant structural changes in banking in my eighteen years as an analyst." Still, change isn't always good, and experts contend that things could come to a screeching halt if we had a Penn Square replay.

As you can see, these are difficult times for banks and S&Ls. They still have major problems in the traditional areas of banking—problems that are growing rather than diminishing—yet they are beginning to experiment in new areas as well. It is up to you to choose whether you want to be a part of that experiment. You know how well they are doing with their own capital—do you really want to trust them with yours? I'm scared of many bankers. You should be too.

INSURANCE: THEY CREATE CASUALTIES TOO

> The great push to sell insurance to college students is not entirely unlike the selling of ice to Eskimos, except that a lot more insurance is sold that way than ice.
>
> —ANDREW TOBIAS

Remember the bank casualties? Insurance is safe and conservative, but insurance companies make casualties too. I have a client who's sixty years old and reasonably conservative. He wants to forget his investments, just leave them to the pros. And for better or worse, he trusts people. After several years, I questioned him more about his assets (I don't pry if clients seem reluctant to discuss their finances) and found he had an annuity, a mutual fund, and an insurance policy all bought through a major insurance company.

After analyzing them, I told him his annuity had been paying 3 percent below most competitive policies, that his "growth" mutual fund had practically stood still for the past five years (when most had at least doubled), and that his insurance policy was costing about twice as much as a policy I could sell him providing identical coverage. In baseball that's called "three strikes—you're out." He wanted out soon thereafter.

He was amazed. And shocked that his "insurance products" were not competitive. He'd trusted the big name behind the insurance company and hadn't looked any further than the dotted line. Investors can't take anything for granted anymore.

A Decade of Change

The competitor that has undergone the most profound internal change is insurance. In the past, the huge prosperous insurance companies had few outside challengers, and the insiders knew there was no need to underprice one another to any significant degree. Over the past decade, however, the industry's products have evolved from fat profit-margin items to more competitively priced offerings. When universal life insurance was introduced in the late seventies by E. F. Hutton a major change occurred. Policies had to compete with noninsurance product yields, such as CDs and bonds, as well as provide insurance at reasonable cost. Why? Because universal life was flexible, had fewer fees, and paid fair returns on the cash value in the policy. Whole life never did that. And that's all insurance companies used to sell.

Consumers began asking more questions about pricing and insurance contract nuances that often work in a noncompetitive way. Term insurance also became more popular, as well as more competitive in price. In many instances it is a sound way to obtain insurance. (But it too is less profitable than the old-fashioned whole life policies that built the imposing skyscrapers synonymous with insurance.) People have learned that borrowing (at about 5 percent) from an old policy (that was slowly building up cash value) is a good idea, especially if they reinvest the proceeds at 12 percent. Many policyholders began doing this, and since then insurance has never been the same.

THE INSURANCE INDUSTRY'S STRATEGY: "WE CAN BUY ANYTHING"

In the deregulation climate of recent years, insurance companies have used their huge capital base not to beat 'em, but to join 'em. They've bought a bunch of Wall Street players, mainly brokerage houses, which gave us, for example, Prudential-Bache and John Hancock/Tucker Anthony. Combined, they claim to be financial-service companies. Insurance companies already had the salesmen and assets. Now the trick is to dovetail their pocketbooks with their acquisitions. Most are having problems doing this. Because the sales forces have been left to follow their noses, many agents seem to prefer packaged products, such as mutual funds and partnerships, rather than trading stocks, bonds, or options as a broker does. And most do not want to acquire the necessary licenses, either. But the insurers recognize that the key words are *financial planning*. CIGNA Insurance Company is a good example of a company following an aggressive marketing approach. It is using its broker-dealer and investment adviser, CIGNA Securities, as a centerpiece to go after the upscale market—people with incomes of $200,000 or more and net worths of $2 million or more. Business is brisk. They have increased sales in their own limited partnerships from only $10 million in 1980 to $285 million in 1984.

ALL THINGS FOR ALL PEOPLE

A major strength of insurance companies is that they cover so many competitive bases. Whereas the insurance agent formerly handled estate planning and family risk avoidance through insurance, today that same agent markets various investments and asset planning. Most insurance companies have at least one financial planner salesman in each branch office who sells a variety of packaged products—not the least of which are insurance-related.

The insurance industry believes its agents' greatest strength is their intimate knowledge of clients, something brokers rarely have. Over the years, insurance agents have sat and talked with their clients, filled out their health and wealth forms, and as a result feel they have a much better chance of having these clients accept their recommendations.

INSURANCE COMPANY MONEY MANAGEMENT VERSUS BANKS

Although insurance companies are free from many safety questions now facing banks, they do have one major problem in common. They are notorious for poor performance in managing money. Most indexes show insurance company managed assets, along with bank money managers, consistently underperform independent Wall Street managers and broker money managers. Their mutual funds also tend to have mediocre track records. But, ironically, many insurance companies have finally brought their insurance products to a competitive level.

MAIN STREET: NO PLACE FOR YOUR MAIN MONEY

> My lawyer can sell more of my real estate deals than any real estate broker I can find. He has total client control.
> —A LOCAL REAL ESTATE DEVELOPER

There are a lot of ancillary competitors on the Main Street of every city and town who also want a piece of your wallet. The primary ones are independent financial planners, attorneys, CPAs, real estate developers, general promoters, and even real estate agents.

Attorneys and accountants are changing their approach to the financial service industry. Previously, they offered legal/accounting advice and billed by the hour. Period. Now more and more local lawyer/CPA firms are offering tax shelters, partnerships, lending sources, and even suggestions in placing your stock portfolio with money managers. This is called cross-fertilization. (It's also called greater profitability to the marketers—and greater risk to the investor.) There is more reason to consider "fertilizer" an appropriate term, especially when results from their investment advice are in. One guaranteed result I see is greater fees to your referring professional. The trick is to know why your professional is suggesting a particular investment and how he will be rewarded for his extracurricular efforts.

Here's how it works. A lawyer or accountant creates a partnership for his client, the developer, "allowing" certain other clients to invest in the project. Or an accountant might be compensated by a developer for referring his clients to that developer's partnership. Payments to these referral sources are made under the table or in other strange ways, such as paying excessive hourly billing rates or transferring "free" interests in partnerships in exchange for professional advice. It is difficult to know if or how your attorney/accountant or professional adviser is being paid for suggesting certain deals to you. By all means ask, but you still might never know. Several accountants and attorneys have told me that 10 percent to 15 percent of their associates market partnerships in this manner.

For your protection, any recommendation should be reviewed by another CPA/attorney/broker for a second opinion. Monthly, strange transactions are brought to me by new clients wondering what it is they bought a few years back through their attorney, accountant, or Main Street adviser. I'm not saying that all of Main Street's deals are bad, but they're not all good, and the potential for abuse is high.

Speaking of hidden charges, are you aware that lawyers make commissions as well as hourly fees? Recently I was told by an attorney that lawyers like to make sure their clients take out title insurance on their properties. Part of the reason is safety; part could be greed. It seems that lawyers are paid a commission (around 50 percent of the premium) on title insurance policies directly by the insurance company. They may be billing you for their paperwork time on the policy too. Rarely does an attorney credit your account with the fee he collects (though some do), although these fees won't make him rich. Lawyers call this practice "double-dipping."

I recently had a classic encounter with a client's lawyer. The client, a family receiving assets from a sizable estate, had asked me to meet with an attorney who was helping them with their financial affairs. The attorney admitted to no significant expertise in finance but termed himself a "jack-of-all-trades." I made several recommendations; one was that the consulting group at my firm should do a search for a professional money manager to oversee a portion of the estate's assets. The search was to be free and national in scope.

The lawyer rejected the idea and instead preferred to have a local broker manage the assets. The lawyer said the broker could "generate 13 percent with essentially no risk." I noted T-bills were at 5.8 percent and that such a statement was inconceivable to me. I said that if the broker could actually do such a feat, he could manage my assets. I was then rejected as an adviser. Ten days later I learned that the lawyer's own firm had its pension assets successfully managed by consultants found by my firm.

Lawyers can also be callous. My friend Lenny had a client holding thinly traded OTC stocks. When he died his attorney, saying he was acting for the estate, called and ordered Lenny to "sell everything at the market." Lenny told him that didn't make sense because the client's positions were too large in stocks that traded only about five hundred shares a day. But the lawyer insisted. "I don't want all that paperwork. Sell it today." Lenny called the deceased client's widow, who sided with Lenny, and the stocks were sold over a period of weeks. The lawyer called Lenny back, roaring about being overruled. "You'll never see the assets from those sales because you violated my instructions." He was right. In spite of saving the account a tidy sum, Lenny never got another trade in it. "How's that for justice?" he said.

MAIN STREET MAGIC: FROM THE ACCOUNTANT NEXT DOOR

Real estate developers thrive in Mathemagicland's jungle. Developers have always been in there selling, but now they have enlisted brokers, bankers, attorneys, CPAs, and insurance agents as selling agents. It is not always obvious who is doing what, why, and for whom. I remember well a recent real estate deal I reviewed. A client brought me a new prospectus put together by a young successful developer who had made it by way of the Vietnam war. To him, the jungle was home. He was intelligent, tough, and smooth. His prospectus had fees worse than any deal I'd ever seen. The developer required about $12,000 each from thirty investors in annual payments of approximately $3,000 for four years. The developer himself had invested a small sum, which he would recover completely when the investors bought in. Thus, after the investors put up their money, he got his out. That's because he was to manage the deal cheap.

The deal had problems: Layers of loans were needed to renovate a historic structure into an office building in a growing but still somewhat stagnant city in New England. Leveraged to the rafters, the deal was risky because it had to work exactly according to plan or necessitate raising additional capital from investors to avoid foreclosure.

When I read more closely I saw the real meat of the issue. Upon sale of the real estate, the investors got their money back and 50 percent of the profits. The developer, who had no money in the deal (as opposed to the investors, who had invested all the equity), also got 50 percent. A prime goal of the deal was to generate income for investors, yet the income was *also* to be divided fifty/fifty. I was learning fast how Main Street operated. "Profit splits" do have wider variances, but Wall Street seems almost charitable by comparison. The worst Wall Street profit split I'd seen was 65/35, with 85/15 the norm; the worst "income split" was about 90 percent investor/10 percent developer. Although the Main Street deal did offer the usual large tax benefits, it was like a racehorse carrying a three-hundred-pound jockey.

Curiosity got the best of me, and I called the developer and asked when he expected this deal to be sold. (He had released it for investors to review about two weeks earlier.) I expected him to say three or four months. His answer: It already had been sold—in two hours. I was stunned. It was one of the most surprising answers I had ever heard in ten years as a broker. How did he do it? "It's easy," he said. "My accountant makes about twenty phone calls." When I asked what that cost, the developer said he was billed for the two hours, and he gave the accountant all the partnership's business (plus other deals). He spoke vaguely of other perks the accountant received. I now figure those "perks" meant commissions. Live and learn. I already knew Wall Street could sell junk. But this developer and his accountant had not extracted just a pound of flesh—they had taken an arm and a leg. If the investor made money, it was by accident.

At the very least, in a Wall Street deal the brokerage firm acts as a middleman and gains nothing if the developer overcharges. The firm loses clients when the clients lose money. Thus the Street provides a filtering mechanism from the excessive charges that many Main Street deals have.

DISCOUNT BROKERS

Even though as a full-service broker I innately dislike discount brokerage firms, I admit they serve a purpose for some investors. In some instances, they are much cheaper than a full-service broker—especially for such basics as a onetime stock trade. Say you inherit fifty shares of IBM from an aunt and you want to turn that certificate into cash. You can sell your shares, take the money, and run. Or if you want to buy a no-load fund, go to a discount broker—a full-service broker considers a pure no-load fund a waste of his time.

But keep in mind that discounters may not be as cheap as you think on markup items such as OTC stocks and nonlisted bonds, and that no-load mutual funds often have other fees attached to them. In addition, discount brokers can have minimum transaction charges that are sometimes greater than their full-service counterparts. Finally, if you're going to reinvest any portion of the money, you should go to an experienced full-service broker for guidance. I know of a discounter who spent his evenings in the library in order to "advise" a client who was calling back the next day.

MY ADVICE TO THE INDIVIDUAL INVESTOR

Eventually the competition will be weeded out—by survival of the fittest—and in that battle capital will be king. In a decade or less we will probably be operating in the land of giants when dealing with our investments—for better or worse. At least technology will improve the bookkeeping.

In my chapters on tax shelters and mutual funds I will discuss at length the pros and cons of each of these types of investments. But remember, in order for your knowledge to work for you in any investment, you will need to deal with a knowledgeable salesperson who knows fees (obvious and less obvious), track records, and alternatives, and who either provides or can find good sources of quality investment support. If the banks and insurance companies can't manage their own investments better and are now a hybrid version of a 1970s broker and his decade-old ideas, then consider: They may be in competition for your money, but in terms of expertise and track records they're not really in the competition at all.

Chapter Seven

FINANCIAL PLANNERS: "LET US REHABILITATE YOUR FUTURE"

> Your purpose is to get up before those people and
> confuse them. And step two is to create a dependency.
> —WELL-KNOWN FINANCIAL PLANNER AT A 1984
> INDUSTRY CONVENTION

My business is prone to selling frenzies. About seven or eight years ago the buzzword was *financial planning*. Overnight a new challenge had been created, a new product was being introduced. It happens all the time, but this was different. The firm knew this would be a major product for years to come, so it wanted everyone to sign up for a course, read some books, and take several exams.

Mass training sessions on estate planning, taxes, and insurance needs were attended by almost the entire office. I was impressed with the logic of the idea, but I was on vacation that week, so I missed the first round of the educational barrage. I also had reservations about the seminars because I felt the topics might prove too complex to be understood in the time being devoted to them.

Two months later, scores of my fellow brokers had framed diplomas proclaiming them financial planners. No doubt their new knowledge was better than no knowledge at all, but the process scared me. While fortunately my associates can rely on our New York department, which produces quality plans for our clients (for which the broker is mainly an intermediary), other smaller brokerage houses or independent planners do not have such large-scale resources.

Financial planning has obvious merit because it forces people to focus on their financial affairs. Therein lies the appeal of the financial planning industry. Planners know most people don't think of estate planning, retirement, taxes, or college educations when they are struggling to pay their first mortgage. As income rises, expenses do too—the second house and mortgage payments are both larger—and long-term planning still seems far in the future. But a financial planner will tell you the time for planning is now. He wants you to earn the salary and pay the mortgage but leave the planning to him—for a fee and/or commission. He will analyze your financial needs, create, revise, and redesign the plan as circumstances change—again, for a fee.

Sounds logical? Yes. In theory. But are you prepared to take his financial advice just because he's dressed in a three-piece Brooks Brothers suit? Put the same tip in the mouth of a cigar-smoking tout at the racetrack, and people are looking for the exits. I am constantly amazed how many intelligent, well-educated investors simply take a financial planner's advice without inquiring, "Just how professional is this professional?"

FINANCIAL PLANNING: A PRODUCT, NOT A PROFESSION

The race is on: Wall Street, banks, insurance companies, and independent planners are all competing for your attention in this new financial planning arena. The stakes are high. All participants know that financial planning involves access to an investor's entire financial situation and therefore, except in a fee-only situation, it is a superb way to capture assets. This hidden agenda is the primary goal of all financial organizations, because once the asset is "captured" it is only a matter of time before it will create a fee. (And later re-create a fee.) In order to "capture" your assets the participants have to convince you that they are the most efficient, prudent, and knowledgeable and can offer you the widest range of products and long-term service—usually their own products and services. Rub a financial planner hard enough, and the insurance agent or broker or lawyer soon begins to show through. For example, one study analyzed various financial plans and discovered that five out of eight recommendations by the Aetna insurance company involved insurance. Seven of eight recommendations by IDS/American Express were IDS products. Not surprising.

Despite attempts by the financial planning industry to foster an image that side-steps the stigma of selling—usually associated with insurance agents and brokers—such self-serving posturing, as advisers rather then salesmen, is not always valid. Financial planners, like their cousins the insurance agents and brokers of Wall Street, often receive benefits for selling their wares. For example, last year Oppenheimer Management Corp. sponsored a sales contest for financial planners, brokers, and others who sell its mutual funds. The following is a list of prizes awarded to financial planners for attaining various minimum sales levels:

FINANCIAL PLANNER SALES CONTEST

$100,000 and 5 sales	Casio pocket color television, or Cobra cordless telephone, or Simac II Gelataio 800 ice-cream maker
$250,000 and 5 sales	Sony compact disk player, or Canon PC 10 personal copier, or Panasonic microwave/convection oven
$500,000 and 10 sales	Sony Video 8 camcorder, or attache case with $1,000 cash, or Waterford crystal barware
$1 million and 10 sales	Honda scooter, or IBM PC laptop computer, or Sony rear-projection videoscope TV
$3 million and 10 sales	Blackglama mink coat, or IBM Personal Computer XT, or Sony entertainment system
Grand prize: Highest total over $5 million and 10 sales	Porsche 944 turbo, or Jaguar XJ-S, or Corvette coupe or convertible

Wall Street Journal, 11/24/86, reprinted by permission. Copyright © Dow Jones & Co., Inc., 1986. All rights reserved.

It all comes down to one thing: Financial planners (FP's) are after your money. That is why you are better off thinking of financial planning as a product rather than a profession. Especially when a company asks for a "piece of your future." They really want a piece of your wallet. Your "future" is big business for them.

SELF-REGULATION: AN FP'S DREAM OR A CLIENT'S NIGHTMARE?

In spite of all the "letters" financial planners print on their business cards, the professional financial planner is not licensed because there are no licenses. He is not regulated because there are no regulations. And furthermore, the federal government doesn't care about his dealings because it doesn't know who he is or what he's dealing in.

As a result, there are quite a few FPs who live on Caribbean islands or in Switzerland and whose fat bank accounts have other people's money in them.

To regulate the process of becoming a financial planner would require an amendment of law. According to an SEC representative, the Investment Advisers Act of 1940 would have to be amended before an organization like the SEC could begin certification or regulation. This doesn't seem likely for quite some time. In fact, one lawyer and former chairman of the Chicago Estate Planning Council feels that it will never happen because "the breadth of the field effectively prohibits any regulation."

The SEC says that out of an estimated 250,000 financial planners, 10,000 are registered investment advisers (so-called RIAs), a designation that is acquired by only disclosing one's background and finances and taking a brief exam. The chief of the office of disclosure and adviser regulations at the commission said, "It's not a credential and it's not a degree." The SEC also objects to the use of the initials *RIA* on business cards and letterheads, no doubt because it implies regulation and expertise.

How does someone decide to become an FP? Well, take a relative of mine. He's in his eighties, retired, but he still wanted to work at something. He soon discovered two things he could do without a license: marriage counseling and financial planning. He debated awhile—and golf finally won. Maybe your financial planner was considering golf, but threw out his back and became a financial planner by forfeit.

Recently, a document was awarded to Boris "Bo" Regaard of Tampa, Florida, identifying him as a certified financial planner and a member of the largest association of financial planners. Bo has a few weaknesses: He can be bought for a meal or two, and he pauses frequently near fire hydrants. He is in fact part poodle and part schnauzer and had been registered by John Gargan, a financial planner, to prove a point: "Just because a person calls himself a financial planner doesn't mean that he is one."

EDUCATION: A FINANCIAL PLANNER CAN TAKE IT OR LEAVE IT

In the absence of government interest or regulation, the industry has attempted to educate and regulate itself. This is better than no regulation at all, but have you noticed a lot of chicken coops in this book with a grinning fox on guard outside? Recent *New York Times* articles cautioned people that financial planning is "still a pretty fragmented industry. And there has to be consumer awareness when there is no regulation and review." Nor is there a "long-recognized, degree-granting pattern" of education in planning. The best-known educational progams are coorespondence courses. Industry organizations have been in existence since the sixties and differe in size, background, bias, cetification requirements, and credentials.

The Institute for Certified Financial Planners is the best-known of the organizations and represents students and graduates of the College for Financial Planning. Recently, it had 23,000 students enrolled in an eighteen-month correspondence course costing $1,800. Since 1972 it has certified over ten thousand CFPs. Of late, the designation CFP, now conferred by the college, was handed over to the control of the International Board of Standards and Practices for CFPs. Now any college or university qualifying under the board's standards will be able to confer the CFP. Several universities now award an undergraduate degree in financial planning, but they are the exception, not the rule.

The American College in Bryn Mawr, Pennsylvania, which was originally founded to train financial employees specifically in insurance, now has an adjunct consulting program that takes four years to complete and graduates chartered financial consultants (ChFCs). American College also has a master of science in financial services degree for planners who have taken advanced courses.

The International Association of Financial Planners (IAFP), founded in 1969, has 22,000 members in ninety-seven chapters throughout fifty states and fifteen European countries. Ninety-three percent of its members are eithcr licensed insurance agents or insurance brokers, and 51 percent have a license to deal in some or all forms of securities. John Cahill, chairman of the IAFP, states, "We're currently in the process of developing what we call the Registry, which includes a test, plus minimum standards and guidelines."

The IAFP's guidelines include: (1) three years in practice as a planner; (2) a degree from a regionally accredited educational institution with a financial planning cirriculum or a law or business degree; (3) an interview; (4) written references; (5) thirty hours per year of continuing education; and (6) an agreement to abide by the code of ethics and bylaws of the IAFP. As of 1988 about 1,000 people had qualified under these guidelines. Does this make you feel a little better? It leaves only 21,000 more to do so, or 95 percent. The IAFP is also the organization that certified Bo. The industry has a long way to go. You may be better off with Bo.

There are other organizations: the National Association of Personal Financial Advisors is a fast-growing group which charges fees rather than commissions. Another new organization, the International Association of Registered Financial Planners, based in Tampa, Florida, is striving to set high standards for a small select membership.

TOO MANY FINANCIAL PLANNING ORGANIZATIONS: TOO LITTLE CONTROL

To be fair, many of the above organizations have rigorous guidelines for qualifying as a financial planner, for graduating from their programs, or for being listed in their registries. And they are sincere in their intentions. But the range of standards only serves to point up a major problem: There is no single organization to coordinate qualifications and regulatory needs of this fast-growing industry. Even the president of the College for Financial Planning admits, "Financial planning is not a profession. . . . In my view, financial planning is an emerging profession."

There is another major problem with self-regulation. The very organizations claiming to set high standards for their accreditation are themselves being supported by companies (for example, an insurance unit of ITT Corporation) that are pushing their own financial products. These companies contribute to advertising campaigns telling the public when and how to select a financial planner and promise prizes, such as a trip around the world, to top salesmen. Obviously, the financial planners who belong to some of these organizations are under pressure to sell certain products. The buyer—and loser—might be you.

Meanwhile, the abuses are numerous. One financial planner from New Hampshire lost $6 million of his clients' money after telling them his real estate partnerships were buying shopping malls and properties only in New England—as opposed to thousands of miles away. His clients felt safe with him because they were close enough to know the properties they were to own. But there was a major problem: His New England pyramid collapsed because he hadn't bought any real estate, but their money was gone nevertheless.

An Arizona financial planner invested $1.1 million of a client's money in a worthless scheme to develop and market the meat of a genetically superior rabbit. Other abuses include bogus money market accounts, Ponzi schemes (selling pyramids), and fake real estate partnerships. The Council of Better Business Bureaus estimates that con artists pretending to be financial planners have defrauded people of $90 million from 1985–1987. The council and the North American Securities Administration jointly issued a nationwide alert, warning consumers of an "epidemic of fraud and abuse currently plaguing the financial planning industry."

I feel that someday this lack of regulation will change. But for now the potential for disaster hangs over the situation like an overly inflated balloon. People are baring their financial souls to these "professionals" and following their recommendations to the letter. They may be playing financial Russian roulette.

WHAT MAKES A FINANCIAL PLANNER TICK? HIS PAYCHECK

Financial planners tell you they are doing you a big favor—getting your financial life in order. Maybe. But their first motivation is money. In 1986 planners earned an average income of $60,000—taking care of your money and their wallets. There are three distinct ways they charge you for their services, and each method has its own process and perspective.

Fee-based planner. It is easiest for a financial planner to print up business cards, rent an office, and enter the field at this level because he does not usually have the securities license(s) required in order to sell securities to his clients (and thereby gain a commission too). Instead he charges either a flat fee for a plan or an hourly fee, depending on the scope and complexity of the plan. A fee-only planner claims objectivity and no conflict of interests since there are no commissions involved. The fees for these plans can vary from a few hundred dollars to thousands. Hourly fees range from $75 to $100 per hour and may quickly add up to more than a client might have paid in commissions.

Commission-only planner. This planner makes his profits only from the commissions on products purchased in carrying out the recommended financial plan. Therefore, he is usually associated with brokerage firms or insurance companies. The rationale behind this system is that implementation is a necessity of financial planning—commission fees will be generated no matter where the plan is eventually executed, so why pay fees over and above the commissions that will eventually be charged during implementation? On the other hand, be wary if too many product suggestions are from the planner's firm.

Fee and commission planner. The third form of planner makes his profits from both fees and commissions. It is not unusual for a major brokerage firm to "farm out" the proposal phase of the plan to a third party, such as an accounting or law firm, which then creates all or part of the plan for the client. The fee often represents this farm-out procedure, but not always. Sometimes fees are levied purely for profit and reflect the widespread belief that "you get what you pay for." As one bank official put it, "We make them pay." Remember that the fee and commission planner is not always who you might expect. While banks may charge significant fees for their plans, they also collect commissions for real estate partnerships, profit/commission on CD investments, and also provide insurance products and stock trading for additional commission income.

FINANCIAL PLANNERS: GLORIFIED SALESMEN

Insurance Companies

Insurance companies were the early entrants into the financial planning arena through their marketing of life insurance policies. In fact, there was a time when an insurance policy was almost the sum total of everyone's financial plan. Until just recently, however, many experts have felt that the insurance industry has managed to fumble the ball. The major companies have been slow to diversify their efforts and to add mutual funds and other basic investment vehicles to their inventory of products. With the deregulation of the financial services industry in general, insurance companies are now moving into money management, stock brokerage, venture capital management, equipment leasing, and even real estate syndication. However, in spite of aggressive advertising campaigns to the contrary, insurance companies are still perceived as narrow and staid. A recent study on financial planning conducted by *Research & Forecasts* found that only 5 percent of the 1,130 adults interviewed would turn to an insurance agent for financial advice—even though the majority still expected to purchase their insurance from an insurance agent.

Although the overall results of this study had to be discouraging to the insurance industry, it is counting on its basic product—insurance—to pull it into the 1990s with a large share of the financial planning market. Insurance is still the primary product in most plans, in part because so many planners (independent and affiliated) have insurance licenses and are marketing policies because they can make big bucks through the policies' high commissions.

As Andrew Tobias pointed out in *The Invisible Bankers,* the insurance industry employs three times as many people as it takes to run the postal service. That's quite an army pushing financial planning. Recently several major companies have purchased large brokerage firms, and more mergers are anticipated. Because of their massive financial resources and purchasing ability, insurance companies are changing their emphasis from insurance sales to the sale of other financial services through their new subsidiaries. Many insurance companies now offer a computer analysis of an investor's financial situation for a moderate fee of $100 to $300. That's the "teaser." They then sell the investor insurance policies and annuities as part of a personalized financial plan. That's the profit.

Banks

As the last arrival in financial planning, banks are attempting to duplicate services offered by brokerage firms. They now offer a variety of services at various costs and are promoting planning programs to the smaller investor through a computer analysis for as little as $80, much like their competitors. But they are also after bigger game. For example, Bank of America offers a special financial planning service to key executives of large corporations for a fee of $7,000 to $10,000. These plans are described as "strategic" plans and often utilize bank-related products, such as jumbo money market deposit accounts and estate trust services. This is worthy of note, because banks (and attorneys, CPAs, and independent planners) who describe themselves as fee-only planners (and therefore more objective) still manage to find ways to offer product suggestions that add to their own bottom lines.

Given all those sick loans south of the border and east of the

Greenwich Meridian, banks' bottom lines are in need of help these days, so they are marketing the necessity of a plan in concert with their oft-emphasized image of stability and safety. It is interesting that such image reinforcement comes at a time when banks are failing at a rate exceeded only during the Depression. More than forty banks have failed recently, and seven hundred more are on the "problem list" of the FDIC. And the FDIC ought to know—for as banks will tell you, the FDIC is there to insure them. I certainly doubt the FDIC can cover all those losses if all seven hundred go under. Makes you remember that your deposits at FDIC-insured banks are covered only to a degree—$100,000 per depositor. If you have more than $100,000 at some of the problem banks, you are a risk taker for sure. I'd rather deal in stock options for my risk capital.

The great rivalry shaping up in financial planning appears to be between banks and brokers. Both are competing actively for the upscale market and offer less expensive services to the middle-tier market. The First National Bank of Kansas City has opened its own financial planning department and offers services from $250 to $500 for its standard program, and charges a minimum of $2,000 for its upper-tier program. An accepted guideline for middle-tier is income under $125,000 and/or net worth of under $1 million. Upper-tier is income over $200,000 and net worth over $2 million. The ranking of clients who are not clearly in either category is left to the individual FP.

Wall Street's Brokers as FPs

Wall Street firms claim that their services and brokers are the best in the financial planning industry. Shearson Lehman/American Express was among the first to label its brokers "financial planners." Merrill Lynch now calls its brokers "financial consultants," and Prudential-Bache has spent a large portion of its advertising budget marketing itself as a financial planning source, asking for a "piece of your future," as well as the commissions from helping you plan for it. Most large firms, such as Shearson and Merrill Lynch, offer several forms of financial plans depending on your income and net worth, and the financial complexity of your assets. Hutton has been involved in this area for almost a decade. It also provides counseling, investment implementation of your plan, and follow-up consultations, which are usually free.

Wall Street maintains that because its brokers have day-to-day dealings in a variety of investment areas, they are better able to provide a more experienced, diverse service. Brokerage firms are spending large sums training their brokers and advertising their financial planning services. They argue that they are in the field to stay because they are already involved in all facets of the business, whereas newly arrived competitors will stay in the field only as long as their recently acquired services are profitable and competitive. It is a legitimate argument, but only if your AE/registered representative/broker, now dubbed a "financial consultant/planner," has been trained for that specific role.

Independent Planners: For the Price of a Shingle

When you use an insurance company, a bank, or a broker, you at least know that your adviser has had some background in finance and some education in financial planning. This is far from true of independent planners. Anyone who hangs up a shingle can be a financial planner. And many are. Remember Bo—he's the one with the tail.

Independent planners have many faces. They can be attorneys, CPAs, or independent insurance agents who charge from as little as $100 to as much as $10,000 a plan. They usually describe themselves as fee-only planners, but they sometimes make additional fees from the sponsors of large investment projects that they have offered to their clients. Occasionally, these fees are in the form of an illegal bonus. It is difficult to know how frequently compensation is paid to independent planners, let alone whether it is legal or not.

INTERVIEW SEVERAL FINANCIAL PLANNERS BEFORE YOU JUMP

If you are going to buy a financial plan, you should take the search for the right financial planner very seriously. His advice may be with you for a long time. Plan to interview three to five people over a number of weeks. Ask friends and business associates for names. Many top brokers and planners report that their new business comes almost entirely from referrals. If this doesn't work, consult the industry's organizations.

On the surface, especially in terms of fees and motivations, the major participants seem quite similar. So the real question is: After

Table 7.1 / AUTOMATED PLANS OFFERED BY MAJOR COMPANIES

Automated financial plans generally consist of a standard text into which a customer's particular data, ascertained through a questionnaire, are inserted. The computer then makes calculations of projected needs and generic investment recommendations based on the data. The results are mailed to the client or presented during a meeting between planner and client, at which time specific product recommendations may be made. The following list of plans was compiled by Jeffrey R. Lauterbach, an associate editor of Financial Planning, the leading publication in the financial planning industry. A member of the Georgia Bar, he studied automated plans in depth for more than a year and has written extensively about consumer financial topics since 1976. Overall ratings are based on objectivity, readability, goal orientation, and the general usefulness for an aware, concerned consumer of the information contained in the plan and supplementary materials.

	AETNA PERSONAL FINANCIAL ANALYSIS, Personal Financial Security Div., Aetna, 151 Farmington Ave., Hartford CT 06156	CHEMICAL BANK PERSONAL FINANCIAL PLAN, Financial Planning Dept., 52 Broadway 11th Floor, NY NY 10004, 800/243-6226	MERRILL LYNCH FINANCIAL PATHFINDER, Merrill Lynch Financial Planning, 25 Broadway, NY NY 10004, 800/221-3844	PRUDENTIAL-BACHE TOTAL FINANCIAL PLAN, Prudential-Bache Service Center, P.O. Box 5002, Clifton NJ 07015, 800/654-5454	THE CONSUMER FINANCIAL INSTITUTE PERSONAL PROFILE & PROJECTIONS REPORT, The Consumer Financial Institute, 288 Walnut St., Newton, MA 02160, 617/965-9652	E. F. HUTTON MONEY ALLOCATION PROGRAM (MAP), Personal Financial Management Dept., 26 Broadway RM. 1132, NY 10004, 212/742-5253	IDS PERSONAL FINANCIAL ANALYSIS, 5◻ IDS Tower, Minneapolis, MN 55402, 800/IDS-IDEA
Cost	$250	$70*	$250	$0	$175	$150	$250
Turnaround	2 weeks	3 to 4 weeks	1 month	24 hours	3 weeks	2 weeks	2 week
Delivery method	agent	mail	mail	broker	mail	broker	broker/agent
Income group suitability	$30,000-$100,000	$25,000-$100,000	$40,000-$140,000	$50,000+	$25,000+	$25,000-$70,000	$30,000-$80,000
Availability	nearest agent	through NY office	nearest office or phone	nearest office or phone	phone	nearest office	nearest office
BASIC SUBJECTS COVERED & HOW WELL							
Personal financial statement	G	F	F	G	F	F	G
Personal budgeting	O	G	P	O	F	F	O
Education funding	F	F	G	F	G	G	F
Survivorship/Estate	F	F	G	F	G	G	F
Retirement	F	F	G	F	G	G	F
Disability	P	P	G	F	G	G	F
Other Insurance	P	P	G	O	G	O	O
Investment alternatives	O	G	F	O	G	G	O
OTHER AREAS COVERED							
Tax estate	Y	N	Y	Y	Y	N	Y
Non-investment planning strategies	Y	Y	Y	N	Y	Y	Y
Alternative risk assumptions	N	N	N	N	N	Y	N
Short-term planning goals, e.g. vacation, boat, home	N	Y	N	N	N	Y	Y
Overall rating (1-10)	5**	7**	8**	4**	9	9**	6**

* $60 for Chemical customers
** "Personal consultations included with plan may substantially increase its value.
G = good   F = fair   P = poor   O = no coverage
Reprinted from the Washington Post, November 4, 1984.

the fees are paid and the homework is done, who really offers the best product? The reports usually look professional; some are even leatherbound. But it is not the length or the looks that makes a good plan. It's the quality of the plan and the ease with which it can be understood. One independent study was published in the *Washington Post* in late 1984 by an associate editor of *Financial Planning,* the leading publication of the financial planning industry. The study took place over a period of a year and focused on the less expensive, basic automated plans of banks, brokers, insurance companies, and independent planners.

While this analysis did not cover all potential sources for a less expensive plan, it is a fair start in terms of understanding how to judge a planner's services. An important caution: Many planners leave several items unreviewed, thereby reducing the effectiveness of the overall plan. They also make mistakes, so review your plan for errors. An extra zero in or out or misplaced decimal points can make a big difference. Ideally, a financial plan should review an individual's entire circumstances. Partial reviews can be misleading and/or counterproductive—like taking a physical exam with your hat, socks, and sunglasses on.

WHO NEEDS FINANCIAL PLANNING?

Most investors do not understand what planning is, who provides it, and why it is of value. A trade magazine, *Registered Representative,* recently conducted a survey in conjunction with an article on financial planning. Over half the people who responded had never heard the term *financial planning* before. About 3 percent said they would see a broker for planning services. About 1 percent said they would use their accountant. A majority said they would go to a bank for advice, in spite of the fact that few banks offered the service. In general, the respondents knew almost nothing about the subject. Which proves that the market has nowhere to go but up—because financial planning is a necessity. And chances are you need it too.

Most planners feel that any individual earning a minimum of $30,000 per year is a candidate for some type of financial review, and probably a financial plan. Under those guidelines, a lot of people qualify for help, and you too are probably in that category. SRI International has conducted a study of American households, and here's what it found:

— There are 7.1 million households in the United States whose occupants have pretax earnings of $30,000 or more. Of these, over 50 percent have a net worth in excess of $200,000.

— About 90 percent of these affluent people do not consider themselves experts in managing their own financial affairs.

— About 99 percent of these people do not have written comprehensive financial plans.

Obviously, to date, few people have actually worked with a financial planner. You might be among the 99 percent who have not yet taken that step. If this is true, you should consider beginning to search for a financial planner—a good one—to analyze your financial situation and put your financial affairs in order.

WILL A FINANCIAL PLAN SAVE ME MONEY?

One firm analyzed its 1983 middle-tier program to determine how effictive it was in terms of dollar savings. A client qualified for this program with an income of $25,000 to $100,000 and a net worth of up to $500,000. (Being above or below those figures would change the type of program the client was offered.) The following is a typical middle-tier client profile.

Age	47 years old
Income	$120,000
Net worth	$450,000
Funds available for investments	$125,000
Number of children	three
Occupations	Business executive, doctor, lawyer
Investment characteristics	Taxability and growth

Clients who use the middle-tier program, costing $2,000 on average, were estimated to have gained the following savings:

Federal income tax savings	$13,000
Education savings via prefunding	$30,000
Federal estate tax savings	$45,000

As you can see, the savings from planning in the above three areas far outweighs the initial $2,000 fee.

TOO MANY PLANS: HELP!

There is a lot of confusion out there regarding the complexity, availability, and marketing of financial plans. Remember four-legged Bo? Well, my dog Egbert is not a planner, but he has been prospected by several. Because Egbert has his name attached to a few of my ventures, he's made it onto mailing lists. He's been offered all sorts of plans, at varying prices, and can't make up his mind. I suspect he's waiting for the first planner who guarantees Milkbones for life. He is a prime example of how plans should reflect a client's needs.

With so many different plans available today it is difficult to appreciate the various services a planner offers for the price. Most financial planning departments and even the independent financial planners have levels of plans that vary according to the complexity of your financial situation and the anticipated changes that may occur in the future as to salaries, inheritance, and so on. When you are interviewing a financial planner also ask him or her to advise you about what level of plan in terms of complexity and work on his part your situation requires—and approximately how much it will cost. Most planners have program summaries that take into account client parameters, fees, and services provided at various levels. Review a few. Use this as a starting point to understand what is available and for how much.

If you feel you may need a plan but hesitate to commit much time and money immediately, the basic computer analysis is a good start. Several extremely basic ones are even free. Obviously, there is no way a computer plan can give you the fine-tuning that a more expensive plan can. It's like comparing a Chevy Nova to a Rolls-Royce. Nonetheless, if you're looking for basic essential transportation, a Nova is going to get you there. While they aren't the Rolls of the industry, these computer plans will force you to look at your financial affairs in greater detail. They will lay out for you what you ought to be aware of—your assets and your liabilities—and they will usually note glaring weaknesses and points needing prompt attention and action, such as a need for a will, insurance policies, or college funding planning.

Don't be too quick to look down on the cheaper basic computer plans. Even in the $1,500 to $2,500 range, 60 percent of the more lengthy reports is made up of computer-generated information.

Computer interfacing is very common in almost any financial report. The litmus test of the industry is: If your report comes back within six months from a major planner, a sizable portion was probably computer boilerplate. Complex plans take money and time.

WHAT IS THE PROCESS FOR DOING A FINANCIAL PLAN?

Once you have selected a financial planner, in order to produce a comprehensive report both you and he must put in good quality time.

— First, you must determine which level of plan is most suited to your situation.
— Next, the planner will ask you to gather information on your financial situation and to fill out a questionnaire that will be used as the frame of reference during your meeting. A complete gathering of all relevant data *prior* to initiating the "discovery" period is critical. The questionnaire is usually from six to twenty pages in length and asks for such information as all relevant insurance policies (disability, life, casualty), past tax returns, portfolio listings, and company or personal retirement fund information.
— At this point, you and the financial planner meet to review materials; this conference lasts from about one to four hours, sometimes longer.
— Finally, the financial planner presents you with his analysis of your financial situation and his recommendations for providing you and your family a secure financial future.
— Now the selling begins in earnest.

DOES A FINANCIAL PLANNER NEED TO KNOW EVERYTHING?

Yes, almost everything. The more the better in all cases. The following are typical questions that are covered in a quality report. If you feel the questions apply to your financial situation, yet they have not been reviewed by yourself or your advisers, then you need a financial plan that will address those areas in detail.

TYPICAL FINANCIAL PLANNING CONSIDERATIONS

Investment Planning

Do you have an investment philosophy?

Do you have defined investment goals?

Have you been introduced to various investments and services available in today's marketplace?

Have you worked with any investment advisers before?

Insurance Needs

How much life insurance do you and your spouse now have?

How much do you and your spouse need?

Does your present policy allow for estate settlement costs? Family needs? Transfer of property or business interests?

Does your home have adequate insurance against replacement needs?

Is your personal liability coverage sufficient and up-to-date?

Retirement Plans

Have you and your spouse made any plans for retirement? Investments? Or pension plans?

Will your company pension plans cover all your retirement income needs?

Have you evaluated the various methods of pension fund distributions together with various target retirement dates?

Will you be able to maintain your present standard of living?

Do you know what you can expect from social security?

Does your health insurance coverage remain the same, or will it change?

Estate Planning

Have you and your spouse made wills? Are they up-to-date?

Do you have a clear picture of your assets minus your liabilities?

Do you know what your death will cost your estate and heirs?

Have you considered testamentary trusts, gifts, and charitable bequests?

Does the surviving spouse have adequate liquidity of assets and a livable income?

Business Planning

If you are an independent businessperson, have you considered the corporate form of organization?

Upon your death, how will your business be disposed of or transferred to partners or family members?

Do you wish to use or enlarge potential fringe benefits as corporate owner?

Do you need key man insurance for your company or private venture?

Are you adequately insulated from lawsuits for malpractice, bankruptcy, etc.?

I TOLD THE FP EVERYTHING: NOW WHAT?

After you have had an interview with a financial planner and answered the preceding questions, either in a written form or during the meeting, he will analyze the information. This assessment will be presented in reports that contain the following:

— a profile of your financial situation. This is a summary of all pertinent data, such as net worth, income, relationships, attitudes, etc., in order to provide your financial adviser with an overview of your financial affairs.

— an analysis of this data. The breakdown is presented much in the manner data were collected—estate, business, tax and retirement needs, and interrelationships.

— specific recommendations for making the most of your income, assets, and tax bracket, and for achieving your financial goals.

The reports average between one hundred and two hundred pages, depending on the level of plan you have requested. Net worth statements, income schedules, expense schedules, cash flow statements, income tax computations, and an updated investment program (recommendations) are typical items included in their texts.

YOUR FINANCIAL FUTURE INCLUDES A FINANCIAL PLANNER'S FEE

Financial planners are not selling plans for humanitarian reasons. They're doing it for money. As they plan your financial future, they are also enhancing theirs. Studies in the marketing of planning show that most clients put their plan into effect through the group that created it.

If you go to a financial planner who recommends that you buy a mutual fund, chances are you will buy the fund through him. The same applies with securities and insurance. That's the payoff. One multiservice financial firm's estimate showed that the average upper-middle–tier plan created about $4,500 in commission revenues. Further analyses showed the revenues came from the sale of the following:

Tax shelters/direct investments	30%
Stocks	23%
Insurance	18%

Mutual funds	12%
Professional money management	10%
Annuities	5%
Bonds	2%

The above list doesn't begin to cover the complex world of financial planning, but it does illustrate my greatest concern: The analysis of your situation might be done thoroughly and well, but if it is poorly carried out or lacks objectivity and a clear sense of purpose (*yours*, not the planner's), much of the plan's potential for a positive effect will be lost.

This is also not to say that fee planning without commissions is the answer. There are too many good investments worth the price of those commissions. And there are too many independent planners who are getting under-the-table fees for pointing you in an investment's direction. They might provide a good financial plan—but can they put it into effect? The investor must oversee all phases in the execution of his financial plan. As Yogi Berra said, "It ain't over till it's over."

PUTTING YOUR FINANCIAL PLAN INTO ACTION

You all know the cliché about the person who can't see the forest for the trees. He sees the trees—the parts of something—but he fails to see the forest. He never gets the big picture.

Well, the person who goes to the financial planner can't see the trees because he is dazzled by the forest. He meets with the financial planner, fills out questionnaires, and is given personal service. Finally, the financial planner presents him with a plan—a forest. The client is amazed that this forest—profile, analysis, and recommendations—belongs to him. And since it is his forest, he doesn't bother to inspect the trees.

Trees matter. The trees are your potential investments. Remember that a financial plan is but another financial product. The whole is equal only to the sum of the parts. Your plan is made up of complex strategies and investments, and each one matters—whether it is a mutual fund, an insurance policy, or a trust document. Each recommendation should be executed with care, which is why the financial planner has such great power. And why the stakes are so high in this new industry. I'm amazed at how many people totally accept the recommendations of a financial planner—on everything. They don't know if he's a tree expert, or if his trees are healthy—they just think the forest looks good.

YOU OWN A PLAN: NOW WHAT?

Buyer beware: A financial plan is a good idea. But once you get one, take it home and read it over carefully. Then ask yourself these questions:

— Are there any mistakes/misunderstandings in the plan report? (They do happen.) Do I understand the plan?
— Does it include everything it should cover?
— Has it stated my financial goals and objectives clearly?
— What is this plan trying to sell me?
— Is my financial planner an expert in the areas he is suggesting for investment? Will he do follow-ups later?
— What are the alternatives to what he is trying to sell me—and to him?
— If he is a commission planner, are his recommendations too slanted toward certain products?
— If he is a fee-only planner, might he be receiving a bonus from someone for pointing me to a particular investment? This practice is not as rare as you might think. Many a real estate partnership has been spawned in such a manner.
— Do the recommendations require too much overseeing, such as stock monitoring, tax shelters, estate planning devices, or gifting plans?
— Is the plan too complex? Can I work easily within the guidelines?
— Is there a built-in review process?

Financial planning can give you a more secure future. Presently only 2 percent of the population over age sixty-five feels financially secure. With an intelligent use of financial planning this percentage can grow. And you can be a part of it. But there is another side to this coin.

The area of financial planning is also creating the new gold rush. Prospecting has reached all-time highs, and *you* are the virgin territory being staked out for financial planning claims on your assets, your 1040, your future W-2s, and eventually your estate (because your plan will likely generate income for your planner long after you don't). While you're around, make sure that you remain in charge.

Chapter Eight

PROFESSIONAL MONEY MANAGERS: MAGICIANS OF THE MARKETPLACE

> It takes twenty-five dollars and an active heartbeat to
> become a money manager.
> —MONEY MANAGER SEARCH SPECIALIST

Several years ago, my old desk partner, Lenny Leftover, was asked
by the office manager to help out a loser rookie broker. Norman
worked hard, made hundreds of calls, but he just couldn't get people
to do business with him. Norman couldn't close; he didn't "ask for
the order." When Norman resisted Lenny's tutoring, Lenny in a fit
of annoyance threatened to prospect Norman's mother away from
him. He picked up the phone and called information in Norman's
hometown. Just as Lenny was dialing his mother's number, Norman
relented. He promised he'd listen to Lenny from then on.

Lenny gave Norman his duties for the next sixty days: He was to
call prospects for appointments, attempt to sell nothing on the
phone, schedule appointments for three people to visit, and say
nothing during the meeting. The only guideline: Norman was to
prospect clients using professional money management (and mutual
funds for smaller clients) as the recommended investment. The three
people who showed up at the client's door were Norman, Lenny,
and a wholesaler/representative for a money manager. Lenny and
the wholesaler did all the talking. Norman was only allowed to nod.
If Norman said anything, the prospecting assistance program would
end, and so would Norman's career.

Norman called like crazy and made appointments . . . period.
These three musketeers covered the streets of Boston. The results:
Norman made out like a bandit. Lenny covered lunch money and
has his memories. And the wholesaler—who looked like Robert
Redford—dated at least a third of the secretaries of Norman's cli-

ents. Today, Norman is a Big Producer, and the rookies all want to know how he did it.

HOW MANY ZEROES IN SIX BILLION

Today, there is about $2 trillion in the hands of professional money managers—the only thing as large and growing as fast is the U.S. government's total debt. The amount of money under management is equal to the value of *all* stocks listed on the NYSE.

Money management has proven itself a growth industry. The fees to manage this money are over $6 billion annually. It is also estimated that money managers control 60 percent of all stocks and bonds in America, and the commissions from such management are even larger than the management fees. Sound like big business? You bet. But you would be more surprised to know how the investment decisions of these managers affect everyone—not just their clients.

WHAT DOES A MONEY MANAGER DO?

First of all, a money manager should not be confused with a financial planner. A financial planner addresses a client's entire financial situation and offers advice on such diverse topics as insurance policies, taxes, investments, college expenses, etc., and then works within a plan to achieve certain financial goals. The money manager, on the other hand, has a much narrower role. He manages a client's money by creating a portfolio of investments from a variety of products commonly found on Wall Street—such as stocks, bonds, and T-bills. He then oversees that portfolio, buying and selling when he sees fit.

The largest number of managers work for bank trust departments and insurance companies. Both of these participants market themselves as conservative and attempt to attract accounts through their image of size and experience. Independent manager firms and brokerage firms are the other major forms of money manager. Most independents are scattered throughout the country but have varying degrees of ties with brokerage firms.

HOW IS WORKING WITH A MONEY MANAGER DIFFERENT FROM WORKING WITH A BROKER?

The major difference is that you are literally placing your money in a money manager's hands and telling him to use his own judgment.

As a norm, managers do not have to consult with you on buying or selling your portfolio because you have given them the power of discretionary trading (something I tell you to avoid with brokers). That is a prime example of how much power a money manager has.

WHO USES A MONEY MANAGER?

Typical clients are trusts, pension accounts, and wealthy individuals. The smallest of managed accounts normally has assets of at least $100,000, although a minimum of $250,000 is quickly becoming the norm. A more common size is $1 million or more. Some large pension funds worth billions diversify their assets by employing the services of as many as fifty to one hundred different money managers and regularly fire the poor performers.

Speaking of "fire," I remember one broker who worked with an M.D. who was a burn specialist. The client referred to his patients as "crispy critters." He'd joke that his medical practice had become secondary to trading stocks. He gave his broker the private number of his operating room and insisted that the broker call him with quotes, but dial in saying it was a "medical emergency." My friend didn't approve of talking to the doctor under those circumstances, knowing he had a "crispy critter" on the OR table, so he eventually persuaded the doctor to sign up with a money manager. As a result, phone calls stopped and the OR was left in peace. The doctor's patients and his portfolio are both doing better.

IF I'M A LITTLE GUY, DO I SKIP THIS CHAPTER?

No. This is a gigantic business that affects all who have mutual funds, bank deposits, government securities, IRAs or Keoghs, pension plans, or insurance policies. The managers of money oversee these huge pools of money—money that affects everyone's future, yours included. So if you care about your retirement income, you should wonder who the professional money managers are who are tending your store, and how well they are performing. People are beginning to take notice.

The consequences of using a weak manager can be disastrous, as *Business Week* has pointed out. "If a pension fund underperforms the S & P 500 by two percentage points a year, that compounds to 10.4% over five years and 34.6% in 20." That means if you are forty-five now and want to retire at sixty-five, your retirement fund could have one-third less to draw from if it is in the hands of the wrong managers—due to a mere 2 percent per year.

Another reason to continue reading even if you're not a millionaire is that you may be in the $100,000 category sooner than you think. The market has done well lately for a lot of people, and many IRAs and Keoghs are now sizable portfolios. Yet too many qualified or soon-to-qualify investors are either losing money because they don't have enough time to manage their investments adequately, or their money managers/brokers are underperforming the averages. One final reason to forge ahead is that several advantages of professional money management can be made available to the smaller investor.

SEPARATING THE GOOD FROM THE BAD

A good money manager adheres strictly to an investment philosophy no matter what the market is doing. He has a consistent and relatively long track record, for at least three years, preferably five or ten. He has access to other managers' and brokers' information and gossip and sifts out important details. And his reported results reflect his true management results, not "doctored" ones. But the latter point isn't always guaranteed. More on that later.

I know a successful manager with an enviable eleven-year performance record. He devised his theories as a professor at a major university. When he found the answer, he left to make his fortune. He believes that stocks with yields of 6 percent are buys and at 4 percent are sells. These figures are arrived at after he uses various filtering standards, such as financial stability, solid earnings, and earnings forecasts for the upcoming twelve months. When a stock passes these tests, and a few more, the manager buys those with yields of 6 percent or so, and when they appreciate such that the present yield has been reduced (through the higher stock price) to 4 percent, he sells. He has been using this model since he started his business. He is very disciplined and has access to timely information. But his concept, actually, is quite basic. I've found this to be true of many excellent investment programs over the years.

Ask your adviser/broker to locate a manager who uses good basic concepts and is disciplined and informed, and you'll probably end up with a good manager. At the very least, you'll know your consultant did enough homework to justify his recommendation.

Managers such as the above accept $100,000 accounts and also manage "pooled" accounts made up of smaller contributions ($50,000), thereby using their investment philosophy to benefit many investors, but on a less individualized basis. Some brokerage firms offer unit trusts, with $1,000 as the minimum investment, that employ philosophies similar to those of the large individually managed accounts. Some of these trusts have produced excellent returns. Thus, there are various ways to profit through "managed" money even when you aren't a millionaire.

ANOTHER SELF-REGULATED BUSINESS

Managers are required to register with the SEC, but there the regulation, if it can be called that, stops. The SEC doesn't require track records to be reported, nor does it tell managers how to calculate those records. *Mandatory audit* are two words foreign to this profession. As a result, you'd be amazed how much time some managers spend in Mathemagicland. Managers exercise self-regulation just as financial planners do—the fox is working overtime again. The Investment Counsel Association, a trade group, prints minimum standards, but they are not binding. This group represents only a fraction of the 11,146 investment advisers in the United States—a number twice the 1982 total. All this can account for "selective performance" reporting.

PERFORMANCE: MORE MAGIC THAN PROFITS

In a recent advertisement, Metropolitan Life proudly proclaimed that it had attracted over $5 billion in new pension funds assets in 1984. That brought its total managed portfolio in pension and tax-exempt funds to over $40 billion dollars. The message: Follow the leader into our fold. Indeed, most large assets are handled by insurance companies and banks. They have convinced the public that because they are very large and a lot of people use them, then they must be good. Sometimes. Banks and insurance companies, like Metropolitan Life, are big, but as a group they often produce subpar results. Their median performance statistics almost always underperform the averages, and certainly underperform successful managers.

It is difficult to discuss "average" performance, however, because the players involved are not required to list results with those who seek to compile them, such as SEI Funds Evaluation Services, or the *Piper Report,* the primary monitors of money managers. So guess who doesn't? Right, the poor performers. Even when managers do publish track records, the data can be misleading. Managers often report statistics from a "model portfolio" that reflects only a small portion of the accounts they manage. Sometimes the fine print mentions this, often not.

One Boston money manager, Mark E. Spangler, built a client base of 150 people whose managed assets totaled $25 million. He's been charged with lying about his academic credentials, forging an Arthur Young audit letter, and making false claims of returns of +86.4 percent for one year. He wasn't discovered until a would-be investor asked for an audit report, was instead sent the forged letter, and then did his homework. The manager's name had appeared on a list of the nation's top five money managers. Obviously, no one had checked up on him before. John Smith, president of Lowery Reports, Inc., was quoted in the *Times* as saying, "Many managers just send in reports to consultants which publish it, and consultants vary widely in how much they check. Some don't check at all. Some require evidence of a manager's performance." But slowly statistics are becoming more sought after. Massachusetts doesn't yet require registration of money managers, but a bill requiring registration is expected to pass soon. No doubt because of Spangler, but there were already victims.

A former broker at my firm who has since started an investment consulting firm interviewed more than eight hundred money managers. He said he has yet to find a manager who admitted to being in the bottom half of the SEI Funds Evaluation Services survey. Obviously, several out of eight hundred must have been below average, but they don't have to admit it or show any evidence to the contrary.

KNOW THE ULCER FACTOR

Track records also can be misleading because they are merely a measure of past years' average performances. Some managers attain good returns for five years but need to pass out air bags for the ride along the way. For example, one manager can average a 20 percent return by making his clients 40 percent in year one and then 0 percent the following year. Another manager averages 20 percent by gaining 18 percent one year and 22 percent the next. The average degree of difference in return during periods studied that varies from the quoted average annual return is called the "annualized standard deviation." I call it the Ulcer Factor. You should use a manager who supplies you with both statistics—return and deviation (variability of return). If he doesn't, drop him like a brick. The less the deviation and the higher the rate of return, the fewer ulcers you are likely to get.

Thus, we find ourselves wondering about a $2 trillion industry (in controlled assets) whose track record is questionable at best, and in which no one is requird to post, in any uniform way, results for public review (least of all for prospective clientele). And most of the money being managed represents your retirement kitty and mine. So where can you turn for information?

The best guidepost for evaluation of this profession is to compare managers' results to the general averages (indexes) in the areas they are dealing in. That's another way of saying let's compare the brains of money managers to the luck of the Dart Throwers. In an analysis done by *Business Week* in 1985, the Dart Throwers won the performance comparison in all cases, even for varying periods of time. The figures came from SEI Funds Evaluation Services, a major force in collecting data on the money-management industry. But this service doesn't work unless it is voluntarily given results—or can find them. Alas, poor performers tend not to provide results, nor do managers who have gone out of business because of poor results. And while results may be screened, they are not often audited. Therefore, these disappointing figures are actually inflated because they represent only those managers who have less to hide or are simply the survivors. The SEI Funds' evaluation of money managers versus the Standard & Poor's 500 Index is shown in Table 8.1, opposite.

One may conclude from this table that money managers are getting worse at their profession. Adding insult to injury, the more conservative method of management for fixed-income accounts also under performed the Shearson Lehman/Government Corporate Bond Index (SLGCBI). The index's 1984 return was 15 percent. Only 29 percent of the managers followed by the SEI beat that mark; 71 percent failed. For the period 1982–84, the averages were 17.6 percent. Only 41 percent beat the averages in that period; 59 percent failed. Finally, for the past decade the SLGCBI produced a 9.6 percent compound annual return, yet only 40 percent of the man-

Table 8.1

S & P 500	Percentage gain	Percent of Managers Who Outperformed Index	Percent of Managers Who Underperformed Index
1984	+ 6.3	26	74
1982–84	+16.6	32	68
1980–84	+14.7	45	55
1975–84	+14.8	44	56

Figures based on data from *Business Week.*

agers out-performed that pace, with 60 percent failing. Thus, in our examples, *no average* was beaten by the majority of professionals, no matter what their philosophy—aggressive or conservative—or what the time period. Which is why more and more executives responsible for pension funds and trusts are questioning professional managers.

A GOOD RATE OF RETURN

Even considering the "pre-Crash" powerful markets of 1985 and 1986, an acceptable return for me and my clients is an annualized rate of about 15–20 percent over five years. After all, money doubles every four years at that rate. The level of deviation that I consider acceptable with the above rate of return is 10 percent to 15 percent. In English that means a manager who averages a 20 percent return could have a bad year as low as 17 percent and a good year as high as 23 percent. (A 15 percent deviation of the 20 percent average is 3 percent. Add or subtract 3 percent from the 20 percent return for its extremes). Not a roller-coaster ride, and no ulcers. I can find better returns, but the risk and just the ride alone may be too much for the average investor, let alone me.

FEES: MORE DEEP POCKETS

All forms of money management create varying degrees of overhead, which must be covered by fees. An aggressive manager will have more transaction costs because of his higher level of activity. Most money managers charge 1 percent of the first $1 million underman-agement. It drops to about .5 percent for most accounts over $5 million. If an account is $25 to $100 million or more the fee may drop to

.33 percent, retroactive to all dollars under management. Managers who accept smaller accounts usually have a minimum dollar fee (about $1,500), which makes the percentage charged to the smaller account greater than 1 percent. Some managers have been known to charge as much as 2 percent, but that is rare and should be a cue to look elsewhere.

"WRAPPING FEES": A NEW TREND

A new and evolving fee in the field of money management is the wrap fee. So far the wrap fee is applicable only to assets handled by a broker in conjunction with a registered and broker-approved manager. The wrap fee can be structured in two ways. In the first, the fee is directly charged to the client's portfolio by the broker for only commissions (not management and trustee fees) and is a percentage of the managed portfolio's value. The fee is determined at the beginning of the year and billed quarterly. The second way "wraps together" the manager's fee, commissions, and sometimes even trustee bookkeeping. But, as usual, beware of excessive wrap fees.

The benefits are obvious. If the client's portfolio is moderately to actively traded, such a fee structure is very competitive, unless the account receives significant discounts on commissions. In addition, sometimes a broker can exert leverage to have the management fee reduced if he has referred other clients to the money manager.

If the wrap fee is either not used or not available, money managers should be able to negotiate some level of discount from a broker due to the large level of trading and size of the accounts the manager typically trades through the broker(s).

HOW MONEY MANAGERS AFFECT THE MARKETPLACE

An aggressive manager can turn over (trade) as much as 70 percent to 100 percent (or more) of the assets in a portfolio per year. Some managers will buy and sell an entire portfolio of a tax-free pension plan ten times or more a year. (That's a 1,000 percent turnover.) There is little wonder that the overall marketplace has become much more volatile—this volatility reflects the professional, institutional money managers moving their security positions in and out. The pressure to perform combined with the tendency to evaluate managers on a quarterly basis has intensified the volatility in securities trading. Many large pension funds and trusts openly tell their managers that the bottom-level performers (usually the bottom 15 percent) will be fired either each quarter or each year. For example, according to *Business Week*, United Technologies Corporation has a $4 billion pension fund run by thirty-seven managers. Each year the company fires several of the poorest-performing managers.

Such pressure causes managers, especially large institutional managers, to "dress" their portfolios at the end of each quarter by selling poor-performing stocks so they needn't list these specific errors for all to see. The losses are still reflected in total assets, but the names of the culprits are not. "Sick stocks" are commonly sold with a vengeance—with managers frequently acting in concerted panic. All this exacerbates the selling wave and the ensuing drop in a stock's price.

Many individual investors have been caught in the revolving door as they see their stock being sold off in sharp drops, primarily by scared institutional money managers who might feel their jobs are in jeopardy. This is agonizing to the small investor left with a sudden drop in the value of his hard-earned portfolio—how did it happen so quickly and why to such a large degree? And it is ironic that these managers often guess wrong. But wrong or not, they can leave a bloodbath in their wake. In fact, money managers are often accused of following the "greater fool" theory: Onto whom can they unload an unpopular security to flush it out of their own portfolio? The problem is that institutions need each other because the public is no longer a big enough player to take on their transactions. Especially in panic situations.

The future holds little hope for the less volatile markets of the old days. Most experts realize that we are now in a market almost totally controlled by institutions, or as the late stock market guru Benjamin Graham is reputed to have said, "Institutional investors are merely taking in each other's dirty laundry." Surely, the statistics do not bode well for John Doe Investor staging a comeback. In 1965 individuals accounted for 85 percent of the trading activity of the New York Stock Exchange. In 1984 that percentage had dropped to 11 percent, and it is not expected to rise again. Money managers today are estimated to control two thirds of all shares issued in American publicly traded corporations. Almost all activity in the tax-exempt bond market has been left to professionals. If you are a small investor and trade your own portfolio, it is going to be increasingly difficult for you to keep afloat as the waves made by the money managers get higher and higher.

Let's look closely at how so few are controlling so much: Including newsletter writers, there are over eleven thousand investment advisers registered with the SEC, and new applications are being filed at the rate of two hundred per month. Nevertheless, only fourteen hundred advisers manage portfolios of $100 million or more. And there are over 45 million shareholders of U.S. securities. If we assume that the big portfolio managers control the action (in view of the fact that 90 percent of the NYSE volume is institutional), then only 3/1000 percent (or .003 percent) of the players are calling most of the shots. (That is not math from Mathemagicland.) It is a clear case of the last inch of the tail wagging the dog.

An example of this trend can be found by examining the growth in corporate and labor union pension funds. The size and value of these accounts have grown *tenfold* in one decade. Most of their money is, and will continue to be, managed by professional money managers. And likely managed badly. Illogically, even the weaker managers seem capable of survival because the institutions don't know where to turn. According to *Business Week,* "David L. Babson & Co., stuck in the bottom half of the performance rankings for most of the last 10 years, still manages almost $1 billion in institutional equity funds." With managers charging about .4 percent as a minimum fee, Babson must be earning $4 million or so per year, maybe more. For a mediocre performance, at best.

THE MANAGER HUNT

I've talked to a lot of individuals and also managers of trusts or pension funds who readily acknowledge that their money managers are performing poorly—but they don't know how poorly in comparison to other managers, nor do they know how to find more competent ones. The process requires research and double checking. And often advisers hired to find them are imprecise, biased, or incapable of doing the research. Here's a story from my past.

It was my second year in the business, and I was off to a flying start with several good clients who liked the market. But my stock picking and my firm's research department were producing only so-so results. Fortunately these clients qualified for professional management because they had $100,000 in their portfolios. Plus the idea sounded sophisticated to both my clients and me.

One day our office had an impromptu sales meeting for Walter Bird, a prodigal broker who had left the firm before I came. Bird was a smooth character who had gone into "wholesaling" a professional money management firm (which he claimed to partially own) for big profits. ("Wholesaling" meant he solicited middlemen—brokers, lawyers, accountants—to refer their clients to his money management firm. These referrals are usually profitable to both wholesaler and middleman, but not necessarily to their clients.) In retrospect, I should have wondered who the big profits were targeted for. But I was a rookie and didn't know any better. Bird had been well liked in the office and sounded like a knowledgeable guy. His firm's track record seemed OK, so I referred several of my clients to his managers. Later, I lost three quarters of them because of Bird's company's poor management performance.

The moral of my story is that many middleman referral sources (brokers, lawyers, accountants, etc.) may limit their research to their friends or whoever has bought them drinks, rather than how well their referrals manage money. Some sources recommend only their own in-house managers. Banks and insurance companies, as well as many brokers, are famous for this. Even a consultant's homework may be limited to managers with whom he has an "agreement." Finding truly neutral consultants is a real problem.

WHAT IS "SMART" MONEY DOING?

Given the dismal performance of most money managers the obvious question is: What is "smart" money doing? Or "scared" money? There are several answers. From a corporate standpoint, many companies are leaving the management of pension money to the individual employee. With this situation the company makes a formula-based payment to an employee's retirement account. The employee then can select one or more of several investments and/or managers through which his money is invested. In this arrangement the employee is bearing the risk and responsibility for the management of his money. In the old method of pension planning the corporation was at risk to pay the employee a certain level of benefit upon retirement. Or they didn't have a pension plan at all. If poor management depleted the pension plan funds, the corporation itself had to cover the pension payments. Today many corporations are choosing a more passive investment philosophy in order to be deemed a "prudent man," and thereby avoid lawsuits.

TWO SOLUTIONS TO MEDIOCRITY: INDEX FUNDS AND PERFORMANCE FEES

One answer to poor manager performance is the growing use of passive index funds which reflect indexes such as the Dow Jones Industrials and Standard and Poor's. In the past few years, index funds have become quite popular. Their managers create funds that attempt to mirror the averages that everyone follows. People investing in these funds believe, probably because of several bad experiences, that most managers can't beat the averages. (My statistics prove the same thing. And remember my earlier example of a pension fund that is in danger of being 33 percent smaller than it need be.) Thus, these investors reason, if you can't beat 'em, join 'em. Major companies, such as AT&T, are committed to using an index fund as one of their passive pension planning strategies. According to *Business Week*, AT&T plans to index 50 percent of its equity pension funds. And it is not alone. In the last ten years, index funds have grown in size to more than $60 billion.

Index funds sound like an easy answer, but they also have drawbacks. Part of the problem of using indexes for comparison is that, unlike the index funds, indexes operate without costs. In order for the index fund to mirror the index, it has to outperform the index to break even after paying for its overhead of managers, offices, and so on. So, while its goals may be more modest, the index fund's basic problem is similar to that of the managers whom you seek to replace—it's forever short.

For my clients, I say why cry "uncle" and turn to these funds? For one thing, even the averages can underperform well-timed alternative investments, so they are not the end-all standard for your investment dollars. Besides, good managers *are* making money for other people. Your attitude should be, "Let's find them."

There is a new strategy that ties fees to performance and may benefit investors who still hope to find a good money manager. Under this method, fees depend on manager's performance, rather than on a percentage of the managed assets. "Performance fees," as they are called, put a manager on notice: If he does well, he'll be paid well. If he does poorly, his fees will reflect this—and if he continues to underperform the competition, he'll be out of business. For some time managers have used performance-fee schedules for individual accounts, but increasingly pension fund sponsors, who account for $1.5 trillion in pension fund assets, are saying no more flat fees. That's a lot of money and a lot of clout. There are details to be worked out—like what index to use to determine performance and what percentages the fee should be—but at least change is in the works. Performance fees are logical and long overdue.

WHO SHOULD BE LOOKING FOR A GOOD MONEY MANAGER?

To determine whether you need a money manager, answer two questions:

1. Do you have at least $100,000, but preferably $250,000 to $1 million or more?
2. Do you want to be involved with the stock and/or bond markets?

These questions require more thought. Consider whether you can tolerate potentially violent price swings in your portfolio (and thus your assets). Can you, in the case of the typical managed stock portfolio, accept income that is consistently less than that of a money market fund or a bond portfolio?

HOW TO HIRE A MANAGER: A HIKE THROUGH MATHEMAGICLAND

The good managers are out there. Some have been providing clients with returns in excess of 20 percent annually, with very minor fluctuations in their returns, for long periods of time. They are the twentieth century's version of the gold mine. Somebody is using them; somebody's financial adviser or broker found these managers for their clients. Are you one of the lucky ones? Probably not. The odds are against you because there are so few excellent managers in the pack—they're hard for even consultants to find. But using a consultant is still the best way to go about it.

First of all, avoid the Walter Birds and the hot tips of your golfing pal who suggests you use the local money manager. Being local is not a requisite in a manager who handles securities being traded on Wall Street. You wouldn't eat only fish just because you live near the ocean.

Researching the Managers

A few firms have good consulting systems that provide complete and accurate analyses of many managers. The best firms have reviewed and filed the track records of one thousand or more managers in their computers and closely monitor as many as three hundred. They can input your investment philosophy and find several managers that have good records with reasonable levels of deviation (remember that Ulcer Factor).

This review of managers should be more comprehensive than subscribing to monthly or quarterly publications listing rankings of several managers they follow. A few brokerage firms and a select few consultants, acting as a third party, can audit and/or analyze the records of managers they recommend to make sure their performance statistics reflect all of their accounts, not just the successful ones. You don't want to be misled by "model" portfolios, which are nothing more than profiles of managers' best accounts.

Research typically analyzes the past five years', three years', and prior twelve months' results, plus portfolio turnover, deviation standards, and investment philosophies. Aggressive managers are compared to other aggressive managers, and conservative to conservative, depending on a client's own investing style. The amount of assets under management is also a key point. Are they spreading themselves too thin? How many accounts does each manager manager? Do they stick to the philosophy requested by the client? You also want to know if performance results include normal expenditures, such as commissions, management fees, custodial/trust fees, etc. They are usually excluded, with the sometime exception of commissions, and their inclusion can lower the performance levels as much as 1 percent to 3 percent.

Finally, an adviser's review should include on-site visits and monitoring of key personnel for changes and departures. They should not make recommendations based solely on past performance. On-site monitoring is critical. If key managers leave the firm, it is imperative to know who is now making decisions involving your money. Management companies don't advertise when key people leave. Another consideration is a management's name change. This is frequently done to dodge a bad track record. The manager attempts to bury a bad past by burying an old name. The new name supposedly allows poor managers to start record keeping anew.

Some brokerage firms do not charge for this service, although they thoroughly expect that the brokerage commission business will be done through them. Manager search consultants can help you find the better managers and even negotiate with brokers to avail you of the cheapest commission charges.

The *Wall Street Journal* recently listed firms that provide in-depth research for finding professional money managers. Examples cited were: SEI Corporation of Chicago: Rogers, Casey, Barksdale of Stamford, Connecticut; and Evaluation Associates of Westport, Connecticut. *Piper Report* is another well-known source. Fees for a complete manager evaluation/search depend on client need and account complexity. For example, on a multimillion-dollar account (to even billions) that involves research of equity, bond, and money market managers, fees could go as high as $20,000–$50,000 per year. Try to determine up front what the expenses might be and attempt to locate any additional or hidden fees. Some consultants have annual update charges. And some managers receive free trips for doing their commission business with some brokers. On the whole, these consultant search firms are doing something right because they are often rehired annually by their clients—which speaks well for them.

The client's biggest concern should be the depth of the consultant's investigation. Stay away from consultants who have few sources or affiliations, under one hundred. If the managers are being truly monitored, the more the merrier, because this allows for a greater probability of finding a manager with a good record and similar philosophy, perhaps even a dozen or more in your geographical locale. Though it is difficult to do, look for hidden conflicts of interest—if there are any. As a consultant, I could care less who is eventually selected by my clients as a manager. The choices I suggest are so varied that they can be labeled completely unbiased. I do have my favorite managers, but they are favorites only because they have successful track records; that is the extent of my bias. Finally, I suggest you review the following with your consultant before any money manager's staff begins work on your portfolio.

Here are some questions to ask your consultant.

ON SELECTION OF MANAGERS

How many managers are you affiliated with for client referral?
How far in the past does your review into managers go?

How do you locate your manager recommendations?
Do you charge for this referral service?
How much do your managers charge?
Do you monitor personnel changes, rather than simply the performance statistics of potential managers?
(If referral is by a broker): Do you offer wrap fees in addition to normal commission charges? Do you discount them?

ON PERFORMANCE AND TRACK RECORDS

How do you gather your managers' statistics? Do you monitor and average all his accounts into one performance figure? Does the manager break down statistics by account size and philosophy? Does he *exclude* any accounts from his statistics—such as high-risk ones or poor performers?

Do you provide a statistical analysis for your recommended managers, addressing the level of deviation in performance (Ulcer Factor) as well as simply the performance?

Do performance results include normal expenditures, such as commissions, management fees, custodial/trust fees, etc.?

If I am dissatisfied with my money manager, when should I fire him? (Talk to the consultant who recommended the money manager. The consultant should already be monitoring the negative situation and making new suggestions. The release is done by a letter.)

After you have met with a consultant, asked questions, and established that you would like to use his services, he will probably present you with preliminary findings on several managers whom he feels would handle your account well. Ask him to explain his reports (often in the form of graphs) and to discuss the finalists with you face to face.

YES, SOME MONEY MANAGERS WILL MAKE YOU MONEY

Professional money managers are like many other products on Wall Street. They're not usually as good as they sound, but if you look hard and ask questions, you'll be surprised how good some of them are. Get second opinions on everything. Check with brokers, other managers, and friends, and interview the managers. Look for personal rapport with your manager. Upon finding your manager(s), consider and suggest using a broker who provides reduced commissions for your sizable managed account, but also make sure he provides good execution of trades. Will the manager oversee this process without charging you a fortune?

I have a lot of respect for good money managers. They have kept some of my largest clients happy and made a lot of money for all of us. But the real challenge is finding a good one. Remember that you are deep in the valley of Mathemagicland, a place without maps or street signs. The Walter Birds of this land are trying to give you directions, but you have to ignore them and use the questions I have provided to find an adviser/broker/money manager on your own.

Chapter Nine

ECONOMISTS, GURUS, AND HEADLINES: NOBODY'S PERFECT

> If all the economists in the world were laid end to end
> they still wouldn't come to a conclusion.
>
> —GEORGE BERNARD SHAW

I like to see economists agree on prognostications or trends, because that leaves me with only one variable: timing—when to go the other way. The last time I made a killing in the market was July 1984 when everyone and his economist were sure that high interest rates would not only persist, but go higher. I felt we were within ninety days of the peak. I was wrong—they broke down in two weeks and went down hard and fast. My clients and I cleaned up—although I reminded them we were still guessing. Being humble never hurts, but don't expect humility from economists.

WHY FOLLOW ECONOMISTS?

For one thing, if you buy stocks, mutual funds, or other risk-oriented investments, those who manage them are still heeding economic theory. So before you are convinced of an investment's viability, consider whom your professionals listen to and how wrong economists can be.

One of my habits is to squirrel away financial magazines and newspapers to reread at a later date. A *Newsweek* cover story from 1982 carried the titles "A Break in Interest Rates," "How It Affects You," and "Wall Street's Wildest Week." The front cover sported a huge percent sign. The text of the article included a chart showing the "Outlook for Interest Rates" reflecting the then prime rate and six expert economists' opinions as to where It would be at year's end, only four months away (not a very long-range forecast).

Of the six economists, three guessed the rate would rise. (The prime rate actually dropped from 13.5 percent to 11.5 percent), or a level of reduction of 15 percent in only four months.) Two guessed the rate would experience a minor to moderate reduction—a 3 percent and a 7 percent decrease, respectively. Only one economist anticipated a substantial drop, as actually happened. And he predicted a 25 percent reduction, versus the actual 15 percent. Nobody was very close, and half were dead wrong, even though they were asked to forecast ahead only four months. Yet these economic estimates and predictions were receiving enormous attention—and misleading many. The bank economist was most off the mark, even though you would expect him to be better than average at predicting interest rates.

According to *Newsweek*, the Big Three forecasting firms—Data Resources, Inc., Chase Econometrics, and Wharton Econometric Forecasting Associates—haven't fared any better with their tons of data, hundreds of equations, and mainframe computers crunching all the numbers.

HOW MANY ECONOMISTS CAN YOU NAME?

The economist-as-celebrity is here to stay. Economists like John Kenneth Galbraith, Henry Kaufman, Edward Yardeni, David Stockman, and Milton Friedman have become personalities in financial news and on our TV screens because, whether we like it or not, they affect our lives, and so do their theories. Keynesian theory was replaced by Monetarism, which is giving way to a third major school, New Classical Economics. Proponents of these theories regularly sit on the boards of corporations, roost in the hallowed halls of ivied universities, affect the decision-making of government, are members of the Council of Economic Advisers, and even reside in the president's cabinet. Ironically, it is this last factor, the economists' affinity for government, that makes their forecasts so frequently wrong.

GOVERNMENT TIES: A NOOSE AROUND ECONOMISTS' NECKS

A basic problem for economists is that they must base many of their predictions on information derived from the world's largest economic morass—the U.S. government. Consequently, because the U.S. government doesn't even know how to keep its books, no one knows what is going on. A recent article in the *Wall Street Journal* quoted Congressman Joseph J. DioGuardi, also an accountant, as saying, "I'm appalled at the way we account for government spending around here. We're using a Mickey Mouse, cash basis accounting system." The government's own comptroller general, Charles A. Bowsher, agrees. It seems the government does not recognize, on an accounting basis, its assets, liabilities, and future obligations. It just keeps its checkbook open, pays the bills as they come due, and borrows when the checkbook runs dry.

This can't continue forever; at some point the government is going to have to put its finances in order. Until then, however, economists will keep making estimates based on a set of facts and figures that have as much stability as a flask of nitroglycerine. For example, the government is particularly unwieldy for forecasters because of its large numbers. The budget is $1 trillion and the debt is $2 trillion. That's the good news. As Morton Egol, a partner at Arthur Anderson, points out, several important items aren't even on the government books, such as future social security obligations. He estimates that the government actually has a negative net worth of $3.4 trillion—$2 trillion higher than anyone in Washington will admit.

There are other headaches for economists—like the economy's volatility. Heretofore, the Federal Reserve controlled interest rates, but today it merely attempts to. The dollar is no longer fixed. It floats all over the place, affecting everyone's else's currency as it moves. The prime rate used to be boring to watch, an unimportant indicator because there was nothing to indicate. From 1934 to 1947 the prime never changed—not once. Between 1947 and 1978, over thirty-one years, the prime changed 143 times. From 1978 through 1984, six years, the prime changed 112 times. Add to this equation our huge underground economy, estimated at 15 percent of the GNP, and you'll begin to understand all the factors—and fictions—that an economist must take into account. But do they? No wonder the late Frank H. Knight, noted economist, said, "I have been increasingly moved to wonder whether my job is a job or a racket, whether economists . . . should cover their faces or burst into laughter when they meet on the street."

ECONOMISTS: AN ENDANGERED SPECIES GOING THE WAY OF THE DODO BIRD

The closer you look at economists and their recent bad calls, the more they seem like an endangered species running out of survival techniques. Those who listen to them do so at increasing risk. At a news conference in 1985, President Reagan commented on long-term forecasts by saying, "Frankly, I pay no attention to them." He went on to say, "There isn't an economist in the world who can do that [estimate what the government's spending and revenue are to be in the next four years] and accurately tell you what you are going to need down the road." Shades of David Stockman in the *Atlantic* and his rumored reference to "the ridiculously wrong" budget projections. Harvard economics professor Dale Jorgenson says, "Economists have made disastrous calls." As a matter of fact, he gives economic forecasting a failing grade. "I wish I could say economists are powerful thinkers and can tell what's going to happen. But they haven't the slightest idea and never had."

The Council of Economic Advisers makes its share of errors. In 1983 it predicted that the GNP would grow by 1.4 percent. Actual growth was 6.4 percent; that is an error factor through underestimation of 78 percent. The next year, economists revised their projections upward, predicting "excessively strong" growth. Yet real growth plunged from 10.1 percent in the first quarter to 1.9 percent in the third. Am I making my point? Recently, when former Treasury Secretary Donald Regan was asked if he was ever an economist, he replied, "I've been called bad names before—but economist?"

GURUS

> When you lose on the stock market, don't blame the bulls and the bears but the bum steers.
>
> —ANONYMOUS

Gurus belong in carnivals, but instead they operate, for the most part, out of newsletters with circulations of ten thousand or more. Annual subscription rates range from one $100 to $500 per year. Many subscribers are veritable disciples—for a while. Once a newsletter has caught on, gurus make enormous profits after paying the

printer and post office. Most newsletters focus on a form of investment or cultivate a fear that is their signature: gold, commodities,
inflation, depression, or a faltering U.S. dollar. Their credentials vary
from real (quite a few have graduated from Wall Street as economists,
analysts, or money managers) to nonexistent. But they are all superb
salesmen. Other tools for success: a good PR manager, a flamboyant
personality, good guesses, and most importantly, investors with
trusting personalities, bad memories, and little inclination for homework.

Some gurus, like Henry Kaufman, go on staff with major firms but
do not sell anything. They can't accurately be labeled gurus, but they
have the same fanatical following. Kaufman was the chief economist
for the prestigious Wall Street firm of Phibro-Salomon. He presided
over a staff of ninety, made four or five major speeches a year (which
were later published by his firm), and edited a well-known weekly
newsletter, *Comments on Credit*. During my first few years in the
business I watched markets fly up and down based on what he
predicted. I soon realized he was wrong a lot of the time and ignored
him, but his popularity continued. Finally, in 1983, *Business Week*
reviewed his record over six years of major predictions, and what it
considered a dozen major "calls." Henry's score: seven successes and
five goofs. Close game? No. Put another way, Kaufman's judgment in
twelve major predictions over six years was one better than a coin
toss. And when he was wrong, he was very wrong. Here is *Business
Week's* table of misses:

Table 9.1/ . . . BUT HE HAS ALSO MISSED SOME BIG TURNS

	Forecast	Outcome
Aug. 26, 1980	Increases in the prime do not signal a return to a 20% prime.	All rates began spiraling up-ward, and the prime rose from 11.1% to more than 20% in December 1980
Dec. 21, 1980	The prime, at 21.5%, will keep rising to between 22% and 24%. There will be no "deep dive" in rates because the economy is too strong.	The prime immediately fell, touching 17% briefly in April, 1981, and has never hit 22%.
Aug. 31, 1981	The prime, at 20.5%, will hit 24% to 25% by year end	The prime started dropping a month later, and by year end it was down to 15.7%

Forecast	Outcome
Jan. 5, 1982	Rates will spurt to near-record highs in the second half of 1982	By the end of 1982 rates fell to lows unseen since the second half of 1980
May 9, 1982	A recovery in the second half of the year will push rates to their 1981 highs	The second-half recovery never materialized

Data: Salomon Bros., Data Resources Inc., BW

Source: Reprinted from the February 28, 1983 issue of *Business Week*, by special permission. © 1983 by McGraw-Hill, Inc.

Note that twice, when the prime rate was at the dizzying level of 20 percent, he said it would continue upward to 24 percent or 25 percent. Both times the prime headed immediately down, but both times the market had already reacted wildly to his predictions. In 1983, "Dr. Doom," as he was dubbed by *Business Week*, was "convinced that the big economic risks are on the downside." That's another way of saying he was negative. Since that time things have been good: the best bull market in modern times, lower interest rates, a healthy GNP, a booming bond market, and a happy Street. Henry has admittedly changed his mind along the way. But why can't great economists see major changes better and well in advance? All the gyrating opinions have to cost somebody money. I know one thing: I lose clients if I tell them to sell a stock and it goes higher four months after they sold. But for some reason, Kaufman keeps rising above his disappointing record. I wonder if he invests in the market.

JOE GRANVILLE

The phone rings after midnight. You answer, and a cool voice says, "I have an early warning for you." It sounds like something out of a spy novel. No, nobody dropped the bomb. However, if you are a $500-a-year subscriber to Joe Granville's "early warning service," you have been expecting this call. That's exactly what happened January 6, 1981. Working for almost eight straight hours, Granville's staff placed some three thousand phone calls all over the United States, to London, Geneva, Stuttgart, and other European cities, and sent out the message, "Sell everything." The next day the market dropped 31 points, costing the overall market 3 percent of its value in one day! (In 1984 the market moved 1 percent in value the entire year.) How can the marketplace justify following one man's advice, losing three times more in one day than it might lose in one year? Another time, the market went up 31 points in a day when he issued a "flash advisory" to buy stocks. Granville called; people listened. "If you follow me, you follow the market—we're interchangeable," Granville says.

One of his followers, Stan Formaldehyde, was a rookie in my office. He and Granville were meant for each other. Stan wanted the entire office to subscribe to the *Granville Market Letter,* which at $250 he couldn't afford to do himself. About a third of the office chipped in, passed it around each week, and spouted out the recommendations to clients. Sadly, Stan got slaughtered trading options on stocks Joe said would crash or rise—Joe often got his directions mixed up. Recently, Lenny told me Stan had been "embalmed" and was no longer in the business.

Joe Granville is not only a market guru, but an evangelist-style entertainer who has mesmerized thousands with his showmanship. And when he was hot, he was very hot. He actually "played" in Las Vegas, sometimes to a crowd of seven thousand, using the props of a vaudeville act: a ventriloquist's dummy, assorted juggling balls, bikini-clad women, a monkey wearing a three-piece suit and holding the proverbial loser's bag, and a piano on which he thumped his own musical introductions. Granville says, "People want to touch me, because everyone I touch I make rich."

Many in his audience became believers and signed up for the *Granville Market Letter.* In the early eighties his newsletter grossed $5 million per year from over thirteen thousand subscribers. But evidently it isn't always his last word. *U.S. News & World Report* pointed out that, ironically, in January 1981 Granville's newsletter was saying buy at the exact time his staff was allegedly whispering sell to the select few who paid a little more for their up-to-the-minute news.

Technical analysts begrudgingly agree that Granville has made valuable contributions to the field of technical market analysis. One is his discovery of a technical indicator he termed On Balance Volume. His real accomplishments, however, were overshadowed by outlandish predictions—for example, he said that an earthquake registering 8.3 on the Richter scale would completely destroy Los Angeles April 10, 1981. It wasn't the first time he was wrong or the last. More recently, in March 1985 when the Dow Jones Average was at 1250 he again forecast gloom. He said the predictions of the

Dow hitting 1400 and 1500 were off by 900 points. He predicted the averages to be at 500 or 600 by mid- to late 1986. One year after he made those estimates, the Dow Jones was at 1800, 500 points higher than when he spoke—and 1300 points above what he predicted. But he still expects to receive the Nobel prize in economics. One outraged broker quoted in *Financial World* said of him, "If a broker made the same claims in front of a public audience that Joe Granville does, he'd be carted off by the SEC in handcuffs, barred from the business forever, and quite probably locked up."

Ironically, Joe and I have something in common. We both have worked for the same firm. He left E. F. Hutton a few years after an article he wrote for our market letter titled "Are the Russians in the U.S. Market?" made Walter Winchell's daily column in 1957 and prompted a CIA investigation. He has also written a book that tells how to beat the game of bingo and was said to be working on a novel in which the Russians and a bad guy named Hunker Bunt try to topple the U.S. economy. I think his newsletter is entertainment enough.

All this is symptomatic of how dangerous gurus can be. Granville and others like him have received tremendous media coverage. They publish hundreds of newsletters, each trying to strike it rich with correct guesses that will turn them into the decade's Wall Street guru—like Granville. The questions to ask are: How did he manage to remain popular despite such large errors, and how has his enormous power affected the market? Lately, he's made enough mistakes to disenchant most of his followers, but perhaps this just means the world is ready for a new guru.

ARMAGEDDON GURUS

There is another form of guru who doesn't pick market moves or analyze interest rate trends; their predictions don't have averages or daily indexes so that one can gauge the extent of their errors. These gurus talk about Armageddon and conjure up images of the Crash of '29.

Anybody remember Howard Ruff, who wrote *How to Prosper During the Coming Bad Years,* which appeared on the 1979 best-seller list for half a year? Ruff was a former actor, singer, and stockbroker who has also gone through a bankruptcy. Perhaps he wanted company. His newsletter *Ruff Times,* which had ninety thousand subscribers, predicted runaway inflation by 1981, riots, shortages and rationing, especially of food, and the failure of municipal and electric utilities. He forecast a change to gold-backed currencies and a major barter economy. Frozen food would be a thing of the past because electricity would be too. He exhorted investors to buy hard assets like precious metals and diamonds. People listened. His colorful predictions were printed on the front page of the *Wall Street Journal*. Companies reported increased sales of gasoline storage tanks, gold and silver, "survival homes," and even dehydrated foods. The owner of Martens Health and Survival Products, Inc., was quoted as saying, "At first, we sold mostly to campers and Mormons—they believe in laying away food for hard times, you know. Now they're mostly to people referred to us by Howard." A young lawyer who agreed with Ruff said of the 1980 elections, "It doesn't matter whether the Republicans or Democrats are in—they all adopt the kind of inflationary programs that are ruining the country. [The election] will just decide who will be the captain of the *Titanic*."

If you listened to Ruff in 1980 and bought a bag of silver coins for $19,000, six years later that bag was worth $5,000. If you bought gold Krugerrands at $15,000, another Ruff suggestion, they dropped to about $8,200. Or maybe you purchased other miserable performers like stamps, antiques, rare coins, or diamonds, or invested $2,500 in hoarded food. Certainly his subscribers didn't anticipate that Ruff would actually create their rough times. Still, Ruff refuses to take any blame for his followers' losses. He gave paperback buyers free coupons to send in for updates to his predictions. If they didn't get his follow-up advice, he says, "I can't be responsible for people who run through stop signs." Ruff is still going strong. And he's persistent. Recently he appeared on NBC's "Today" show and once again said "buy gold." Sooner or later you have to guess right.

Douglas R. Casey's *Crisis Investing: Opportunities and Profits in the Coming Great Depression* was another doom-and-gloom book, like Ruff's, that made a pile of money peddling its author's dire prognostications. He predicted a depression not later than 1983 with roaring inflation, Armageddon, shortages, property confiscations, and the usual bankruptcies. He estimated that gold would rise to $3,000 per ounce. (In 1986 gold was selling for $300 an ounce. That's an error factor of 900 percent.) When *Barron's* tried to talk with Casey he was said to be out of the country. When they reached Howard Ruff, he claimed that his predicted depression was still coming—and that his subscribers had increased to 120,000. I guess somebody still believes.

A NEWSLETTER THAT RATES THE NEWSLETTERS

For the past five years, Mark Hulbert has been rating most of the prominent newsletters—in addition to those by Granville and Ruff—in his own newsletter, the *Hulbert Financial Digest*, which has a circulation of fourteen thousand. His general thesis concerning research is that "(1) It's much harder to beat the market than is generally realized; (2) nevertheless . . . it can be done. And some investment letters do it." However, his research bears out my thesis that these letters have runs of good luck but can't be depended upon for long-term investment advice.

REAL ESTATE: NO MONEY DOWN

The new faces on the guru block are those gurus who claim to make fortunes in real estate with "no money down." In books, tapes, seminars, and TV sideshows they suggest buying property nobody else wants, or can afford to keep, using ingenious bank or seller financing. Ed Beckley does his shtick on late-night TV for the stay-at-home folks who aren't into "Saturday Night Live." He's reduced his course fee from $600 to the bargain price of $295, saying the cost is so low it won't change anyone's standard of living. But it will change his. This fast-talking video salesman claims one hundred thousand course graduates. That's up in Howard Ruff's league and translates into $29 million in revenues, not counting some higher-priced $600 courses. He claims to be the "Millionaire Maker." He at least made one—himself. His fifteen-hour cassette-tape course doesn't adequately deal with the potential for a too-heavy mortgage payment, the recalcitrance or inability of some people to pay their rent, the legitimacy of luring banks into shaky deals, or how to emerge from a resulting cash flow "squeeze play."

John Reed, author of *Sensible Finance Techniques for Real Estate Investors* openly states that "you have to mislead a lending institution and find a dumb seller." Great. Go to jail over the former and find there are few of the latter. Don Rule, a former partner of best-selling author Albert Lowry (*How to Become Financially Independent by Investing in Real Estate*) was quoted as saying, "I don't know any of them who made a fortune in real estate, either before they started teaching or since." And a partner should know.

YESTERDAY'S HEADLINES: A VISIT TO MY CLOSET

The investor who reads financial news assumes that a great deal of research, neutrality, and informed writing are reflected in banner headlines telling us what is going on now and will be in the future. The bigger the headline, the more likely it is that John Doe Broker and Mr. and Mrs. Investor will accept the information and its conclusions. Many articles are accurate. However, others can be very misleading. In terms of impact, the bigger the headline, the more one-sided the conclusion.

How about a jaunt down memory lane by way of my closet—full of yellowed copies of the *Wall Street Journal, Barron's, Business Week,* and *Forbes* for starters. These newspapers are my career albums, providing "still shots" of both good and bad information. Some of the articles are neutral and considered, and others sound like reports from the Gospel. Well, I'm here to tell you that financial Gospel can cost you a fortune.

The following headlines from days past appeared in the *Wall Street Journal, Business Week, Forbes,* and *Fortune.* They represent some bad calls for the years 1981, 1982, 1983, and 1984. They all sent people in the wrong directions. No doubt after the Crash of '87 we'll know more about how bad some articles from 1985 to 1987 were.

October 15, 1981: *Wall Street Journal*, Front Page

BEHIND HOMELY IMAGE OF CONTINENTAL
ILLINOIS IS AN AGGRESSIVE BANK

The lead paragraph of this article states, "The top managers at Continental Illinois Corporation like to describe themselves as modest men whose simple diligence and virtue built one of the best banks in the country." The next paragraph has gems like "The [executives] like to mention that Chairman Roger E. Anderson still prefers a slide rule over a calculator, or that most of the bank's executives graduated from obscure western colleges rather than the Ivy League." The head of banking services is quoted as "attributing the bank's success to 'clean living and hard work.' "

Shortly afterward things started down the tube. Less than two years later Continental Illinois gained a unique distinction. It needed the largest federal bailout in U.S. history. The government had to come to its rescue with $1,500,000,000—that's $1.5 billion—fast, and also guarantee several loans on the bank's books, or the U.S. banking system might have been in real trouble. But the fall 1981 article quoted an unidentified West Coast banker as stating, "Right now, they're the top of corporate banking business in the U.S. I'd stack them with Citibank and Morgan Guaranty." That banker was wrong but strangely prophetic. A few years later, the government wanted to "stack" Continental Illinois with those banks, or any other large one, through a shotgun merger. But there were no takers. The article did provide a few warnings, such as "about 15% of Continental Illinois' $30.03 billion loan portfolio now is in energy loans." The problem is (and was) that few realized at the time that this was a negative point. In fact, clues to future problems were cited as present strengths. On October 15, 1981, the date of the article, Continental stock was selling at 38⅞. By 1984 the stock was 2¾.

February 10, 1983: *Wall Street Journal,* Front Page

FEAR OF INFLATION . . . MANY ANALYSTS SAY NEXT
MOVE IN PRICES MAY BE AN ACCELERATION

This front-page headline called a trend and discussed the reasons it was evident. Experts were quoted and statistics cited, but the call was wrong by a wide margin. Granted, the numbers had been awful for about a decade. For three years straight the United States had double-digit inflation, which was highly unusual and very disruptive. For the four years prior to the article the inflation numbers were:

1982—6.0%
1981—10.2%
1980—13.5%
1979—11.5%

As you can see, 1982 saw inflation fall, but fears remained because even 6.0 percent was still not good. Early in 1983 the *Wall Street*

Journal had us worrying again. Here are the quoted experts. " 'I think we've [inflation] stopped going down,' says Gary Shilling of the consulting firm bearing his name. 'Indeed, the consensus forecast is that the next move in inflation is likely to be upward.' " I hate consensus forecasts. I never know who the "consensors" are.

The article also went on to quote the chief economist of Bear, Stearns and Co. "The Fed . . . has lost substantial credibility and raised the risks and fears of accelerating inflation in the future." Also quoted was the chief economist at Philadelphia's Fidelity Bank. "These price increases suggest that the recent cycle of commodity-price relief has ended." The article also stated that "another major contributor to inflation pressure is the decline in the value of the dollar. The dollar has weakened in most currency markets recently, and analysts look for some further drop in the period just ahead." A falling dollar may have added to inflation, but the dollar didn't fall. It rose 16.3 percent for 1983 and 1984.

The major premise of the article was wrong for two reasons. The first is obvious. Statistically, inflation that year was the lowest in over a decade, at 3.4 percent, and except for 1972's 3.3 percent rate, it was the lowest level in eighteen years. The following year, 1984, inflation was 4.2 percent, and in 1985 it was 3.7 percent. Thus for the three years that followed this article, inflation averaged less than 4 percent.

As a second error, the article caused a great deal of "lost opportunity." By following an erroneous point of view, investors/readers lost the opportunity to act properly or promptly on a major change taking place at that very time—namely the beginning of a substantial and sustained drop in the rate of inflation. In fact, they probably headed off in an entirely wrong direction. This headline, perceived as financial Gospel, is a sad testimony to the fallibility of financial news reporting.

March 13, 1982: *Forbes* Magazine Cover Story

THE GREAT OIL SWINDLE

The lead paragraph of this story begins: "A lot of Americans fooled themselves into thinking the oil crisis was a phony; we are paying a terrible price for that delusion. Many of the same people are now saying that the crisis is over. They are just as dangerously wrong this time." With this and similar statements the article proceeded to pound home not a report on the situation, but a treatise as to why their opinion on where oil prices were headed was valid. After reading the eight-page cover story, I have little doubt that a lot of *Forbes*'s readers went away with a dead-wrong conclusion that may have cost them a lot of money.

The article went on to say that it was "naive and foolish to have the idea that the oil crisis was over and OPEC's days are numbered. Those are dangerous illusions; we entertain them at our peril." I couldn't find the price of oil in the article, but I checked it out. In March 1982, oil was at $34 a barrel. Guess what? It never went higher, but it sure dropped lower. In 1986 it traded under $10 a barrel—a drop of about 70 percent.

What overwhelmed me about this article was the certainty of its presentation, much surer than that of the *Wall Street Journal*, which as we have already noted, goofs too. *Forbes* spoke to the reader's "delusions" that prices may go lower and stay lower. (Mind you, at this time the price had already dropped from $40 a barrel to $34 a barrel, but more important, it was the first sign in years that oil would do anything but inevitably rise.) Now that it had fallen, we were hearing it was practically a mirage. "Oil prices have not permanently peaked." The article further asserted that prices might remain under pressure for one to two more years, but that then we would face another rise—a shock comparable to the skyrocketing prices of 1979 and 1980. "Even if the price drops to $25 a barrel, the crisis isn't over."

Forbes then assessed the strengths and weaknesses of OPEC. It concluded that OPEC would be a menace for quite a while, keeping prices firm, if not climbing. The article stated that "despite the continuing glut and the steady slackening in demand, OPEC is in one sense even stronger now than it was a decade ago." The article also pointed out that "the U.S. government's interest in avoiding prolonged price weakness in oil is especially strong."

Experts were quoted. Yale's Philip Vergeler said, "Saudi Arabia could defend the price on its own. They could go down to 4 million barrels a day temporarily and bring the whole glut process to a stop—on their own—right now." In 1986 Saudi Arabia was thought to be pumping about 2.5 million barrels a day and had been below 4 million for quite a while, yet the price was still down and the glut still status quo.

But the article attempted to be fair. Having quoted an expert from Yale, *Forbes* found another from Harvard. The article stated that "Harvard's Mossavar-Rahmani expects such an interruption in oil exporting to occur in the mid-eighties, either because of a political disruption or because of a decision to cut back production, a shock he figures could send prices into the $70 to $80 range." That expert was halfway right. There was a cutback in production by the mid-eighties—because of a lack of demand for OPEC oil. The price at that time was $10 a barrel, a long way from $80. So much for the experts.

The article also warned readers not to feel comfortable about trading a compact for a gas guzzler. And it was confident about its closing comments too as it quoted energy expert Melvin Conant. "Price changes in oil will not be gradual, not orderly or gradual. There will be the same kind of surging we experienced in the seventies." The final statement of the article read, "The oil crisis is over? Who's kidding whom?" How many readers who read this article and acted on it are laughing now?

April 30, 1984, June 25, 1984, and October 1, 1984: *Fortune: Fortune's* Forecasts

FADING HOPES FOR SLOW INFLATION

WHY INTEREST RATES WILL KEEP SOARING

THE DROP IN INTEREST RATES IS OVER

I've combined these three articles because they all have similar themes, and they all appeared in the same column, "The Economy," of *Fortune* in the same year. This was not a great year for *Fortune*'s forecasts. For, obviously, inflation did stay slow and seemed to get even slower after the first article appeared in April 1984. Interest rates didn't "keep soaring," nor was the drop over in October 1984.

The June inflation article predicted "the honeymoon is ending as costs and prices creep up across the board." It projected several trends, all erroneously. "The cost of energy . . . will stay level at best from now on." It said that gasoline prices, which had started to fall at that time, would "reverse direction." And its call of the inflation rate was way off the mark. It expected the Consumer Price Index "to be increasing at a 6.5 percent rate by this time next year." Despite the fact that it also said that its forecasting error, if it made one, would be to underestimate the rate of inflation, the 1985 rate was about half what it predicted—3.5 percent.

The other *Fortune* articles dealt with interest rates. They stated that rates would soar, but having said that and then observing rates continue to drop, they then said rates would stop dropping. Wrong again. Both short- and long-term rates averaged 2 percent more in 1984 than in the following year, 1985. Meanwhile, the articles stated that "bond rates are likely to reach new peaks . . . and short term rates may pass 13% as the U.S. pays the price for trying to invest more than it saves." (Treasury bills averaged 9.5 percent in 1984 but dropped to 7.5 percent in 1985.)

Yet the lead paragraph of the June *Fortune* article called for the opposite. "Short term rates will probably rise at least another three percentage points in the next year or so." The same article also offered seemingly irrefutable logic that "a 2.5 to 3.0 percentage point rise in U.S. rates will be necessary just to maintain foreign savings inflows at their recent $65 billion annual rate." In retrospect, maybe "the $65 billion annual rate" just wasn't that important—because none of what *Fortune* predicted happened. Nevertheless, the article said that "as much as a 50% rise in short term interest rates (5 percentage points) may be required to keep inflation in check." But inflation ended up easy to keep in check, going down almost 20 percent, and rates never went up, let alone by 5 percent.

The October article assumed inflation was speeding up, so therefore rates would go higher also. That only adds strength to the axiom that one bad guess leads to another. The same article expected a weak economy ahead, yet 1985 proved to be a good year. What had a bad year was *Fortune*'s guessing.

May 18, 1984: *Wall Street Journal*, Front Page

BATTERED BONDS. FIXED-INCOME ISSUES PLUNGE,
AND MANY FEAR THE DECLINE ISN'T OVER

Another front-page headline pointing to a trend. This was a follow-up one year later to the preceding article. It too was dead wrong. The lead paragraph would scare anyone out of the long-term bond market. "If someone tells you it's a jungle out there, the chances are he's in the bond market." The story didn't get cheerier. "I think in this decline, just about everybody stuck his head out of the foxhole and got shot at at least once," said a vice-president for fixed-income investments. A $500-million pension fund manager complained, "If the volatility keeps up, I wonder if there's going to be a long-term bond market at all." A Los Angeles junk bond dealer said, "Treasuries are supposed to be such a good, safe place, and they've been going up and down like a yo-yo. . . . When's the last time you saw high-yield bonds drop three points in one day?" The answer—in a market that's about to be a screaming *bull* market. The vice-chairman of Prudential Life was quoted as saying, "Everybody's getting scared about what's coming."

Sure enough the shock arrived. In less than sixty days after the article appeared, the bond market started the greatest, most sustained rally in modern times. After two years, in 1986, it was still rising. Anybody who went the opposite way from this front-page headline made a fortune fast.

The point is, the commentary and experts' opinions discouraged this by quoting the negative news of the day to a maximum. Its timing was poor, and it was wrong. But the greatest sin was that the article had center stage on the front page.

YES, KEEP READING THE FINANCIAL NEWSPAPERS AND MAGAZINES

Newspapers want to sell news, and bad news is better than dull news. But the investor/reader and broker/reader have to keep in mind that front-page prognostications are by no means more accurate than the articles on page two or any less fallible than the analysts, economists, and gurus who are quoted to help give the news more background.

I took you on these forays into past headlines and articles to show you that even the best newspapers and magazines can be wrong in their predictions. This doesn't mean that you should stop reading them. Instead you should read everything you can on a particular investment area or subject that interests you. And finally, be slightly suspicious of everything, no matter what the subject, the source, or how powerfully the case is made. Keep in mind that when you are reading an opinion or forecast that you are reading a guess. A little lack of respect for the "experts" may go a long way toward saving you money. Nobody bats 1.000 in the major leagues—or on Wall Street.

Pitfalls on the Road to Profits

Chapter Ten

MUTUAL FUNDS: SOMETHING FOR EVERYONE

> Unless trees grow to the sky, we are going to end up
> with investors who are furious.
> —CHAIRMAN OF A MAJOR MUTUAL FUND GROUP

Funds are Wall Street's most popular product these days. Yet it wasn't always that way. Markets have been skyrocketing of late, but not every year will be a 1985 or a 1986. Thirty percent annual gains in the averages are a "once in a generation" occurrence. Read this chapter with that in mind. *Excess* is a word held in reverence and fear by those who know the ways of Wall Street. Remember the old saying, "There's no free lunch."

No area of Wall Street is more prone to using the magic of mathematics than the mutual fund industry. It is a tribute (perhaps a dubious one) to the power of Wall Street that 1985 sales of mutual funds totaled $70.8 billion—in spite of some large fees, weak track records, and a confusing multitude of choices. In fact, few areas of investment have enjoyed the growth, image, and popularity of mutual funds. By 1987 there were over 27 million shareholders in mutual funds (excluding money market funds) investing over $600 billion dispersed among more than eighteen hundred funds. Sales in 1983 alone increased 155 percent from 1982 to more than $40 billion. As a product this is a brokerage industry's dream come true. But is this investment right for you? Emphatically yes in many cases, but unfortunately no in many more. You must learn the difference.

FAST CARS AND FAST NUMBERS

Let's run through a typical scenario: You have money you want to invest before your husband buys his Ferrari. But you've been mugged too often by a broker's stock recommendations, so you decide to go with a professionally managed investment: How about a mutual fund? Relief: Your decision is over. You sit down at your current broker's desk; he pulls out a slick red brochure with exciting-looking charts. The figures sound great, the charts look like a rocket launch, and you're sold. Seven years later you wonder why you did it. You haven't lost a lot of money, but you haven't made much either—and the Ferrari is still in the dealer's lot, or maybe in your broker's driveway. What went wrong?

The first thing that went wrong is that you assumed a mutual fund is the answer to everything—as if they were all alike. In fact, not all growth funds are created equal, and the same applies for income funds, balanced funds, etc. I frequently recommend mutual funds to my clients, but only after I review and compare a number of critical factors, including the studies done by my own firm's mutual fund department. This double review is a crucial step before making an investment because it helps take the magic out of the math.

MATH, MAGIC, AND MARKETING ON WALL STREET

For now, let's look at excerpts from a mutual fund brochure (like the one in the above scenario) distributed in the industry to help market this product—to you. I hope you are ready for some shocking figures!

This shiny brochure describes a hypothetical investment of $10,000 over the twenty-five-year period from 1959 to 1983. The assumptions are: The money was invested among thirty-five mutual funds whose objectives were growth and income; and all dividends and capital gains were reinvested to buy new shares whenever distributions occurred.

To the brochure's credit, it mentions that the hypothetical fund had its ups as well as downs. But it proudly emphasizes that "an investment of $10,000 made on January 1, 1959, would have grown to $82,465 by December 1983." Visually, the graph (see chart 10.1) of the funds' performance looks like a plane taking off up, up, up into the sky.

The brochure goes on to say, "In addition, the compound rate of return during that period would have been 8.8% per year—an extremely attractive rate compared with alternative investments ... even after allowing for initial sales charges and expenses." The bro-

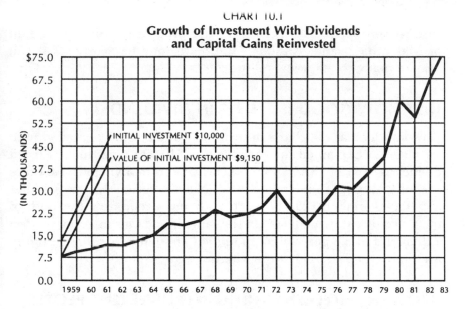

CHART 10.1
**Growth of Investment With Dividends
and Capital Gains Reinvested**

chure also states that "over the 25-year period, the funds [invest-ment] would have paid $15,917 in dividends. Additionally, a $10,000 investment would still have been worth $35,682 at the end of 1983." (See chart 10.2.) Sounds great. But is this your American dream?

Let's do some further analysis. Properly so, the brochure goes on

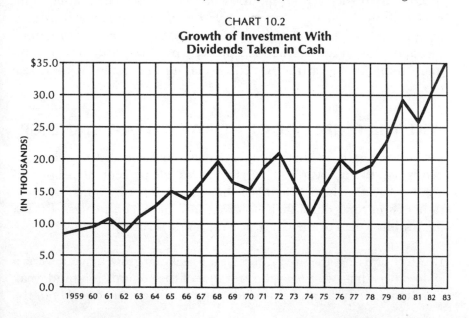

CHART 10.2
**Growth of Investment With
Dividends Taken in Cash**

to say that, "Past performance, of course, is no assurance of the future." Fair enough. But the rest of this brochure reminds me again of Mathemagicland. Although the math may be "correct," it can also be made to tell a few tall tales.

JUST HOW GOOD IS $15,917 IN DIVIDENDS?

Now let's look at the charts in terms of numbers and related growth statements. Explained another way, a $10,000 investment earned dividends of $15,917 and grew, exclusively from dividends, 1.6 times the initial amount invested. Sounds okay. A second way to say that is: $10,000 grew to $25,917, in total. Sounds good, too. But both of the preceding statements mean the same thing: Our investment paid a dividend of 3.8 percent compounded annually. But that certainly isn't going to put a Ferrari in your garage.

GROWTH: DIFFERENT THINGS TO DIFFERENT PEOPLE

The brochure maintains that after you received all that cash through dividends and spent it, you still had $10,000 turning into $35,682. That's called the growth. After all, you should be getting growth because you bought growth funds. But growth, and beauty, are in the eye of the beholder. Another way to analyze the growth to $35,682 is to shorten the math. It equals 5.2 percent annual compound growth. In summary, you've taken your dividends in cash and made Ford payments (some anyway), and your money gained through growth an average 5.2 percent per year. But whose summary sounds more attractive, the brochure's or mine? Mine is real too.

WILL THE TRUE LEVEL OF GROWTH PLEASE STAND UP

Let's look again at chart 10.2, "Growth of Investment with Dividends Taken in Cash." (This is the way 90 percent of people invest—they take the dividends of their stocks in cash and enjoy them rather than compound their holdings into more certificates.) I think the middle years of the chart deserve some scrutiny:

1. After starting the investment and seeking growth, you were a loser the first two-plus years because of the commission (and weak management didn't help either). In fact, after only one day in the

fund, your initial investment of $10,000 is only worth $9,150. The difference is in your broker's wallet.

2. Follow the line on the graph through 1963. After five years, you made only 10 percent total overall growth, or less than a 2 percent compounded rate, for half a decade.

3. After a decade you finally doubled your money, a compound rate of 7 percent, but thereafter your investment went down again and, allowing for two brief exceptions in time, took an additional ten years (what's another decade?) to get to where you started ten years earlier. Put another way, you gained some gray hair over those ten years, but your fund gained nothing!

4. You unfortunately lived through year sixteen when the market fell precipitously. At that point you had owned your funds for sixteen years, and they provided an annual compound growth rate of merely 1.7 percent. Your $10,000 investment had grown only through "growth" (management expertise) to $13,000. If you had bought the fund for a newborn daughter, by her sweet-sixteenth birthday sour might have been a better term.

5. If the chart had been compiled two years earlier, stopping at twenty-three years (in 1981) instead of twenty-five, it would have "died" at a market bottom, rather than being bailed out by the market's sharp rise. That's also called "leaving them smiling." By 1981, the rate of growth was 4.2 percent, or $10,000 growing to only $26,000, over twenty-three years.

You should be shaking your head. Does all of the preceding sound as good as turning $10,000 into $82,465? Don't all raise your hands at once.

IS 4 PERCENT OF ANYTHING A GOOD SURVEY?

First of all, the brochure gives no indication of how the "anointed" funds were chosen—I would have liked to be a bird in one of the square-rooted trees in Wall Street's Mathemagicland for that important meeting. The brochure merely states that 35 funds were selected as a sample. But it also said there was a total of 860 funds. Granted, there were fewer to choose from twenty-five years ago. Nevertheless, that means the preceding charts and figures were based on about 4 percent of funds in existence when the brochure was distributed.

Second, what does the brochure mean when it says that the rate of return takes in "successful and less successful funds?" Certainly the researchers are too savvy to use the top 35 funds, but they probably chose funds at least close to the top. Doesn't that make you wonder how the average fund did? Next, how good is 8.8 percent annual compounding over the time period versus other unexplored alternatives? The brochure offers no answers, right?—even though it states that this "is an extremely attractive rate compared with alternative investments." And finally, what is the source of this very authoritative-sounding information?

As footnoted in the brochure, the charts were prepared by the "Investment Company Institute," a "central intelligence agency" for the mutual fund industry. They are legal, but they could be biased. And they are good at what they do—supplying data on the mutual fund industry—supportive data in order to sell. Now all the average investor has to do is hesitate a moment and then learn how to interpret this data or find unbiased sources of information, such as the Wiesenberger Investment Companies Service "Management Results," Standard & Poor's, and Lipper Analytical Service. They are good sources and quite complete for anyone who wants details. I have listed them in Chapter 13, "Financial Publications: Favorites of the Pros."

APPLES TO APPLES: INVESTMENT COMPARISONS

Performance

While past performance is never a sure indication of future results, most investors are looking for good performance figures and, I might add, most funds are trying to perform well. From 1974 to mid-1984, according to Wiesenberger's research based on following a group of 540 funds, the average growth fund increased 168 percent. Potential sales charges were not considered when calculating performance, and reinvestment of all capital gains and dividends was assumed. That sounds good on the surface. But what do the numbers really mean?

As a final statistical foray into analyzing the growth/track record of mutual funds, let's closely examine that performance during those 10½ years as it compares to alternative investments. To do this, I have prepared the following table, which is an analysis of several popular investments or major investment indexes. This table lists both the total percentage gain made by the investment or index over the 10½-year period as well as the annual rate of gain, compounded. Thus, we are able to compare the track records of these alternative investments, usually omitted in most sales literature, to the track record of the growth funds.

After further research I found that if we ignore the Consumer Price Index (inflation), alternative investments in half the following areas outpaced the return of growth mutual funds.

Assuredly, the gain of 168 percent was very good versus the Dow Jones's increase of 93.2 percent, and Standard & Poor's 500 Stock Index rising 116 percent. In this regard it is obvious that mutual fund management can have a proven worth in at least exceeding the performance of the averages. Yet that still doesn't help the investor sort through choices to find the best investment for his money.

But first more results. One would think that if you take risks, you are entitled to greater rewards, especially over a long period of time, say, 10½ years. Not so. It seems investing can never be that easy or logical. Note the following:

—The funds that had growth with income did better than growth funds overall (194 percent versus 168 percent).
—The most conservative, the income funds, did best, rising 210 percent.
—The worst group was the balanced funds (141 percent), showing that you shouldn't try to be all things to all people (at least not during those ten years).

Table 10.1 / GROWTH FUNDS VERSUS OTHER INVESTMENT ALTERNATIVES

Investment	10½-Year Gain	Average Percent Year/Compounded
Growth Funds	168%	9.8%
Moody's Corp. bonds, Baa	227%	12.0%
Prime rate	210%	11.4%
Moody's Corp. bonds, Aaa	186%	10.6%
Growth funds	**168%**	**9.8%**
Commercial paper, 3-month	160%	9.5%
U.S. Treasury, long-term bonds (over 10-year maturity)	154%	9.4%
U.S. Treasury, 3-month T-bills	138%	8.7%
Consumer Price Index	111%	7.4%

As you can see, the way funds define themselves isn't always an indicator of how they will perform—which further complicates the investor's decisions. Judging by the above results, you now know to question "what's in a name." At least for the above decade growth was a way to have your money grow, income provided more than that when judged overall, and balanced was the least effective, although one might have felt he or she was covering all bases with a balanced purchase. Maybe the names will hold true next decade, contrary to how they performed in the last one.

The Most Popular Funds

For now, let's focus on the growth fund area that is the most popular fund arena and representative of why people buy mutual funds. (It is also the most quoted area for funds' performance figures.) Again, according to Wiesenberger's study, from 1974 to 1984 the funds' average growth was a respectable 9.8 percent, compounded annually. But, in analyzing our 9.8 percent figure, consider this:

—that dividends represent 3.9 percent of the 9.8 percent growth
—that management's skills were responsible for 5.9 percent of the
  9.8 percent growth

Not terrible, but probably not as fantastic as you originally thought. Perhaps you now see how difficult it is to pick the best funds from among so many choices. And half are below average. When I think of mutual fund analysis, I remember a saying my mother told me when I was figuring out whiffleball batting averages. "No matter what the subject, you can be sure if there is more than one, half are above average and half will always be below average." And half of all mutual funds strike out—and are therefore below average. They just don't advertise it.

Compounding Your Costs and Losses

Upon a further analysis of our decade's example, if you were to demand a minimum growth level of 8 percent annually (even with dividends and gains combined), you would need more direction, and luck, to find a fund that met that relatively modest requirement. You can further apply reality to the Wiesenberger study by including the sales charge of 8.5 percent charged on load fund purchases of $10,000 or less (they didn't, although it was a common occurrence, especially before the recent growth in availability of no-load funds). When an 8.5 percent fee is figured in the performance of growth funds (due to the compounding of those immediately lost sales expenses), the gain is not 168 percent, but actually 145 percent. That substantial drop changes the annual rate of return from 9.8 percent to 8.8 percent.

I have not considered no-loads in my analysis because during the time period of our example they were much less common than today. One can gain a greater appreciation for their benefits, however, when analyzing the above for loss of growth because of initial sales charges, especially when the loss is compounded over time. (More about no-loads later.)

How Much Does a Sales Charge Really Cost?

The following table is similar to our preceding table with the exception that our growth funds' return has been corrected and recalculated with the assumption of a $10,000 investment incurring the maximum sales charge of 8.5 percent. With the return dropping from 168 percent to 145 percent, many things now change. Let's look.

Table 10.2 / GROWTH FUNDS (INCLUDING MAXIMUM SALES CHARGE) VERSUS OTHER INVESTMENT ALTERNATIVES

Investment	10½-Year Gain	Average Percent Year/Compounded
Growth Funds	168%	9.8%
Moody's Corp. bonds, Baa	227%	12.0%
Prime rate	210%	11.4%
Moody's Corp. bonds, Aaa	186%	10.6%
Commercial paper, 3-month	160%	9.5%
U.S. Treasury, long-term bonds (over 10-year maturity)	154%	9.4%
Growth funds*	**145%**	**8.8%**
U.S. Treasury, 3-month T-bills	138%	8.7%
Consumer Price Index	111%	7.4%

* Reflects return after 8.5% sales charge.

With our new table, all but U.S. Treasury bills beat the funds' gains. And the T-bills were beaten only by a minimal amount—145 percent versus 138 percent—or 7 percent, with no risk. The risk factor is important here: When you consider the possibility or probability of buying a fund that underperforms the mean/average mutual fund (after all, 50 percent of all mutual funds did just that—underperform) choosing a riskless investment like a T-bill and accepting a slightly smaller gain seems somewhat appealing. If you don't choose T-bills, there are only two things left to consider: Where are interest rates going in the future, and what is the stock market going to do? We're back to guessing again.

In fairness, several of the above long-term bond indexes, such as Baa or Aaa, grew much better than comparable investments, but the bonds themselves are sometimes valued at less than their original purchase price, and therein lies another potential for loss. This table did not take that possibility into consideration. One justification is that although the bonds can go down, they are also contractually obligated to pay their original value back, in full, at some predetermined time (except for the rare case of default). Thus, there would be no loss. No mutual fund does that.

Finally, the most important aspect of the above table is knowing what the returns were for several alternative investments, good or bad, in comparison to funds, and knowing that comparisons are possible. Every investor should consider this information before making an investment decision. Yet the probability of seeing comprehensive comparisons, especially when not advantageous to the seller of the investment, is unlikely when dealing with Wall Street or Main Street—which is more reason for you to study my Appendix of Tables and Charts.

SIZE AND PERFORMANCE

Better Can Mean Bigger, But Bigger Can Mean Different

Recently a major firm's mutual fund department report stated that among 385 funds it followed (that had survived the past ten years), 13 funds had gains in excess of 1,000 percent, and 68 funds had gains of 500 percent to 1,000 percent. Those annual rates of return are handsome, and not levels investors are accustomed to achieving. But a note of caution: Many of the funds that have done well are no longer the same size or have the same degree of agility they had when they created their terrific track records. Yet they are selling their past performances to today's investors, few of whom pay much attention to the fact that eight to ten years ago their fund had only $200 million in total assets to invest/diversify—and now it has $2 billion. But isn't bigger better, you'd like to know? Not always. Let's follow a successful fund to see why.

Ten years ago, a fund's managers bought shares of several small OTC stocks, each with .5 percent of the fund's assets. By establishing those investment positions the fund excelled because its stocks rose. Today, ten years later, that same fund has $2 billion, not just $200 million. Its size has increased because of management gains and the sales of new shares. Making profits draws attention, and attention is money in this business. But with such large funds to invest, just .5 percent of the portfolio would buy *all shares* of the small OTC stock the managers liked years ago. They can't buy all the shares of a company. They don't want to own and operate companies—so they don't. After all, what do they know about genetic engineering? They are forced to manage money differently. They buy stocks that are large enough to absorb their large positions, like GE, GM, and AT&T. That kind of stock picking is quite different from buying unique small gems of stocks that can be located anywhere, on the American Exchange or OTC, not just on the NYSE. Those atypical selections were part of their past portfolio and past performance. But now that the fund has changed its style of investing, you have to worry about today, not the past. Even when key managers who made your fund great leave, the fund name often stays the same.

Size presents another problem. When a crisis occurs and you have an elephant-sized investment in something like Union Carbide, the elephant can't dance out of its holdings as quickly as a smaller fund. When the disaster happened in Bhopal, India, the floor traders from one major mutual fund were standing at the sell window for three days trying to dump their position. They had to "ease out" because selling their entire position in one day would have obliterated the stock. Smaller funds were out of it in a half day. Needless to say, the stock had dropped steadily by the third day.

Let's Create a Fund

Let's form a fund—The Diversified Hoola Hoop Fund—because you're clairvoyant. You sense that there is a reemerging fad with strong traits of longevity. Oscar the Grouch just sang a song with a hoola hoop around his waist. Kids are buying them like crazy. Companies are springing up everywhere, manufacturing hoops of various weights and sizes. Musical hoops. Fluorescent hoops for evening use. Hoops that will float. People need professional help in sorting out which hoop company is the best investment. People need a new mutual fund. You create one—The Diversified Hoola Hoop Fund.

Soon the stocks of your carefully chosen companies skyrocket; your fund soars with their success; management fees and operational profits fill your pockets. But there's a problem. When the Hoola Hoop Fund gets larger it can no longer invest in the same Hoola Hoop companies because even a small percentage of its fund could *own* some of those companies. You like hoops, but you don't want to be president of a hoop company that produces them. So the HH Fund now has to look around for new companies, slightly larger companies and slightly duller ones, like Kat Toys and Kitty Litter. The world needs Kitty Litter, although it isn't quite a fad. The fund does well; its HH reputation is still bringing in new investors. You make *Forbes*'s Honor Roll, and the next year you are a Wiesenberger champion. There's a new problem: The fund has grown so large that it is juggling too many stocks from too many companies. Now, in order not to own Kat Toy companies, you buy the stock of larger companies—GM, AT&T. They're boring and dull, but at least you can't end up owning them. You and the other managers yearn for wilder times. You decide to sell HH. You make reservations for the islands and pack your favorite floating hoops. The sale of your HH Fund goes through. You make a bundle. The new owners love the Hoola Hoop name and want to keep it. They admire the track record and need the name to advertise the fund. They pay you well for it. Half your key personnel leave for the islands with you; half stay. People are still buying the fund like crazy—but suddenly everything has changed. Better did mean bigger, but when you got too big you got very different.

The moral is: Learn to look for changes in your fund's size, investment style and policy, and its managers. They are potentially dangerous to the continued success of your fund.

DO YOU KNOW WHERE YOUR FUND'S ORIGINAL MANAGERS ARE?

Like your HH Fund, funds that have done well over the years usually have wealthy fund managers. Some are now sipping wine on their yachts and no longer manage the fund that is advertising their past exploits. Or perhaps they remain with the fund, but only part-time—after all, owning a yacht takes time too. If so, the investors only hope is that the fund's new players are as good as the old. Or they depend on a broker to warn them that this "name" fund is not what it appears. Funds have been known to sell out their entire operation, as American Capital Funds did, but the buyer (the new seller to investors) keeps the name of the fund intact. Remember our Hoola Hoop Fund. It would have been harder to sell if we had changed the name. But the islands were calling.

PROFIT MOTIVATIONS

Why do mutual fund managers want people to invest in them? Quite frankly, they want a tiny piece of all that action—over $500 billion, excluding money market funds. Money market funds have the same objective; however, they simply seek a smaller percentage take.

I used to walk racehorses when I was fourteen years old (I lived two miles from Monmouth Park racetrack), and all this reminds me of how a racetrack operates. The track wants to increase betting because it receives a portion of each bet. Likewise, mutual funds have their take:

—Funds impose an annual charge of .5 percent to 1.5 percent for investment advisory services, depending on the fund.
—Some funds take a small percentage of the initial sales charge, with the major portion going to the broker.
—Some funds charge a redemption fee when a client sells his shares. It is seldom more than 1 percent and often less. Sometimes there is no redemption fee. But if the fee is levied, it is one more expense to the investor and profit for the fund.
—Some no-load funds charge withering withdrawal penalties of 5 percent to 6 percent decreasing to 0 percent over several years.
—Some no-load funds have no withdrawal charges but may have significant annual advisory charges taken from the fund's assets each year.

To be fair, many of these fees cover expenses such as reports, secretaries, office rent, and printing costs for brochures. But if the fund operates efficiently, and most do, then a sizable portion of all charges can safely be labeled the profit motivation for running a mutual fund.

THE BROKER'S MOTIVATION

Why is your broker trying to sell you a mutual fund? The obvious answer is that a percentage of it will show up in his paycheck. But:

—Does he really know how to explain the various fund choices and subtleties of each that are relevant to your situation?
—Does he know how to direct your money most advantageously within those specific chosen areas, such as outlining the benefits of a "family" of funds?
—Does he just want you to buy an investment that could immediately make him almost eight times more in fees than an equivalent stock purchase?

Don't be shy about trying to figure out what your broker's motives are.

THE PAYOUT: A FAIR DEAL

Another potential negative in buying mutual funds is the inordinately high payout (percentage of the commission actually paid "out") to the broker. It is often 50 percent—in contrast to a 35 percent to 40 percent average level for many other investment products, such as stocks or options. Some firms now use a payout schedule that cuts this back to between 40 percent and 45 percent, unless the fund is sold by a Big Producer. For example, on a "load fund" $10,000 mutual fund order the commission can be as high as 8.5 percent, or $850 to the firm. Of this, the broker receives $425 (50 percent) net. As the order size increases, the sales charge decreases, so at $25,000 the sales charge is 6 percent, and the 50 percent payout nets the broker $750 in his paycheck. For example:

$25,000	×	6 percent	= $1,500	× 50 percent =	$750
investment		commission	p/c	payout	broker's paycheck

Does this reflect fair compensation? Yes—especially when you remember that a mutual fund sale is a one-shot fee. In addition, your broker ultimately would have made more money selling you 100 shares of stock to be traded over the course of, say, ten years. Recently the industry has tried to address the disadvantage of the one-time fee and, starting in 1983, some funds pay brokers a tiny annual "trailer" fee, based on the client remaining in their fund. (On a $100,000 investment the broker may receive an annual fee of $100.) You won't notice this fee because it is paid by the fund, not billed to you as an investor. There is also no commission paid to the broker upon sale of the fund. As noted above, occasionally the client is charged a 1 percent (redemption) fee for selling, and certain no-load funds have withering withdrawal penalties. Neither the redemption fee nor the withdrawal charges end up as commissions to your broker. Lastly, initial sales charges above 4 percent are becoming less commonplace with the advent of the no-load/withering withdrawal penalty funds.

THE PURE NO-LOAD FUNDS

The debate continues over the value of using mutual funds with no sales charge, a common trait of newer mutual funds—they have no front-end loads. However, many no-loads often have deferred sales charges in the form of withering withdrawals—a back-end load—if they are sold by brokerage firms, banks, or insurance companies.

Even as a stockbroker, I must admit that no-load funds with good track records should be investigated. When purchased under proper circumstances, these funds can be a good deal. For example, if you stay for three to five years in a fund such as a withering withdrawal penalty fund, you eventually avoid all or most delayed sales charges. Therefore many clients choose not to cash in their assets in a fund for several years. In addition, almost all withering sales charge funds (back-end load) allow access to your income from the fund at all times without any penalty. And many no-loads have excellent track records. I sell them (no load/withering withdrawal funds) to clients every day.

But a note of caution: Even no-front-end and -back-end load mutual funds charge annual fees. These fees vary and can undermine your original intent to save money. Track records for no-loads also vary as much as they do for load funds. So why save on sales charges just to invest in a poorly performing fund? Performance is more important than fees.

NO-LOAD DOESN'T MEAN NO COMMISSION

Finally, keep in mind that most full-service brokerage firms offer several no-load funds. As a matter of fact, brokers make almost as much money on no-loads as they do on loads; it is just a different compensation arrangement. But to find out more about the funds and their fees, you have to ask the experts—experts who mainly get paid for selling items with fees attached to them. Maybe that's why a recent statistic by one major firm showed that the average mutual fund order was $15,000, yet only $1,500 for direct-mail no-load funds. Take note: The big money seems willing to pay the fees, if levied. And better performance might be part of the answer.

Before buying a no-load fund, there are key points to consider that make load funds (or no-loads that have withdrawal penalties) highly competitive with no-loads:

—If you are a large investor, your initial fees decrease the more you invest.
—If you plan to add to your original investment within twelve to fifteen months, you can take advantage of the "add-on" contract provision called "breakpoint." This allows you to increase your investment later but immediately receive a lower sales charge based on the total amount to be invested over time.
—When dividend and capital gains are reinvested, there is never a sales charge.

To find out the true bottom line on performance and fees of the no-loads, you must consult neutral investigative sources—Standard & Poor's and others, or read the fine print yourself. Several newsletters also follow their track records. But your broker or banker won't sell you a no-load fund if they can help it. Here you must be your own expert, but if you want to take on the task, the savings can be worth it. If you do buy a no-load/withdrawal penalty fund, plan to keep within the limits to avoid the penalty and thus pay no sales charges—ever.

TRADING FUNDS VERSUS EXCHANGING FAMILY MEMBERS

Investors don't regularly move from one fund to another; they shouldn't either. Occasionally a broker might attempt to "trade" a client into another, "better" fund and gain another big commission. But this form of abuse is discouraged by major firms and rarely occurs. In fact, when a broker "trades" a client from one fund to another he has to admit to this in writing on the new purchase order ticket. (A "trade" is different from transferring money within the same "family.")

THE <u>GOOD</u> NEWS ABOUT MUTUAL FUNDS

I've spent the first part of the chapter advising you to be wary of mutual funds; now for the good news. Historically speaking, mutual funds have been around for years—since the early twenties. Through periods of terrible markets and national crises, their number gradually increased from seventy in 1940 to around fifteen hundred today. The last ten years have shown the best levels of growth, overall, since the funds were first monitored. The last two years have been explosive. That reflects a better market environment, to be sure, but it is also true that the best-managed funds continue to substantially outperform the major stock market indexes. The industry has learned from past mistakes, and natural selection (i.e., "survival of the fittest") in effect has shaped the structure of funds as we know them today. So let's examine the reasons for buying mutual funds in today's marketplace.

Mutual Funds Have the Protection of Government Regulation

Since the passing of the Investment Company Act of 1940, the government has been overseeing the mutual fund industry, and abuses today are rare. Fortunately, such government regulation is a form of protection for the investor.

Track Records Are Evaluated by Neutral Sources

The track records of mutual funds, which can be presented in Mathemagic terms in sales brochures, are more realistically presented in several neutral sources such as Standard & Poor's, Wiesenberger, and Lipper Analytical.

Diversification of Assets Reduces Risks

I'd rather own twenty municipal bonds in a municipal bond fund than hold one bond and have Murphy's Law a few years later present me with a notice of default regarding my lonely lemon bond. If the same lemon bond were held in my municipal bond fund, I would lose one twentieth, or 5 percent. Professional management and such diversification cannot help but eliminate the risk of having your egg in one bad basket, which can happen should you go it on your own.

The Funds Are Professionally Managed

The fund managers watch stocks, bonds, and their subgroups, such as utility stocks, with a multitude of resources that only a multimillionaire could duplicate. But that multimillionaire wouldn't have the managers' contacts. While professionals can be less than spectacular, I've seen many a solo client do much worse than a poor fund.

Shares Are Liquid and Can Be Sold for Cash Quickly and Easily

Buying (and selling) your mutual fund is the same as dealing with a stock or bond. The shares are quoted daily as to price. One buys and pays in five business days, or one sells and receives the proceeds in five business days, sometimes less.

Funds Have Low Investment Minimums

For this reason, mutual funds are excellent for IRAs, Keoghs, and children's custodial accounts. Many funds allow as little as fifty dollars to be invested.

Funds Eliminate Excessive Trading in an Account

Investing in a mutual fund eliminates the temptation for a broker to create more sales commissions through excessive trading of your account. This is a powerful argument for mutual funds, although it is impossible to calculate the savings derived from it. Nevertheless, it is possible to recognize how funds limit the possibilities for trading abuses.

The Menu of Services Is Varied

—Distributions of dividends/gains can be reinvested into the shares of the fund you hold or any other fund offered by the adviser/manager of funds you are presently invested in, without any sales charge. For example, depending on the fund, a service frequently offered provides automatic depositing of your fund's dividends directly into another "family" member's money fund, on which you can write a check and collect excellent rates of interest until your check clears. Your paycheck can be set up for direct deposit into most funds, too.

—Quarterly statements are issued, more frequently if activity justifies, at no charge.

—Fiduciary record keeping for retirement plans, IRAs/Keoghs, and pension and profit-sharing accounts is provided either free of charge or at a nominal rate.

—Brochures describing the fund's philosophy, services, and even its track record are available from many sources. And mutual fund track records are audited, unlike those of professional money managers.

—Once your money has been invested in a fund, the fund has a vested interest in seeing you remain, due to annual fees, potential for reinvestment of funds, and capital additions.

All of the above factors benefit the fund as well as the investor. Indeed, it is an advantage to the investor and the manager that the goal of each is the same: excellent overall performance.

PERFORMANCE COUNTS

Another reason I recommend this form of investment is that there are some very well-managed funds, funds that I feel over a reasonable period of time have and will outperform popular alternative methods of investment, including your broker and/or his firm's ideas. An examination of the returns of the top performing funds shows results that are truly superb. In the following table, I have listed the top fifteen funds' gains (as reported by Wiesenberger from January 1976 to March 1986) together with their respective sales charges.

Note the Fidelity Magellan Fund ($6.0 billion in size) would normally have been listed as a top performer, but it was not given a rating for having had a change of either management or policy in 1981.

As I said earlier, one firm recently tracked thirteen funds with gains in excess of 1,000 percent and sixty-eight with gains from 500 percent to 1,000 percent plus. The object now is to find them.

Table 10.3 / TOP-PERFORMING MUTUAL FUNDS

Name	Percentage Gain	Sales Charge	Fund Size/ $Millions
1. Twentieth Century Growth	1,365	1% redemption	975
2. Quasar Assoc., Inc.	1,355	none	187
3. Evergreen*	1,246	redemption fee	589
4. Twentieth Century Select	1,232	none	1,738
5. Lindner*	1,194	none	411
6. American Capital Pace	1,127	load	2,102
7. Sequoia*	984	none	667
8. Fidelity Destiny	951	load	1,117
9. Over-the-Counter Securities	940	load	197
10. Value Line Leveraged Growth	939	none	270
11. Weingarten Equity	892	load	200
12. Amev Special	876	load	130
13. Acorn	851	redemption fee	382
14. Nicholas	842	none	955
15. Mass. Capital Development	811	load	923
Fidelity Magellan	—	load	6,037

* Closed to new buyers.

FUNDS, FUNDS EVERYWHERE

The diversity of ways to invest your money within mutual funds, and especially within a fund's family of alternatives, makes mutual funds particularly attractive. One can switch from an aggressive philosophy in a fund group to income or "balanced" funds or both—at a moment's notice, normally for no charge. It is not commonly done, but the choice is yours.

Types of Funds

Below are the types of mutual funds being sold today as referenced by the Investment Company Institute.

Growth: a fund whose primary objective is long-term growth of capital. Principally invested in stocks with growth potential. This form of growth fund usually has greater concentration in blue-chip companies such as AT&T and GE, not just any form of growth stock.

Aggressive growth: a fund seeking maximum capital appreciation through the use of techniques involving greater-than-ordinary risk, such as borrowing money in order to provide leverage, short selling, hedging, options, and warrants. Also invests in "wildcat" companies that could strike it rich. A common investment would be OTC stock of high-tech companies and small corporations in general.

Growth and income: a fund whose aim is to provide for a degree of both income and long-term growth through, for example, a combination of IBM, convertible bonds, and utility stocks.

Balanced: a fund that has an investment policy of balancing its portfolio, generally through a mixture of bonds, preferred stocks, and common stocks.

Option/income: The fund's objective is to seek high current return by investing primarily in dividend-paying stocks on which call options are traded on national securities exchanges. Current return generally consists of dividends, premiums from expired call options, net short-term gains from sales of portfolio securities on exercises of options or otherwise, and any profits from closing purchase transactions.

Income: a fund whose objective is current income rather than growth of capital. Basic investments are bonds, utility stocks, and convertible bonds.

Corporate bond: a mutual fund whose portfolio consists mostly of corporate bonds, with emphasis on income rather than growth.

Municipal bond: a fund that invests within a range of tax-exempt bonds. The fund's objective is current tax-free income.

Short-term municipal bond: These funds invest in municipal securities with relatively short maturities. They are also known as tax exempt money market funds.

Money market: Also called a liquid asset or cash fund. A fund for immediate income and high investment safety through the purchase of high-yield money market instruments such as U.S. government securities, bank certificates of deposit, and commercial paper.

Specialty funds: These funds are of particular interest because of their amazing diversity. Examples are gold, international investment, insurance and bank stock, tax-exempts, U.S. Governments, diversified precious metals, health care, electronics, marine/oceanic investments, aviation technology, international bonds, individual foreign funds, and high-technology funds. In fact, over the years various investment areas, such as a fund to harvest the wealth of the oceans, have even become fads. This fund invests in companies hoping to profit from the sea through exploration for minerals, oil, energy—you name it.

Actually, this example is not so bizarre when you consider that some people on the Street believe that market cycles can be predicted by sunspot activity. The market is supposed to rise when sunspot activity is on the increase. This belief is based on comparisons of known levels of activity on the sun's surface to known levels of performance of our down-to-earth stock market.

The sunspot theory is topped by the consistency of the Super Bowl Axiom. According to Wall Street analysts, history has shown us that when an original NFC team wins the NFL's Super Bowl, the market will rise. Whereas if an AFC team wins, we'll go down. It has worked in eighteen of the twenty Super Bowls for which results are in, or 90 percent of the time. When Frank Gifford leaves television, he should take a shot at being Wall Street's next guru. With theories like these it is difficult to question the logic of a specialty fund, oceanic or otherwise.

TWO MAIN TYPES

There are two primary forms of funds—closed-end and open-end. Closed-end funds are just that in terms of the amount of shares they may issue to the public. The shares trade on exchanges and are normally priced by supply and demand at slightly less than their book value. Through mid-1984 the seven closed-end funds followed by Wiesenberger Services were selling at 4 percent below book value. By the end of 1985, closed-end funds represented only $8 billion of the investment companies' total value of $500 billion.

Most investors associate open-end funds with mutual funds. These funds continue to offer shares to the public in an "open-ended" fashion. They grow larger with the public's investment of additional funds and through reinvestment of dividends and/or capital gains. At times, specific funds, as well as funds in general, become less popular. When this happens, the funds receive investors' requests for redemptions (sales) and are forced to liquidate (sell) some of the securities they have purchased for investment. This is an example of the negative influence of institutional pressures in today's marketplace.

Funds account for a huge segment of the institutional marketplace. The funds sometimes have to sell their positions because the market has dropped and investors/managers are either disappointed or scared, or both. In a down market in which mutual funds sell to meet redemptions, the market slides faster and further, helped along by the big sell orders of the funds that must meet those redemptions. They sell their stocks to create cash to pay investors. It's an ugly circle, but a fact of today's marketplace.

Another positive attribute of funds is their ability to buy and sell a stock for as little as two cents a share. This low cost of trading increases the likelihood that funds will change their shares around more often than you and I. They can do it cheaper and therefore justify doing it more often. As a result, when they sell they sometimes "mow over" an individual investor's portfolio. If you've owned 100 shares of IBM at $150 a share for four months, and then suddenly the big funds sell, IBM is going to get killed. Your IBM stock could drop to $125 in one week. Whether a fund's action is right or wrong is secondary to the fact that it can clobber a stock by simply unloading it. Nobody, including the funds, will know whether they were smart or dumb to do so until long after the fact. But they will definitely leave the individual investor mumbling about how and why his IBM was swamped in the wake.

Perhaps one of the most intriguing changes in mutual funds is the growth in availability of no-load mutual funds, especially through commission brokers. In 1987 over one-third of total mutual fund sales was done by no-loads. Despite my previous warnings, a free "entrance" into a fund that has a good track record can be a good deal—especially if it is being monitored by your broker's firm. I discuss such a fund in a later chapter, "The Right Stuff." For the record, Wall Street is aware that people don't like the terms *commission* or *sales charge* and continues to try to eliminate these words from the investor's vocabulary—while at the same time creating new ways of disguising them.

YOUR BROKER'S ADVICE

At this point you have been warned about the pitfalls and alerted to substantial advantages of mutual funds. If you now want to invest in a mutual fund, what's your next step?

First, you should look for a knowledgeable broker and ask his advice. Also, you can send for prospectuses from various funds, but beware of the "mathemagic" they use to make their fund sound wonderful—imminently capable of buying you that Ferrari. I still find that in spite of all the information included in a prospectus, I can only partially evaluate a fund by reading one. So ask a broker his advice. He probably has additional information that can help. But remember, it is crucial that your broker recommend a fund that reflects your long-range goals—not his. How can you ensure this? In order to better judge your broker's suggestions when he pulls out a slick, red brochure with sexy charts, ask the following questions:

1. What type of fund(s) should I invest in? Growth, income, balanced, specialized, etc., given my situation, age, income, etc.?
2. Is the fund a load or no-load? If a no-load, does it have withdrawal penalties, and what are they?
3. If it is a load, what is your charge for a purchase of X dollars?
4. What are the fund(s) past one-year, five-year, and ten-year records?
5. What is the yield of the fund? Is the yield "net" after all fees, especially management fees?
6. Has the fund's size changed significantly (grown larger?) over the years?
7. Is today's management the same (relatively) as the management that was responsible for the past track record?
8. Does your company approve of and monitor this fund? (If so, ask for some research.)
9. Is the fund a member of a family of funds within which I can transfer my money? If so, at what charge, if any?

By the way, if you're still concerned about performance, buy (or ask your broker for) a copy of *Standard & Poor's Stock Guide*. Turn to the back section entitled "Mutual Funds." It follows almost all funds. Find the column titled "$10,000 Invested" over a given period of time (usually five or six years). That column tells you what that same $10,000 is worth today. Take some time and compare different funds from this section. Now you're comparing apples to apples.

WHO SHOULD BUY A MUTUAL FUND

When someone asks me if there is a profile of the perfect mutual fund investor, I always answer no. This investment is so varied and flexible that it can be a lot of things to a lot of people—from a millionaire to the person with a small IRA, from the sophisticated investor to the amateur. So, although I can't give you a mutual fund investor's profile, let's see who some of these investors are:

—people who want to take some slight risk (by choosing a growth fund, etc.) to outpace interest rates available from banks. They are willing to invest their money for at least three to five years, preferably longer.

—investors who hold IRAs or Keoghs or pension funds—from only $500 up to $1 million or more.

—investors who appreciate diversity and don't feel entirely comfortable investing with equities, hence risk investments, through their broker or on their own.

—people who believe in track records. Mutual funds, properly researched, provide clear-cut records of past performance, something a newsletter, banker, or broker rarely does.

—an investor who believes the market will outperform alternatives, but has been burned in trying to do so himself. While rare, the truly excellent funds provide superb results from a rather tricky environment. They deserve a lot of credit for this.

—investors who want to leave well enough alone. They want to invest their money, take notice of quarterly statements, and hope for good, long-term results. They like having the record keeping done for them, a service not offered by many close alternative investments.

—people who do not want their accounts to be churned or do not want to pay a sales commission. Mutual funds avoid churning because they lack a commission upon sale, only on purchase. Sales charges can be avoided by no-loads, although remember those withering withdrawal charges.

—investors inclined to invest in the securities marketplace but who want to walk before they run. The various "sector" or specialized funds help educate investors about industries and trends, while a professional watches over the nest egg.

If you can relate to any of the above cameo profiles, consider mutual funds as an investment area for your money. Once you and your broker have done all the homework, you will have an excellent investment with above-average potential for gains. Mutual funds have withstood the test of time and the marketplace and have evolved into a solid investment vehicle, capable of providing safe and substantial gains. Success is really a question of going beyond the magic to the math.

One last word: Despite the easy money made in the marketplace in 1985 and 1986, and reflected in mutual fund performance, remember that every year is not a 1985. If the marketplace kept up the 1985 pace for an extended period of time, everyone's money would double every 2 ½ years. The Roaring Twenties would look dull by comparison. Be sure to examine all mutual funds within the perspective of the last decade. Even in '85 and '86 many funds did not beat the averages. Did your fund make more than 60 percent from 1985 to 1986? The averages did just that.

(Author's note: The above paragraph was written in early 1987. By the end of 1987 many people had learned an expensive lesson, as the quote at the beginning of this chapter ominously foretold. Remember the irony of these events the next time any investment, including mutual funds, looks to be *very* attractive.)

Chapter Eleven

TAX SHELTERS: BEFORE AND AFTER THEY CHANGED THE RULES

> I'll sell a tax shelter when I hear about one that pays its investors their money back, let alone a profit. So far I've never heard of a single one."
> —FORMER ASSOCIATE, SIX YEARS AFTER HIS FIRM
> BEGAN SELLING SHELTERS.

Billions of dollars in tax shelters have been sold by Wall Street and Main Street. However, when Congress came up with sweeping tax reforms in 1986, it seemed as though tax shelters were doomed to extinction. In general, investors were already unhappy with their performance, so nobody really mourned their loss, although lots of people mourned the billions of dollars shelters took with them when they sank.

What toppled the Shelter Empire? Nothing.

Tax shelters still exist. The laws have not outlawed them, merely changed them. They offer fewer tax benefits than before, and they still make promises they cannot deliver. Look around at today's programs. These quasi-tax-sheltered investments are being marketed as unique and sophisticated products when they are simply remodeled packages containing many, and sometimes all, of the negative attributes of their predecessor cousin. One syndicator was quoted recently by the *Wall Street Journal* as saying, "Clever people in our business will come up with all sorts of wrappings for the same old stuff." Indeed, the new generation of partnerships has many of the same high fees in the same confusing prospectuses, similar unrealistic assumptions—and in too many cases they will produce the same poor results.

In the 1970s tax shelters were marketed as relatively high-risk investments aimed at areas of the economy in which the government wanted to stimulate growth. For example, in the late seventies our country wanted to avoid huge importations of oil, whose high prices were crippling our economy. Tax incentives to encourage domestic oil exploration made sense. *Voilà*. Billions in oil shelters were sold. But the heavy emphasis on oil exploration at a time of peak demand turned out to be the wrong time to expand. Interest and exploration costs skyrocketed. And we all know what happened. Some programs even fouled up on fundamentals. They found *no* oil. The next time tax laws change, remember the investment consequences of partnerships from years gone by. Experience is a good teacher. Just don't pay too much for it.

CHANGING TAX LAWS EQUALS CHANGING SHELTERS

In terms of reducing your income taxes, consider your tax return as divided into three parts: regular income from wages and salaries; investment income from interest, dividends, and investment gains; and lastly "passive income"—the type that comes from partnership investments, such as tax shelters. There are ways to reduce each of these three distinct areas.

The best way to reduce your salary income is to have a home mortgage and deduct the interest payments on the mortgage. Tax shelters can't help lower the taxation on your salary anymore.

Investment income can be reduced by deducting interest paid on loans other than your mortgage up to a maximum of the total of the interest, dividends, and capital gains you take in. But this is a poor way to reduce your taxes—spending money on interest to negate the positive flow of interest, dividends, and investment gains.

Passive income can be reduced by using the good, old-fashioned tax shelter deductions—against good, old-fashioned gains and income generated by those same partnerships you purchase. Actually, you should thank Uncle Sam because he is forcing us to invest in partnerships with economic merit, not merely tax-saving merit. We therefore have to be more discriminating, because if our partnership investments aren't successful, then the deductions they generate will be wasted. In the past there were a lot of "dogs," but they stayed out of the pound because they had tax-saving merits. No longer. If you can't find a shelter that will make you money, skip it, for it isn't really a shelter—it can't shelter what it doesn't make.

Meanwhile, today's products are being made to sound more enticing, conservative, and capable of creating what they now must—gains and income—than ever before. But they haven't really changed much at all. To understand today's products we must clearly understand yesterday's. My review encompasses the following:

—definitions of the players in a partnership
—descriptions of fees and where they can be identified
—an analysis of some past programs—and why they failed
—investment situations to avoid
—the mathematics of shelters—the magic in their math

All these areas are important to understand before investing in today's programs. So consider the following not a history lesson, but an investment lesson for today.

THE TAX SHELTERS IN MY LIFE: A DECADE OF DISAPPOINTMENT

I admit it: I get emotional about tax shelters. The list of bad memories they have given me is longer than Wilt Chamberlain's arm. In fact, the only blot on my career was a suit brought by a client upset by the poor performance of some shelters. The case was settled out of court, but it has never been settled in my mind.

A shelter was also responsible for my largest investment debacle. It was a real estate investment that had been recommended by several Wall Street real estate experts. They said the project had a competent developer and a sound economic footing. (I'd now adamantly debate both points.) My clients, friends, and I lost tons of money and were constantly aggravated throughout the investment's unnecessarily prolonged life. I know now that from the outset the investment hung on the edge of a freshly dug grave.

I've had only one positive experience with a tax shelter. No doubt its success can be attributed to my partner, who's tall, dark, and handsome, with brown eyes and dark brown hair. He stands six feet nine inches tall from head to toe, and has broad shoulders females swoon over. When we're together he gets all the attention. He does have one unorthodox habit—the tendency to run around in circles, taking his partner along for the ride. But he is also goal-oriented, self-sufficient in business, and earns an excellent salary. I'm most jealous of his private life. When I was single I did all right, thank you, but he manages to seduce at least two dozen gals a year, primarily from February to July. He also has four legs and a tail. His name is Lordly Love. He's a thoroughbred racehorse owned by a partnership, Egbert Farm. My dog, Egbert, and I are the sole partners.

Egbert is the best sponsor I've worked with, and Lordly Love by far the best "developer." (Lately, he's been developing foals through cavorting with all those girlfriends.) I've made a lot of money with him. He's provided straightforward tax benefits, stakes victory purse monies, and now stud fees and progeny values. I want to come back as a famous racehorse stallion in my next life.

Since I don't anticipate another Lordly Love in my lifetime, let's consider all those other shelter alternatives. But we must tread carefully. Why? Because shelters have lost much of their magic. Recently, as sales slowed, the industry has tried to stop the decline by changing its old names to some newer ones: "tax-advantaged investments," "private placements," "special offerings," "syndications," and "direct investments." Though some partnerships have been better designed, less fee-laden, and better researched, they are hardly the norm. And their prospectuses are as confusing as ever. It's still tough to tell the good ones from the bad ones. Congress may be doing a better job of saving investors from themselves and their shelters than we realize.

THE SHELTER SOCIETY: LESSONS FOR NOW

In the past I bought and sold shelters because my clients and I wanted relief from the tax man and a decent return on our investments. I discovered, however, that the shelters' assumptions, estimates, and financial projections were usually very wrong. In fact, I can count on both hands the number of deals I know personally that ceased operation and returned the investor a profit. I have been involved in only two projects that returned profits on schedule— almost. Ultimately, most shelters are either late "paybacks," "breakevens," "losers," or dead and buried. Here are a few calamities.

Calamity number one: In a 1984 study of highly touted public oil programs offered by a major firm over the past decade, only 11 out of 116 were expected to return the original cash outlay, or "breakeven." Since then, oil has dropped so dramatically that now probably only 1 out of 116 will be profitable.

Calamity number two: This deal was concocted by a big brokerage firm that liked leasing deals. How about railroad cars? They called them rolling stock (I now suspect they meant their clients' heads). Like most leasing transactions, the cars needed to be used as rentals to pay the partnership's bills. (These cars hauled coal, so a demand for coal was necessary, too.) The cars were also expected to keep their residual value, as outlined in the program's original projections. Problem: If you owned railroad cars, you needed a place to store them. You also needed an assignment so they would be moved out of the yard and used prior to other cars being stored there. If you moved to sign up too slowly, your cars could get buried at the back of the line—for quite a while. Well, it seems these cars were never assigned an "exit visa" out of their yard or were signed up too late. To add insult to injury (and losses), demand for coal collapsed just as the partnership's new cars were delivered to the yard. Weeds sprouted along their rails. The machinery rusted to a soft orange, and the railroad car-leasing industry continued its slump. Finally, the cars idled so long in a scenic New England railroad yard that the partnership went bust.

Calamity number three: You've all heard about how dry the desert is in Arizona. Well, at one time an attractive Phoenix real estate offering was being considered by my firm. We turned it down because of financial hassles and a flood plain report that noted the building was going up in a spot that had flooded fifty years earlier. We did our homework, but someone else didn't. They got washed away by a flood eight months after their investors had coughed up money. Rumor also has it that nobody had bothered to get flood insurance.

Calamity number four: This concerned an oil income fund with a track record for using the "conservative approach." The program managed to drag 183,000 investors (an enormous number) downhill. The fund relied too heavily on the assumption of rising prices. In June 1983 the estimated value (done by a neutral party) of the fund's assets was $1.7 billion. One year later, a new value of $920 million was estimated, or a drop in value of $780 million—46 percent. Shortly thereafter another estimate lowered the appraised value from $920 million to about $860 million. One partner in a suit against the partnership said that a settlement would pay investors only ten cents on the dollar. To add insult to injury, as these events were unfolding, the fund's sponsor disclosed that cash bonuses totaling $1.3 million had been awarded to twelve of the general partner's (GPs) top executives "for outstanding performances." Later the fund also announced it intended to pay its chairman $1.3 million upon his departure and $337,000 per year in retirement benefits for the rest of his life. What do you think? Remember also that sheltered oil income programs will be offered for years to come. Some may be good, and surely some will be bad.

I could go on, but it's too depressing. Besides, I've made my point: The odds aren't in the investor's favor.

WALL STREET'S SHELTERS: IN NEED OF A CEMETERY

Few investors understand partnerships or know how they really work. Most brokers can be included in that statement, and even some firms as well. But the Street isn't about to admit that they have filled kennels with these shelters. This attitude leads to a lot of double-talk: "delayed results," "slow cash flow," "further capital contributions by investors" (often amounting to additional losses, or throwing good money after bad), "the market is soft," "all of the market is slow—oil, real estate, etc." These reasons are cited to sustain sales and encourage a client to continue to trust the system and the shelter he is gaining "shelter" from. But remember: Because of fees, the broker and his firm are ahead on day one. However, the client may be left with no profits and a late return of capital—if he's lucky.

Main Street, through its accountants, attorneys, and financial planners, produces even greater calamities than Wall Street. Main Street's bad tax opinions and poorly designed partnership schemes often cost the investor far more headaches than the taxes he would have paid, especially considering today's lower tax brackets.

But there is hope. Wall Street has been burned along with its clients. It is definitely becoming wiser and more conservative by offering more conservative cash flow programs and eliminating the riskier deals. Some programs occasionally deserve a second or third look.

WHO ARE THE PLAYERS IN THESE PARTNERSHIPS?

The players in the partnership game might be a group of local Main Street people developing the empty corner lot where you used to play pick-up baseball, or a consortium of megabuck developers whom you will never meet. Learn as much as you can about them because who they are does matter. The game may have changed somewhat—but the players haven't.

Developer/general partner: The GP is the person(s) or corporation who assumes responsibility for managing the affairs of the partnership. Legally, the GP signs for debt—loans or mortgages he is liable for should the deal go sour. Limited partners are involved in nonrecourse debt (debt that legally is exclusively the GP's responsibility). Thus, they are responsible only for their invested sum, not the partnership's borrowings, with only a few exceptions. The GP should be knowledgeable, have an adequate net worth, and high standing in the partnership's field. A rookie GP is much more dangerous than a rookie broker. Also beware of the GPs who were successful in one area and are now trying another—with your money. GPs make or break a deal. I recommend partnerships in which the brokerage firm is a "co-GP" and therefore more closely involved with the program—and the risks. Consider avoiding programs merely sold by your broker's firm. It may, depending on its integrity and monitoring system, "love 'em but then leave 'em."

Syndicator: The person(s) or corporation who organizes, manages, and raises the funds for the limited partnership. Normally the syndicator is also the GP or co-GP, but in some cases those duties are handled by a third party who has been hired for fees and/or a percentage of the partnership's profit.

Developer: The person(s) or corporation who manages a real estate project for the partnership. He is usually the GP and syndicator, but may, like the syndicator (above) be a third party for hire.

Broker: The person who sells the limited partnership to investors for a fee. His firm may occasionally be the syndicator and co-GP, but is rarely the exclusive GP and almost never the developer.

Accountant/tax attorney financial adviser: Someone called upon by investors to review the investment merits of a partnership. They are integral participants in the drawing up of the prospectus used in outlining the investment. However, they have been known (especially on Main Street) to receive direct and indirect fees for helping to sell a partnership to investors, over and above advising them about the program. Know what role your adviser is playing before you make your investment.

Appraiser: Sometimes assets purchased by a partnership are appraised as to their "true" worth. CAUTION: Not all appraisals are accurate. My biggest investment error was the result of a lousy appraisal. Later, insiders told me, "If you look hard enough for an appraiser to hit your number, rather than the right number, you'll find one."

Investors: The person(s) or corporation who pay the majority, if not all, of the investment's expenses in the hope of getting their money back with a profit. In most partnerships, money expended by syndicators, GPs, brokers, and developers is refunded immediately once investors have jumped in. Thus, most insiders have time at risk, but little capital, while the investor has spent time and capital. The investor pays fees and shares profits with all of the partnership participants. In most cases, the investor receives the majority of any tax benefits, but generally these may be deducted only to the extent of his investment. Any deductions in excess of the investment will be recaptured in some manner when the shelter shuts down—whether the results are good or bad.

WHAT CAN GO WRONG

We've talked of profits and benefits, so why do I now approach partnerships with such a jaundiced eye? Experience. I've learned that cowardice is the better part of solvency. There are shelter benefits that are immediate and often significant, but these benefits are overshadowed by the potential trouble spots.

Problem Number One: Prospectuses—Hot off the Presses of Mathemagicland

By law, a prospectus must include: program size, objectives, fees, risks, conflicts of interest, and a review of principal participants (general partners). It also tends to include sales projections, past results, and brochures with photographs and charts that show consistent, upward movement for its attractive assets.

This is complicated information, much of it required in order to "protect" the investor. But prospectuses also seem intent on presenting facts and figures meant to confuse with a vengeance. I feel barely comfortable with prospectuses after two reviews. In fact, I know only a few brokers who read prospectuses thoroughly. Instead, most brokers trust their firm's ability to write a concise summary of the deal. Thus, we rely on "summary writers" who seem to understand the program well enough to explain the basics and leave out many details that bore both broker and client—and slow sales. Brokers read summaries, scan prospectuses (sometimes), attend an internal sales presentation, or watch a video on the program, and then go out and sell like crazy.

When an investor invests in a partnership, he is supposed to review the prospectus. But I've had only one client in my career who actually read all the prospectuses I gave him. Most people look at them in a cursory way and give up in confusion or disgust.

Perhaps because of this confusion, people seem anxious to believe what they choose when reviewing partnerships. That's what the GPs want. And sponsors legitimize many contradictory points in a prospectus through assumptions and a personalized style of math. It amazes me that prospectuses correctly labeled high-risk leave investors and brokers with a strong sense of confidence, even complacency.

There is one axiom brokers agree on: The prettier the pictures the worse the deal. I've seen a lot of glossy Wall Street photo albums in my day, and a few years later too many were receiving last rites.

Problem Number Two: Aggressive Assumptions—Don't Take Their Word for It

Assumptions are mathematical and business concepts that underlie the partnership's program. An assumption is also a premise made by your partnership that will, in all cases, make the investment fare better in the future rather than worse. It is actually a guess, and rarely recognized for its full impact on potential returns. Assumptions are the backbone of many partnerships, so they should be valid or reasonable—rather than the sales enhancements they too frequently are. They appear innocuously throughout the prospectus and summaries, and are hard to fully appreciate unless you are cynical or "from Missouri."

No area on Wall Street is more prone to ridiculous assumptions than partnerships. It is hard enough to simply find profitable areas for current investment, let alone extrapolate today's trends, extend them into the future, and end up with an accurate forecast. Too many things change.

Remember how the prime rate went from 6 percent to 21 percent and was supposed to keep skyrocketing? It didn't. Remember how OPEC controlled oil prices, and they were rising? It doesn't and they aren't. Real estate used to go up, and inflation was always worse the next year; it doesn't always go up anymore, and inflation learned how to go down and stay down. Maybe.

The word *maybe* says it all. Assumptions need to have "maybe" added to each one of them, but instead, they are given the weight of the Ten Commandments. In actuality, biased experts are making self-serving guesses/assumptions. But it is the investor who stands to lose the most. I've been there.

I made mistakes in oil shelters along with everyone else I know. I trusted guesses (appealingly called "forecasts") about how well oil programs were going to perform—even the U.S. government estimated higher prices. Exxon, Mobil, and Shell Oil agreed. I remember a seminar given by the president of a major oil program sponsor, who said at the end of his speech, "Anyone connected to the oil and gas industry these days who isn't excited about what's going on is the kind of person who sleeps through sex." "Hey, not us," we all said, "we believe." (His outfit sold about $1 billion in programs, and today it's one step from bankruptcy court.)

Brokers invested and lost money, and our investors lost too. But they didn't know we were guessing, and most of us didn't either. Everybody was trusting assumptions made by the Other Guy. Yet investors lost most of the money. Today nothing's changed.

Some Typical Assumptions

Defining a Trend and Extending It into the Future

This type of assumption defines trends, such as rising prices, housing and rental needs, inflation, etc., and extrapolates from them to calculate future performance. It's almost impossible to accurately define a trend from which to make good projections, but it's even more difficult to peg a proper time frame to all that. How many on the Street thought oil would drop to $10 a barrel when it was $40 a barrel? Within five years.

Lack of Competition: Maybe in the USSR

This is a frequent aggressive assumption that is insufficiently addressed in a prospectus. If your shelter is a good idea, what happens if lots of other people do the same thing nine months after you've spent your money? Unfortunately, you are left in a world with too many apartment complexes or hotels, or perhaps too much oil and gas—and prices fall. Tax-advantaged programs tend to mirror the mistakes of the business world. How often has business's overzealous enthusiasm created overbuilding, oversupply of materials, or, worst of all, an expensive, noncompetitive product such as synthetic oil? Synfuels were financially sinful.

Fixed Interest Rates—Gotcha Again

How good are the economists at forecasting interest rates? Tax shelters often have floating rates of interest charged against their debts, or fixed high ones, whichever is worse, it seems. If the program you buy made optimistic and aggressive assumptions on interest rates, you have another item to worry about when calculating profitability or survival, whichever the case may be.

Estimated Rate of Inflation: No Easy Guess

Shelters often make the assumption that the rate of inflation will be either the same as the present rate, or higher, or lower. Then they assume that it will suddenly maintain a constant level for the partnership's entire life—five to twelve years! Don't they watch the news?

Consistent Behavior of Prices: Are They Kidding?

Far too many shelters assume that a commodity such as real estate, oil, labor, etc., will either rise or fall in a consistent manner over the life of the partnership, despite the fact that the commodity has either risen or fallen frequently and dramatically in the recent past and should not be expected to continue any pace indefinitely without change. Or shelters assume that a commodity will consistently *appreciate* at a fixed rate over the partnership's life, often at a greater rate of increase than in the past.

Honest, Expert Management: You Hope

Has your tax shelter, sold to you by someone you trust, chosen a general partner or a project manager who is asleep at the wheel or playing with the books? There are infrequent cases of dishonest management, but it doesn't hurt to question management's role and past performance history.

Fixed Tax Laws: Not in Your Lifetime

Have you ever asked what kind of tax laws your tax shelter will operate under in four years, when it's only halfway finished? What if new laws are unfavorable? They usually are. You can't divorce a tax shelter no matter how incompatible it and your wallet have become. We all know the laws changed in 1986. People are now paying for that change. And the laws will probably change again before this decade is over.

Realistic Interim Reports about Your Shelter: Tomorrow's Junk Mail

One major firm recently issued a report analyzing the performance of its previously sold oil and gas tax shelters. That's a rarity. An assumption was made at the beginning of the report, dated fall 1984. (The assumption was necessary because the programs analyzed were assumed to be producing oil and gas for years to come—if in fact they had found sufficient oil reserves, which many had not.) Believe it or not, after most of these programs had done poorly because costs had escalated, prices recently had declined, OPEC was in disarray, and not enough reserves were found, the latest pricing assumption still dared to be upbeat. How? The report assumed that oil and gas prices would continue to rise uninterrupted for the next twelve years at 6 percent per year. Thus, oil would soon be at $55 a barrel. A wrong assumption. Only 1½ years later it was at $15 a barrel.

How could this report justify such an assumption when the opposite was true? No one can be sure, but it certainly was easier than facing up to reality by asking "are these good assumptions?" Good research? Due diligence? Or was it self-serving hope, disguised in statistics straight out of Mathemagicland?

A seal of approval from a Wall Street Due Diligence Committee does not make you immune to the forces of the marketplace. Interest rates rise and fall. Energy prices go haywire. All these factors can have a greater impact on your investment than the quality of your sponsor. Yet due diligence and upbeat assumptions encourage investors to feel a bit too comfortable.

The best way I've found to review past results is to have dinner with five or six brokers from other firms and compare notes about the past ten years. Chances are only two can remember selling a winner—in a decade.

Problem Number Three: Liquidity—Off Like a Herd of Turtles

It's easier to divorce a husband or wife than it is to separate from a partnership. This is a problem—you are eternally married to them, especially when the partnership underperforms its original goals. The few shelters that do well either swiftly sell their underlying assets at a good price and close down operations, or pay excellent cash flow to their investors in the interim. But these shelters are rare. In my few cases of completed shelters, the time duration was about six years, and the gains were 30 percent to 60 percent.

Today, and in the past, shelters are/were expected to operate for between seven and ten years and then close down. Some programs are extended because their industries make it difficult to cease operations until the final asset is sold. But it's hard to know that before you buy. Good examples of that sad scenario are oil and gas programs. They were to explore for oil and gas for one to three years, begin cash flow upon successful well production, allow the wells to slowly bleed themselves dry, and finally close down in twelve to sixteen years. Despite the long time frame, most of the payback was expected when the wells were heavily pumping and on stream— usually from years four through ten.

The basic question: Did the programs find enough oil/gas to worry about the rest of the equation? Usually not, so their liquidity problem thereby became moot. Other forms of shelters must run at least seven to ten years to provide anticipated levels and timing of tax deductions.

Wondering where the exits are? How many forms of investments can you name that give little or no cash back for a decade? Very few, because absence of liquidity is unacceptable to most investors. Too many things change: interest rates, popularity of investments, political environments, methods of taxation, and personal needs for cash. Liquidity is an area that is gaining more attention by Wall Street syndicators, and shelter durations of five to seven years are becoming more commonplace.

FEES: A GOLD MINE FOR WALL STREET

If you study various forms of shelters and partnerships, you will find a mosaic of expenses—but you'll have to search for them. These charges are often impossible to locate in a prospectus, first because there is no standard schedule of charges (nor a standard method of labeling as with mutual funds). And second, because shelters are often created by people who want fees, are good at disguising them, and hire excellent legal minds to help them do it.

OBVIOUS—AND NOT-SO-OBVIOUS—FEES

Commissions

A basic fee is the broker's commission, which he shares with his firm. Many people avoid Wall Street–sponsored shelters because the commission, normally 8 percent, is one of the highest initial fees on the Street. As a result, shelters are now being marketed with no commissions. The concept sounds new, like a no-load fund, but remember, "no commission" doesn't mean there are no fees. Today's lunch is not necessarily cheaper than yesterday's, let alone free. In fact, a lesser commission may mean greater fees somewhere else. I know one no-load shelter sold recently that had other (nonsales charges) fees that would choke a horse.

Organizational Expense Fee

This is a fee to reimburse the GP for his accounting, printing, legal fees, travel and entertainment, and various other expenses associated with creating the partnership and bringing it to the marketplace.

If the partnership proposal is rejected by Wall Street or falls through, this expense is usually borne by the GP/sponsor. If the deal is completed and sold out to investors, the partnership refunds these expenses. Many a sponsor has breathed a sigh of relief when those dollars were recouped. While the amounts and percentages represent small numbers to a large partnership, they are sizable to the originators. Sometimes an "acquisition expense" is noted. It reflects a portion of organization expenses and only reflects a greater definition of this general expense area.

Acquisition Fee

This charge is an important potential expense. With an acquisition fee, you, the investor, pay a sum for the sponsor/developer/general partner's perceived expertise in purchasing assets for the partnership. Note that sometimes fees are paid to affiliates of these people. Acquisition fees are levied as the assets are purchased. Normally fees are charged per purchase up to a maximum charge overall.

Management Fee

This is a charge that everyone understands. The question then is: How much should it be, and who determines it? Also, sometimes the sponsor is not paid a management fee, but rather an acquisition fee. Confused yet? It may be by design. When trying to determine how large a management fee may become, look at the initial working capital reserve. The larger the reserve, the greater the chance the sponsor is planning to draw down some form of future compensation from escrowed working capital funds, as well as for general expenses.

Added Costs

An additional area of expense should always be explored by asking the question: Is the partnership buying its assets at a price reflecting their true worth? Or is it overpaying, which adds additional costs from the outset? The key way to avoid a problem is to make sure the appraisal for the partnership's assets is an accurate one.

Back-End Fee, or Profit-Share Fee

This last expense is by no means the least. This fee is known only by its percentage, rather than by a dollar value, and represents a share of profits to be given to the general partner when the shelter closes down. At that point, a properly structured shelter stipulates that first the limited partners are to be paid back all their capital. It might further pay them an additional predetermined percentage for each year they were invested in the program. After this, if any proceeds are left, the general partner and investors share them according to an agreement. From the outset, the general partner's share in this arrangement is outlined as the back-end fee.

If the partnership is large, any percentage share in profits of a well-run program can be a substantial sum for the GP. The real problem is getting the profit to begin with. Usually, the percentage share in profits to the GP runs from 10 percent to 35 percent, but Main Street has some at 50 percent. Wall Street's rationale for a back-end fee is that:

—it reduces initial fees normally paid the GP for finding and creating the project.

—if fees are reduced at the outset, there is more money available for investment.

—the more money invested at the beginning, the greater the basis for a better return.

—the GP's management, with a share in profits as an incentive, will sharpen.

It is true that this start-up equation is healthier for all involved in the partnership, including the GP. More money goes toward the investment at the outset, not to fees. The biggest weakness of the back-end fee is that it is an additional fee, justified by lowering other costs. A fear is that new partnerships will keep the old (higher) fees and also implement the back-end fee, or that back-end fees may increase.

But to be truthful, back-end fees worry me least. I've been involved in only one deal that charged them. Programs just don't turn out that profitable often enough. I'd almost like to pay one.

HOW DO FEES WORK?

Because there is no norm, I have taken a sampling of fees from a popular real estate program. The last time it was sold (by a single firm), sales reached $50 million. The fees in the prospectus, using terms and descriptions I have just given you, are as follows in simple percentages:

Selling commission	8.00%
Organization and offering expense	5.00%
Acquisition expense	2.00%
Acquisition fees	7.75%
Total expenses	22.75%

This means that almost one quarter of the pie in this partnership was served up to the syndicators. All money previously expended by the GP was returned to him, leaving the investors paying all the tabs. An additional item of "working capital" (5 percent) was held in escrow, which pushed the total UNavailable for real estate investment to 27.75 percent. This left only 72.25 percent going in the right direction. So investors who put up $50 million saw about 72 cents of each dollar go where they wanted. Of the rest, $11.375 million was paid out in fees. And $2.5 million was kept in the bank. But even the money kept in the bank had fees collected on it. This is a common shelter fee structure—many cost about 20 percent in total start-up fees. Investors may end up happy with returns, and if so 15 percent of their profit dollars will go elsewhere, as a back-end fee.

One consequence of disguised fees is that investors remain confused longer. If you can't figure out your investment, you don't know if you're being overcharged or have been stuck with a nonperforming dog. Or both. It also postpones the day of reckoning: Do you have a winner or a loser?

Another important point about fees to remember is that they are dollars paid out, and when the money is spent, it's gone—into the promoter's wallet. And those expenses don't go away. If they did, brokers' and developers' initiative would go away also.

TRACK RECORDS: WHY ARE ALL THE HORSES LIMPING?

To move from fees to track records is jumping from the frying pan into the fire. But the real problem is that no one knows for sure just how badly the nation's tax shelters are doing. No one.

There are no centralized organizations keeping tabs on how Wall Street tax shelters have fared. Very few firms provide their brokers with updated information. In many cases, they would just as soon forget because the details are embarrassing. Also, programs that are total losses often aren't promptly recognized. The tendency to hope and pray outweighs pragmatic acceptance of disaster. Investors, too, want to believe. Since they never understood the shelter, a lot of time goes by before the broker has to unveil the results. Inevitably, that's when brokers start prospecting for new clients.

Real estate shelters were the fad of the seventies, but what about the eighties and the nineties? The track records for real estate partnerships have shown better returns than any other shelters. From 1972 to 1983, real estate appreciated 11.7 percent annually. Put another way, real estate investments doubled each 6.2 years. I have insufficient data to say conclusively, but I doubt real estate shelters managed that level of appreciation. And those nice gains were during periods of hefty inflation, which we do not have today. If returns were not outstanding during strong inflationary times, what will they be when inflation goes down? Or stays down? Or if we have deflation?

REPORTING THE RETURNS: CLOSE YOUR EYES AND PICK A NUMBER

Forbes, in a recent article, points out how easy it is to "fool with the averages," or returns, of partnerships. Especially since, as an assistant director of the SEC admits, there is no accepted method for computing yield. In analyzing a tax shelter report, *Forbes* cites mathematics that turn a completed partnership's 18 percent annual return into 42 percent, calling it a case in "financial gobbledygook." Same program, same numbers, different interpretations. "Gobbledygook" is difficult to spell, so I'll stick with Donald Duck's Mathemagic.

Forbes also points out that tax shelters make their claims without recognizing the positive effects of compounding. A bank could play the same shenanigans. For example, if a 12 percent CD grew from $1,000 to $3,100 over 10 years, is that a gain of 210 percent? Or a 21 percent annual rate of interest? (210 percent ÷ 10 years = 21 percent/year.) No! It is the original concept of holding a 12 percent CD for 10 years. But you might hear any of the preceding if the CD was instead a tax shelter. The banks call it as it is: 12 percent. But partnerships may misleadingly claim 21 percent and climb from there— into the trees.

The Internal Rate of Return: Apples to Apples

The fairest way to analyze a shelter is to look for the "internal rate of return." Yet this is rarely used in statistics involved with selling a product. The internal rate of return takes into account when and how much money comes back to the investor, and calculates the average return over the time period. On the other hand, this formula loses its effectiveness when evaluating a fairly new program that is selling all good assets first—thereby showing good returns—but is guilty of holding onto the poorer ones and praying for better days. An early evaluation can prove misleading in this case. But in others, analysis of the internal rate of return would put tax shelter performance on the line. When one sponsor was asked why his shelter didn't use this equation he said it would just "confuse 90 percent of the people, maybe more." Does he think they aren't confused now?

Even the publisher of a respected tax shelter newsletter stated, "With a real estate program, I say, 'Well, this will take me about five hours to read.' Undoubtedly, thirty hours later, I'm still saying, 'How can I get this to make sense?' "

CHANGING THE RULES AS YOU GO ALONG

Another glaring example of how hard it is to evaluate tax shelters involves one of the Street's largest deals. This particular partnership, offered as a private real estate program, reflected a syndication valued at a mere $757 million. That, mind you, was what investors paid to be in the partnership. However, the real estate (the only asset of the partnership) was acquired in a debt/equity package for $428 million. The spread in value was large enough for *Forbes* to title an article, "How to Turn $430 Million into $760 Million."

It seems a brash young brokerage firm set up business in Mathemagicland and came out ahead—immediately. But no one will know for some time how the investors fared. The program purchased nineteen New York City office buildings—such as the Gulf + Western building. Each limited partner paid $250,000 spread over seven years. The brokerage firm managed to sell a total of 1,344 of these $250,000 units to 1,250 different buyers. There was the incentive of two-to-one tax write-offs early in the partnership's life, and the expectation of higher rents as well as the buildings' appreciation.

But one must question, as *Forbes* did, the wisdom of investors spending $757 million to buy an asset worth $428 million, even if an additional $120 million is used for repairs and reserves, and another $129 million is set aside for bank interest and insurance payments, among other things. The difference in the above is approximately $80 million. Where did that go?

Most of it went to fees. That's only 10.5 percent of the partnership's value, but it's also equal to 18.7 percent of the original purchase price to the sponsors. Even more interesting, *Forbes*'s estimate of net profit to the firm of $70 million (collected over seven years) represents a fantastic return to a firm that started in 1975 with less than $1 million in capital and only seven employees.

The firm did have a problem when a disgruntled former employee sent a 2½-page letter to hundreds of investors stating that the firm was siphoning off large chunks of money for itself, its lawyers, and its accountants. The letter also warned that one of the primary lenders,

General Electric's pension fund, would be able to grab a large share of the real estate in the partnership. According to the prospectus, the lender (GE) could exercise an option to own 49.9 percent of eight of the choicest buildings, in exchange for forgoing accrued interest of $289 million. This could be done in thirteen years and might prove to be a very attractive option for GE—but a bad one for the investors. When the letter raised eyebrows, the firm offered to give investors their money back, but eventually the deal sold out. The investors were now married to another bride. If the transaction ends with a profit, the firm might make even more money through back-end fees. According to some sources, its profits could range as high as $257 million. All from one deal. This same firm, over the past ten years, has managed to raise $1 billion in equity from investors banding into about 250 different partnerships.

WHAT IS THE MOST INTELLIGENT WAY TO SAVE ON TAXES?

The best way is to buy a house, get a reasonably priced mortgage, and use those deductions against your income. The roof over your head is gravy—and a necessity to boot. As for your capital gains and interest and dividend income, make as much as you can and worry later about paying taxes on it. That's one problem you can live with.

On the other hand, if you want diversity and feel a partnership would complete your portfolio, then start looking around. I recently reviewed an improved fee structure tax-advantaged partnership. It allows 100 percent of the investors' assets to go into the real estate "equity and appreciation" fund. And 99 percent of the cash flow will go to investors. Only 1 percent goes to the GP. A 2.5 percent annual management fee was the only true expense, for there were no other charges—*not even a sales commission.* The 2.5 percent fee was not too far out of line for investors—even large multimillion-dollar institutional investors pay about 1 percent to 1.5 percent per year in fees to similar real estate equity funds. The partnership was much like a mutual fund for real estate. It expected to list its units on an exchange within five years, and appraisals of the investment were to be made quarterly. Even Robert Stanger, the noted independent tax shelter analyst, rated this program AAA+, his highest rating. I agree. There is hope for shelters, but you have to be very selective. Given the lessened benefits of shelters, why go on a learning curve into investments you would not otherwise choose?

MY FINAL ADVICE

If you are considering a partnership of tomorrow, hesitate before you reach for your wallet and remember the following:

1. Partnerships without tax benefits usually offer little more, and often less, than alternative investments, such as long-term bonds. Yet the partnership is less liquid. (Remember to review the performance of long-term bonds in the appendix of tables and charts.)
2. Syndicators will say that their deal is income-providing, even when the level of income is only 1 percent or 2 percent. Income is in the eyes of the beholder. Read the prospectus.
3. With today's new laws, taxpayers gain greater risk and liability when investing in partnerships. "Limited" partners are more at risk when there are notes and debt involved in the partnerships, which allow for increased deductions to the limited partners. Taking on the additional risk and headache for deductions only applicable toward gains made exclusively through partnerships is not intelligent investing.
4. Despite the above problems, syndicators will nevertheless label the new cousins of the old shelters "economic," "new and improved," "safer," and "liquid." It may be possible, but don't take such statements for granted. Shop carefully.
5. Oil and gas partnerships, for example, have been allowed preferential treatment in their ability to generate tax deductions. But remember their past track record of poor results.
6. Some syndication groups have sold past programs that have been severely affected by recent tax law changes. In some cases, past investors are reluctant to pay future obligations as they come due. If investors do not pay, some syndicators may not be able to manage their new programs efficiently. Know what your syndicator sold in the past, and if those programs' hassles will affect the investment you are contemplating today. Being distracted by the problems of past deals has become a common malady for many syndicators.

It is true that both the Street and tax laws have moved toward producing stronger partnerships. The truly abusive deals are almost obsolete. But bad deals will be offered, fees levied, and assumptions made—none in a uniform or clearly understood fashion. If there are tax benefits, consider them secondary, like gravy. Paying taxes may not be so bad after all. You may have less than you want afterward, but you're liquid, you've skipped a decade's odyssey with your wallet, and you'll probably remain sane. The old adage still holds: "Want a shelter? Buy a house."

Self-Defense: Making the Right Moves

Chapter Twelve

THE RIGHT STUFF: INVESTMENTS FOR NOW

> It is a tribute to our persistence, ingenuity, and marketing abilities that we can overcome the poor returns of many of our products. Gentlemen, it's not always going to be fun out there.
> —SENIOR VP SPEAKING TO MY ROOKIE CLASS OF 1973

I've always remembered these words, but I didn't fully appreciate their meaning until years later. This was a rare admission of what goes on on Wall Street. Indeed, I have spent almost two thirds of this book warning you about inept brokers, badly designed products, poor track records, high fees—about all the pitfalls of Wall Street— so by now, you're probably wondering where the exits are.

Surprisingly, my answer is: Stay with Wall Street; it is still the best place for your money.

Brokers sell failures more than we like to admit, and far more often than the public knows. In some cases, both client and broker understand the risks involved, and when a loss occurs, well, that's the breaks. Brokers respect clients who can take a loss in stride, within the perspective of a long, mostly successful relationship. I call such clients Big Boys. They have my deep respect, and I try my heart out for them.

This chapter is the result of my mistakes. It points out what is right with the Street and why it is still the investor's best opportunity for profitable and secure investment. I have narrowed my miscues down to what I think are areas that are *not* error-prone—the positives of my business. The winners. The right stuff. Some products are available in better packages at one firm versus another, and fees and strengths are not uniform. But by and large, these products have a lot of strengths that make even their weak versions worthy of consideration in comparison to other financial products referred to by the speaker at my training class. Good products do exist, and there are competent brokers to help you find them.

The items below reflect the reasons I still like being a broker.

MEDIUM-TERM U.S. GOVERNMENT BOND FUNDS

This fund is for people who want income that is substantially (about 50 to 100 percent) higher than short-term investments (bank accounts/money funds), without a sales charge. These funds are becoming more available and popular, but many investors don't know they exist or how they work.

To begin, these medium-term government bond funds are composed of bonds of about ten-year maturities, or less. Many of these funds have no sales charge, but instead have a "withering" withdrawal penalty applied only when the investor takes out more than his interest income (or 10 percent to 12 percent) in a given year. This penalty typically starts out at 5 percent to 6 percent and gradually drops to about 1 percent over a period of five or six years, after which the investor pays no penalty. Some have no sales charge at all; others have a front-end load.

Most important, these funds are managed not for creating income and capital gains, but for income and price stability—hence they are less risky. Heretofore, bonds owned by individuals and funds would jump around, sometimes down as much as 20 percent to 30 percent. Yet their high yields made them attractive, so people often overlooked their risks.

Now the Street attempts to keep a portfolio's value static—much like a money market fund—sometimes using commodity futures contracts as hedges for giant portfolios, writing calls to generate more income from these portfolios (and at the same time hedge them), periodically shortening the fund's average bond maturity, and employing computers and research staff. This is safer than the alternative of owning bonds in the free-swinging bond market.

So far, the management of these portfolios has been acceptable. While good performance is not guaranteed, results over the past several years have been promising. Essentially, the funds that have sought to reduce their volatility relative to the marketplace have succeeded, except for occasional short-term movements up or down of 1 percent to 8 percent. Given higher yields, government-guaranteed safety of principal, and no sales charge, such temporary and slight fluctuations are acceptable.

One drawback is that the annual maintenance fees can be high. However, even after this charge, the return usually beats alternatives such as CDs, money market accounts, and T-bills. As always, check past track records thoroughly. The other major risk is that the U.S. government will go bankrupt—a risk most people can live with.

Questions to ask about medium-term U.S. government bond funds:

1. What have been the levels of price fluctuation for the past twelve months for the fund?
2. Is there a sales charge? (If so, are there any breakpoints—sales charge reduction points?)
3. Are there withering withdrawal penalties? If so, how are they applied? What are the percentages? What time frames are applicable?
4. Are there check-writing privileges?
5. When are dividends paid? (Monthly, quarterly?) Can they be reinvested in new shares?
6. What is the size of the fund?
7. Is there a minimum investment?
8. Does the fund consist of all (100 percent) U.S. government paper?

ANNUITIES

Over the years I've sold millions of dollars of annuities to clients. And I intend to keep selling them. Tax laws over the years have made them somewhat less attractive, but they are still an investment that makes sense. In fact, the most recent tax changes left their benefits virtually intact.

An annuity is a life insurance contract between you and an insurance company for the purchase of income either now or in the future. The two main forms of annuities are immediate and deferred. The immediate annuity begins a stream of income payments to you immediately. The deferred postpones income payments until a later date. I have several clients who may never annuitize (start scheduled withdrawals). They will simply withdraw funds when they want income, in as haphazard a manner as they choose.

Present tax laws do not tax growth within an annuity until you make withdrawals. Hence the concept of tax deferral. Since the withdrawals are made by you, you control the decision of when to be taxed. Thus, taxation is not an annual affair unless you choose to make annual withdrawals.

My favorite annuity is the deferred annuity. Clients treat it as a glorified savings/CD account, without the taxation—each and every year. Compounding your money's growth at competitive rates without taxation, and without any significant risk, is a good deal.

Despite the bankruptcies of a few insurance companies, annuities are a safe investment. They are overseen by state regulators, who are more suspicious than they used to be (having been scared a few times recently). Besides, banks also have their share of bankruptcies. Just as the government saved the banks, the sellers of annuities and other insurance companies helped cover the failures of annuity companies. No one has lost any principal invested in annuities as a result of these bankruptcies. The most recent and well-known annuity issuer bankruptcies were Baldwin-United and Charter Company. Both have been resolved, and no investor lost money. Also, annuity issuers are rated as to financial strength by A. M. Best Company, whose reports are available to brokers and the public.

Among deferred annuities, there are two primary forms: the fixed-rate annuity and the variable annuity. The fixed rate does what its name implies—offer a guaranteed fixed rate of interest, usually in one-year intervals. The variable annuity is becoming extremely popular, for it is all things for all people and offers a choice of investment styles within the purchase of the one annuity. You may choose one method of investment for all your assets, or choose several and divide your money within the single variable annuity. You can also switch your assets around at any time. You may want to invest in stock/equity funds, bond/income funds, money market funds, or even the standard fixed-rate vehicle. The choices for division of your annuity assets are strictly left to you and your consulting broker. Usually there is a modest service charge per year for bookkeeping your choices, executing switches back and forth among investments, and quarterly (or monthly) investment summaries.

Many of the variable annuities have performed well overall. One has had the following annualized returns since its inception on December 31, 1983, to December 31, 1986:

Components of Variable Annuity	Average Annual Return
Money Market	+ 7.0%
Equity (stocks)	+23.7%
Bond/Income	+25.6%

When you consider that the above growth is without taxation until you make a withdrawal, these performance statistics are truly excellent. Also, if you choose an investment fund that can and then does lose value, the death benefit available to your beneficiary (remember, the annuity is an insurance contract) amounts to whatever total contributions were made to the contract minus any cash withdrawals. Thus, if loss of value occurs, your beneficiary still receives a death benefit as though no losses (or growth, for that matter) occurred. The death benefit is available to the beneficiary income tax-free.

Annuities have up-front sales charges or withering withdrawal penalties. The up-front charges are usually 3 percent to 6 percent. The withdrawal penalties are steepest at the outset, 5 percent to 8 percent, and are typically scaled down over five or six years until they gradually disappear. Withdrawals are often penalty-free if done once per year up to about 10 percent of the account value, although sometimes the 10 percent is allowed only on the original account value, not the present value, which is normally larger. You should thoroughly investigate the many methods of fee-levying that insurance companies and brokerage firms employ—another reason to have a solid broker-client relationship.

Finally, apply the old "Rule of 72" to calculate the years that it takes to double your money. Simply divide your rate of return into the number 72. The answer is the amount of years it will take to double your money (compounding annually)—that is, without considering taxes. For example, if you receive 12 percent from your annuity each year (tax-deferred), then 72 divided by 12 equals 6. Thus it takes 6 years to double your money growing at 12 percent tax-deferred. And it takes only 12 years to quadruple your investment. Remember that on other investments, if you get a certain rate of return and don't account for the tax bite, you will miscalculate your time frame for actual net after-tax returns. One more reason annuities are so popular with my clients.

Questions to ask about annuities:

1. What are the fees to purchase? Is there any sales charge? Withdrawal penalty?
2. What is your fixed-rate annuity interest rate? For how long is the rate guaranteed?
3. What investment choices are included with your variable annuity?
4. What has been the performance record of each of the available investment choices since inception?
5. How large (total of funds invested) are each of your variable investment funds? Too large a fund may be unwieldy.
6. What is your minimum investment?
7. Can you add funds to your annuity after you make your first contribution, or do you have to start another annuity?
8. What, if any, is the annual maintenance fee for your annuity?
9. How much (percentage of present value, or initial investment?) are you allowed to withdraw from your annuity each year before you are penalized?

MUTUAL FUNDS/UNIT TRUSTS

As I pointed out earlier, good funds are available, and their fees can be reasonable especially if you purchase either a no-load fund or a fund with a sales charge of 3 percent or less. But beware of high fees, mushrooming fund size, exiting managers, and fund name changes. Find a good adviser/broker who can help you stay abreast of who's good and why. Check neutral sources for track records: Standard & Poor's, Wiesenberger, and Lipper, among others.

Another form of fund is the unit trust fund. Although it has several of the usual drawbacks, such as up-front sales charges of 1 percent to 4 percent and annual maintenance charges, it is still worth looking at for a variety of reasons.

Unit trusts offer diversity, for they combine investors' assets to purchase large pools of some form of security (municipal bonds, convertible stocks, utility stocks, government bonds, etc.). If you want diversity of issuers and states, as in municipal bonds, it is difficult to acquire these on your own without spending large sums because most municipal bonds are issued in minimum blocks of five $1,000 face-value bonds. However, for $1,000 you can purchase a unit of a large portfolio of many separate bonds, all at more favorable prices because of the unit trusts' large size. And you needn't worry about bad management of assets because management is not ongoing. Securities are purchased at the outset, placed in the unit trust to sit, and the bookkeeping is handled by a bank or neutral overseer. Because there is no trading of the original portfolio, your only worry is that the initial investments were done prudently— today's judgment calls, not tomorrow's. This arrangement has a lot of sanity and logic. What you have today is what you're going to get.

Additional benefits are monthly/quarterly income, as well as automatic reinvestment of income into either a money market fund or new unit trusts. Bonds, for example, may pay interest only every six months, so receiving either quarterly or monthly income from a unit trust of bonds may come in handy, especially if you are retired. In many cases, unit trusts also offer insurance from the threat of bankruptcy or default. This feature is common with municipal bond trusts, which are insured by large insurance companies for a fee. The yields are slightly reduced, but the benefit outweighs that negative. Though diversified, the funds can also provide specialization in several areas, such as unit trusts that contain several issues of municipal bonds, all issued by one state. Thus, these unit trusts are tax-free from the given state's tax on interest, as well as being federally tax-free.

Lastly, some unit trusts offer unique twists in investing in the stock market. The trust selects stocks and then holds these securities for a certain period of time. But no further buying or selling occurs after the stocks are purchased. They are left to sink or swim. As an example, one firm offers a unit trust that operates in an unusual way. Once the portfolio of securities has been chosen (each stock receives an equal investment position), the portfolio is left to perform for twelve to fifteen months, never longer. Then they are sold off, and whatever the results are at closing constitutes the track record of that particular unit trust. The investors' money is returned to them (whether the results are good or bad), and they have the opportunity to join another trust or change to something else.

Thus, with the above form of unit trust you have disciplined selling periods combined with a stylized stock selection approach. Since its beginning in 1974 through the end of 1985, results show that this firm's trust portfolios have provided an annual average gain of about 19 percent versus the Standard & Poor's average gain of 9 percent per year.

Questions to ask about unit trusts:

1. Do I know the actual security portfolio to be purchased before or after I invest? (Is it a blind pool?)
2. What is the sales charge for the trust? Are there any volume discounts?
3. What is the track record of the trust to date? Its yield?
4. How many different issues will be represented in my unit trust?
5. Is there any liquidity for trust units being sold prematurely?
6. When is the expected maturity date for the trust?
7. Will any part of my investment be returned to me prior to the maturity of the overall unit trust?
8. How large is the trust?
9. Who is the trustee for the trust?

PRIVATE PLACEMENTS/DIRECT INVESTMENT OFFERINGS

In my chapter on tax shelters I warned you about the high costs and various risks associated with tax shelters and most private placements offered on the Street. There are, however, a few good ones.

Remember, all private placement/direct offering investments come with a prospectus. As an example of a potentially successful direct investment offering, consider federally guaranteed mortgage funds. Federally insured mortgages were formerly owned by the U.S. government or large institutional investors, who purchased them from the government. Today the government is selling many of its mortgages at competitive auctions, where mortgage funds buy the mortgages—one hopes the better mortgages at good prices. Occasionally, mortgages can be purchased from institutional owners too. If the purchasing is done well, a mortgage may be obtained at a discount from its maturity value, but the mortgage may later be paid off prior to the assumed date of maturity (at the full mortgage value) because the owner wants to convert to a conventional residential mortgage. The conversion comes about because the mortgages were originally issued for purposes of financing low-cost, federally subsidized rental housing. But now, many years later, the low-cost housing can be converted to more conventional forms of housing, as long as the underlying low-cost mortgage from the government is paid off. The profit from conversion overwhelms the cost of paying off the attractive mortgage prematurely.

Thus, you want your fund to purchase discounted mortgages that are likely to be refinanced to conventional mortgages. The developer pays off the mortgage sooner than planned, and a windfall gain occurs to the holder of the discounted mortgage, because the process occurred sooner than anticipated. If your fund is smart at picking mortgages likely to be converted, gains will be made in addition to income derived as the mortgages are held. There are no tax benefits. All income and gains are taxable. But some funds are anticipating returns of between 11 percent and 16 percent and more, depending upon their success in locating premature conversions.

Another strength of this investment program is that good programs have several properties already chosen; thus there is less "blind pool" purchasing—you have an idea where your money is being spent. Some properties and areas are better than others, so a good selection process is crucial. Also, the purchased mortgages and their performances are government-guaranteed, so you always receive the stated rate of return on purchase. And the sales charges and fees are less than in many other prospectus partnership/funds. One firm's version of this investment provides that 95 percent of the investors' money ends up purchasing mortgages. Thus, only 5 percent is "lost," versus other investment partnership programs that "lose" as much as 25 percent or more through fees. There is also ample diversification, for most of these programs are over $100 million in size. Liquidity is often better than the normal partnership, because when the fund is created its assets are divided into beneficial unit certificates, which can be traded like a security on the OTC.

Questions to ask about direct investment offerings:

1. What are the risks? What is the worst that can happen in this program?
2. What is the sales charge?
3. How much of my invested dollar is invested in the actual property?
4. What is the track record for this investment?

5. If liquidity is promised, can the units be sold on the OTC/major market, or solely through the broker's "network"?
6. How can I follow the progress (or lack thereof) of the investment?
7. What is the minimum investment?
8. Is there a discount for larger purchases?
9. Does your firm analyze the value of this program annually?

IRAs

IRAs are IRS-permitted retirement programs. As you probably know, the tax law change of 1986 took away many of the benefits of IRAs, although you can still invest in them. The major remaining benefit is the tax-free growth of the account's assets. However, you can no longer automatically deduct the contribution ($2,000 maximum per working person). Only those people who are not covered by a pension plan at work, who are single, and who earn no more than $25,000 per year, or who are joint filers with a combined income of $40,000 in earned income can take a full deduction. IRA contributions are only partially deductible for those who earn slightly more.

However, before you eliminate IRAs from your investment thinking, remember that disciplined contributions of $2,000 per year, prudently managed and growing tax-deferred, will amount to a sizable nest egg someday, and could dramatically affect your retirement life-style. So if you have an IRA and can afford to keep feeding it, keep reading.

IRAs are a large enough financial force that professionals are devising stock market strategies based on where IRA money may be invested next year. With $132 billion in IRAs as of the end of 1985, the action is where the IRAs are. Those who assume a flood of IRA money into stock mutual funds also expect the stock market to rise. If IRA assets ever leave the markets, things could get precipitously worse around the stock exchanges. Already, many people have plans with over $10,000 in them. These people are learning to shop around. They have discovered that if they want to move an IRA to a more competitive financial institution, they can make an IRA transfer just by signing their name. Wall Street is fighting over these potential transfers, and the new contributions people make each year. In 1984 alone, new contributions totaled $35 billion.

Why are IRAs such a good deal? For one thing, they force you to prepare for gray hair and social security checks. Social security isn't famous for allowing people to retire in style, so any additional dollars squirreled away, providing the potential for tax deductions and whose assets are growing tax-free, are well "spent."

Two good questions: How much can an IRA increase over the years? And what is the best way to have it grow? The following table outlines levels of growth. It also points out that if you invested your money at the outset of each year, rather than at the last permitted moment (April 15 of the following year), your money will grow much faster. This is due to the tax-free compounding of your contributions over the additional time period allowed by the early contributions—15½ months earlier.

For those who get a tax deduction with their investment, the IRA is certainly gratifying, but a tax deduction is only part of the story. Everyone can expect their IRA assets to grow, and therein lies the challenge. Tiny miscalculations as to who is offering the best investments can drastically affect your IRA. For example, the IRS became concerned about poor disclosure of true rates provided by IRA sponsors such as banks, savings and loans, brokerage firms, and mutual fund organizations. Starting in 1985, sponsors had to provide disclosure statements showing how a $1,000 investment at the cur-

Table 12.1 / GOOD FORTUNE COMES TO EARLY INVESTORS

If you invest $2,000 early every year, here's how much more you'll have in your IRA by age sixty:*

Age when first $2,000 deposit is made	Deposits made on the first day of each tax year†	Deposits made on the last day allowable for the tax year‡	Extra interest earned by early deposits
25	$687,236.53	$602,285.90	$84,950.63
30	409,175.90	357,787.70	51,388.20
35	240,173.50	209,184.10	30,989.40
40	137,455.48	118,864.40	18,591.08
45	75,024.57	63,968.98	11,055.59
50	37,079.69	30,604.10	6,475.59
55	14,017.16	10,325.27	3,691.89

* Projections reflect pretax earnings only and assume that the IRA earns interest at a rate of 10% per year, compounded monthly.
† The first day of the 1985 tax year is January 1, 1985.
‡ The last day you are allowed to make an IRA contribution for 1985 is April 15, 1986. Early withdrawals require the bank's consent and are subject to a substantial penalty. Withdrawals made before age 59½ are subject to IRS penalty charges.
Source: Baybanks, Boston, Mass.

rent rate would grow until the participant was age seventy, depending upon the participant's current age. The advertising and disclosure of any rates must be no higher than what the buyer can actually obtain. Why? Because even small misrepresentations of true yields can eventually cost investors a tidy sum.

In a recent *New York Times* article, Joe Mintz, publisher of the *Nroca News Letter,* stated that banks in various parts of the country are "deceiving" IRA investors because the yields on their CDs are less than those indicated on their disclosure statements. This is now against the law. "There is only a tiny difference between a yield of 10.52 percent and a yield of 10.79 percent. But after forty years of depositing two thousand dollars annually, the higher yield can represent a difference of about ninety thousand dollars," said Mintz. In other words, if you were to invest consistently in an IRA that provided 0.27 percent less than a slightly better alternative IRA, over forty years it would cost your IRA plan $90,000. And if you could consistently beat your neighbor's IRA by 1 percent annually, you would have over $333,000 more in forty years. Need an extra third of a million when you are seventy?

Homework counts. An intelligent review of IRA alternatives can produce results higher by at least 1 percent per year. This should be ample reason to investigate competitive alternatives. Although there are many good investments for your IRA money, the problem is that there are many more mediocre and poor alternatives. Don't get stuck in one of these; it will matter a lot some day. When you consider that two thirds of the current work force is employed by small businesses, that 50 percent of all small businesses in America fail after five years, and 85 percent fail after ten years, you will know why people had better plan and add to their own retirement plans. Social security can't do it all, and your employer may not be much help. Getting a good broker/financial adviser and using several of these "Right Stuff" ideas is a good start.

The most powerful attribute of an IRA is accrual without taxation. But don't push your luck by being too greedy. Study the charts at the end of this book. For example, if you look at U.S. Treasury bonds (ten-year maturity), you will see that they have averaged 10.52 percent per year for the past ten years. And Baa bonds have been terrific performers for twenty-five years. I feel that 10 percent to 12 percent per year with insignificant risks will do well against most alternatives. You won't have the best results (do you really know anybody with those?), but you won't have even close to the worst, and you'll be near the top without any ulcers—if you stay with government bond funds, high-income conservatively managed assets, money market funds when their yields jump up to 9 percent to 12 percent (if they ever do again)—and in short keep your cool. When your IRA is over $10,000 in value, apportion some of your IRA into equity funds that have good track records for diversification. All in all, IRAs are for smart, sane, and solid investment strategies, not the hotshot avant-garde recommendations you will no doubt hear.

Questions to ask about IRAs:

1. Do you charge an annual fee to maintain my IRA?
2. Do you have several forms of investment—safe, moderately risky, and risky—for me to choose from?
3. Is there a fee to switch my investments within your selection of alternatives?
4. Would there be a fee if I chose to transfer my IRA from your firm?

UNIVERSAL LIFE INSURANCE

Nobody trusts insurance companies. Most people feel they overcharge for a deliberately confusing product. And often they're right. But insurance, like so many other financial products, is changing—and some of these changes are in your favor.

A substantial improvement in insurance occurred with the advent of universal life insurance, invented in the late seventies by a brokerage firm. It was initially seen as a threat to the highly profitable alternative methods of insurance promoted by the industry, primarily whole life insurance. The battle over whether universal life was "permissible" raged for a while, but it was legal, more competitive, and became enormously popular. Insurance companies now embrace the product and make a tidy profit selling it—which should tell you how uneconomic and fee-laden whole life insurance is. Today about 40 percent of individual life insurance sales is universal life, versus 2 percent in 1981.

Universal life insurance is an insurance policy that provides permanent protection through a death benefit but also builds up its cash value (which can be accessed by the owner of the policy) at current competitive rates. It also has great flexibility for the insured owner/investor. The following are the primary advantages:

1. Insurance protection is permanent.
2. Premiums are lower than whole life premiums because of more competitive returns on the cash value, and the lower cost of insurance rates.
3. Premiums are flexible. They can be adjusted by the owner (subject to policy limits).
4. The cash value of the policy grows tax-deferred, just like an annuity.
5. You have access to your cash value via loans from the policy, usually at reasonable rates.
6. The loans from the cash value enable a policy owner to create income from the policy tax-free.
7. Current rates of interest, more competitive than previously offered by insurance companies, are credited to the cash value.
8. Premium payments may be reduced or eliminated if there is sufficient cash value in the policy.
9. The death benefit of the policy passes to the beneficiary income-tax-free.
10. Coverage is flexible. Your death benefit can be increased (subject to evidence of insurability) or reduced, if you so choose.
11. The policy is guaranteed by an insurance company, so it is quite safe.

Therefore, when you buy a competitive universal life insurance policy, you have an excellent method of insurance and potentially an excellent investment in its own right. But not all universal life insurance policies were created equal—on purpose. Insurance companies that believe they can sell sand to Arabs also try to sell less competitive but more profitable products. You have to know how to spot the differences, and it isn't easy. A recent *Wall Street Journal* article quoted the chief actuary and deputy insurance commissioner for California. "There are so many claims being made about high interest rates paid on policies. But when they subtract all these charges, the yield may not be anything like that." You have to determine the cost of insurance and any other fees the policy may have, not just accept the rate of interest at face value. John Belth, professor of insurance at Indiana University, has stated, "The gross [interest] rate is a sales gimmick." The problem may soon be alleviated by requirements that insurance policies quote a yield index that will reflect all other additional expenses. In other words, a true, net yield, not the fugitive numbers from Mathemagicland.

If, however, a client needs insurance (because he has not included insurance in estate planning, etc.), and he were to buy almost any universal life insurance policy and maintain it over the years, he would in most cases have a reasonably good investment. Even if the net yield is a few percentage points less than the quoted yield. The yields are quite competitive, the cash value growth over the years is substantial versus many other alternative investments, there are significant guarantees, and the cash flow can provide tax-free income (via the loans). Warning: future tax-law changes may impact universal life negatively.

Questions to ask about universal life insurance:

1. What are the up-front fees?
2. What is the quoted rate of interest? What is the approximate net rate of interest?
3. How long is your quoted interest rate guaranteed?
4. What is the minimum guaranteed interest rate for your policy (should interest rates fall)?
5. What is the minimum and maximum insurance coverage I can receive for my premium payments?
6. May I see computer analyses for more than one scenario of payments and insurance coverage offered through your policy?
7. Do I need to take a physical? Will I need to take one later if I wish to increase my premiums payments and/or my insurance benefits?
8. Do you provide free insurance analyses of my present insurance policies?
9. Are there surrender penalties? If so, how much and for how long?

ZERO COUPON BONDS

Zero coupon bonds are relatively new to the financial marketplace, but they are selling fast. Zeroes are bonds that pay no interest to the holder, sell at large discounts from their maturity value, and have fixed interest rates guaranteed to maturity. The most common form of zeros is bonds backed by the U.S. government. But there are also municipal zeros, corporate zeros, and even zero coupon CDs.

The appeal of zeros is basic. You don't get paid any interest, but instead your bond appreciates. The longer the wait for maturity, the more you have bypassed interest, and instead may anticipate appreciation on an annual basis. Since a lot of appreciation occurs (for the preceding reasons) in a longer-term zero, it will cost a lot less on its purchase date. Zeros normally mature at a face value of $1,000 per zero. If your interest rate is higher due to prevailing rates, the zero coupon bond will cost less. That's because it appreciates more (by forgoing an even larger amount of interest) per year, and that level of appreciation is calculated in advance of maturity on the purchase date, which reduces the initial cost/price.

The bonds sport strange nicknames, such as CATS, TIGRS, and STRIPS. CATS and TIGRS are issued by brokerage firms that have stripped off the coupons from the underlying government bonds their issues represent. The process is profitable for brokers who have the savvy to package the standard government-issue bonds and re-sell them as zero coupon bonds. They take their fees for packaging and selling, and even a tiny fee on such a large volume of sales adds up quickly. Over the first three years of sales (1981–84) over $20 billion in zeros were sold.

A negative of zeros is that for other than tax-free municipal zeros, the interest you forgo in cash payments is still recognized by Uncle Sam as having been earned. You earned it in an abnormal growth manner (versus actually being paid), but you have to declare it nonetheless. Therefore you pay taxes from your wallet for interest that is merely a bookkeeping entry and does not surface in your checking account. However, for an IRA or pension account, which accrues all interest tax-free, a zero coupon bond is an excellent idea. Many people (and money managers) use them for such accounts. For equally obvious reasons, tax-free municipal zeros are popular with high tax-bracket investors, to be held tax-free in nonsheltered accounts.

Zeros have other positive attributes. The rate of interest compounds annually, but the principal invested is not the only part that compounds at the guaranteed rate of interest. The interest paid each year also grows at the guaranteed rate and compounds with the principal once it is earned. That is much different from a normal bond, stock, or bank CD. With those investments, when you are paid your interest you receive a check or clip a coupon. What you do with the money you receive is a matter of your ingenuity, and where interest rates are at the time you are paid. For example, if you bought a standard U.S. government twenty-year bond with a coupon of 10 percent, it would pay interest every six months. You might put your interest check to work today at 7 percent. In 1991 neither one of us knows what the rate earned on your deposited interest check will be, but the bond will be paying you 10 percent on your interest proceeds for a long time to come after 1991, guaranteed. In no case can you be guaranteed interest on your interest check at a rate equal to the bonds' coupon rate of 10 percent. Therefore, if you are willing to forgo interest checks, you can count on a guaranteed lump sum on your chosen maturity date.

Zeros have a wide range of maturities for investors, whereas bank CDs (a compounding cousin to zeros) fail that test—the longest CD available is about ten years. Many zeros are available with maturities of forty years. If you happen to want a lump sum to mature from a small initial investment (say, $1,000 or more), you may want a zero. If you need the lump sum after a period of ten years, and if you want your earned interest to compound at a guaranteed level throughout the life of the investment, you must choose a zero. If you need safety, the U.S. government behind your zero presents the safest bet.

Purchasing a zero to create a lump sum of $1,000 upon maturity requires an outlay that seems modest to most investors, especially when the maturity date is long-term. The following is a table for CATS that range in maturity from zero to twenty years and have interest rates ranging from 9 percent to 13 percent.

As with all investments, however, you should know the potential shortcomings of these bonds. Zeros are markup-priced securities. Because the bonds are so low in price, they seem cheap to the unsophisticated investor at almost any quoted price. On the surface, buying something at $130 that will someday mature at $1,000 sounds enticing. But you may be able to buy it elsewhere for $125 per zero. But what's $5, you say? A 4 percent additional commission, better known as a markup. Most people would be upset to pay a 4 percent commission on anything, but they may easily find that difference in the quotations regarding zeros, even from discount brokerage firms that sell bonds and zeros at markups. Recently, clients have been known to question some markups to the degree that they

Table 12.2 / CAT PRICES (WITHOUT MARKUP) BASED ON YIELD AND MATURITY

$ Value @ Years to Maturity	9%	10%	11%	12%	13%	Years to Maturity
20	$ 172	$ 142	$ 117	$ 97	$ 81	20
19	188	157	131	109	91	19
18	205	173	146	123	104	18
17	224	190	162	138	118	17
16	245	210	180	155	133	16
15	267	231	201	174	151	15
14	292	255	223	196	171	14
13	318	281	249	220	195	13
12	348	310	277	247	221	12
11	380	342	308	278	250	11
10	415	377	343	312	284	10
9	453	416	381	350	322	9
8	494	458	425	394	365	8
7	540	505	473	442	414	7
6	590	557	526	497	470	6
5	644	614	585	558	533	5
4	703	677	652	627	604	4
3	768	746	725	705	685	3
2	839	823	807	792	777	2
1	916	907	899	890	882	1
0	1,000	1,000	1,000	1,000	1,000	0

The above values are approximate unless CATS mature on the same day of the year as purchased. Yields are based on semi-annual compounding of interest.

have sued their brokerage firm over alleged excessive markups. Brokerage firms trade zeros on a marked-up basis for the most part, and there is no uniformity to their pricing schedules. But you can be sure that brokerage firms will profit when they sell you your zero. Investors should also be cautious as to premature calling-in of bonds, which is a potential hazard in dealing with municipal and corporate zeros. Here again some homework, and a good broker/adviser, is a big help. Markups and call features notwithstanding, zeros can be a solid and competitive investment.

Questions to be asked about zero coupon bonds:

1. Do you sell several forms of zeros—governments, municipals, corporates, and CDs? What are your ranges for maturities?
2. What is the yield on your most popular government zero? (Compare elsewhere.)
3. Do you provide a market to sell my zero?
4. What is your minimum purchase?

BROKER MONEY MARKET/ASSET MANAGEMENT ACCOUNTS

This form of multiservice account, originally called a cash management account (CMA), was instituted by Merrill Lynch in 1977. It has since been copied and improved by other firms and is the strongest attempt by brokers to replace bankers. First, the account is a checking account with an automatic sweep mechanism. With this, free cash balances from dividends, sales, etc., are "spotted" and put into an interest-paying money market account. You use it for deposited funds, as well as a multipurpose credit card and line of credit (margin) lending source. These accounts are insured by the Securities Investor Protection Corporation (SIPC) for up to $500,000 in securities and up to $100,000 in cash should your brokerage firm become insolvent. Additional insurance is provided through insurance companies, for total coverage to as much as $10 million.

Most asset management accounts offer three forms of money market accounts to choose from: standard money market account, U.S. government securities money market account, and the municipal (tax-free) money market account. The money market account receives deposits, pays competitive rates of interest, and automatically sells shares from the money market account each time any check you write is cashed. You often receive more "float" on your check because the bank the fund uses is not in your state of residence—unlike your local bank. This provides you with more interest income because you are paid interest up until shares are sold from your money market fund to cover your checks, a process that is delayed to your account because your new bank is out of state for the processing of your locally cashed checks.

Another strength is your statement. It reflects activity in several financial areas: the number and amounts of each check you have written, the activity in your securities account, dividends paid on your stocks and from your money market account, charges on your credit card, and any loans you may have initiated. On the other hand, some people find this confusing rather than convenient, and would also prefer to receive their cancelled checks. Some asset accounts do not return cancelled checks, or only on request and at an extra charge. Other firms post the identity of the recipient of your check on your statement in lieu of cancelled checks, which gives you less privacy as well as a weaker method with which to keep records.

Although trading in your portfolio may be standard fare to you, the ease and costs of borrowing through your asset management account may surprise you. You can borrow up to 50 percent of the value of marginable securities by signing a margin agreement, and up to 90 percent of the value of U.S. government bonds or T-bills. After signing for your account and depositing securities as collateral, borrowing is a function of writing a check. It is cheap to borrow from these accounts—and easy. (Interest charges are usually at the prime rate plus or minus 1 percent.)

Fees for the accounts range from one firm's offer of a free first year for their asset management account to the norm of about $50 per year for accounts without credit cards, and up to $80 to $100 per year with a credit card. Judging by banks' monthly fees for their checking accounts, and considering that their interest rates are usually not as competitive as the brokers' money funds, these asset management accounts are worth investigating. At the very least, banks do not allow unlimited numbers of checks from their higher-yielding accounts. Do expect minimum asset requirements to establish the account. Several discount brokers require as little as $5,000 to start an account, and several charge no fees. Many other major firms require around $10,000, and a few demand as much as $25,000.

Questions to ask about asset management accounts:

1. What are the fees for an asset management account, both with and without credit card services?
2. Do the accounts use a credit or debit card?
3. Do you receive cancelled checks back from your accounts?
4. Where is the bank that clears your checks located? Out of state?
5. When are your deposits credited to your account after receipt? (Should be the next day.)
6. What amounts are needed for automatic sweeping of your account, and how often are they swept? ("Sweeping" is the automatic transferring of cash balances created by sales, deposits, dividend payments, etc., into a money market fund.)
7. Ask to see a brochure about the account and a copy of the statement's layout.
8. What are the charges for borrowing? (Also see the margin agreement.)

COMPUTER LINKUP SERVICES TO WALL STREET

A new, realtively unknown service for serious or detail-oriented investors is the computer linkup services provided by several Wall Street firms at a reasonable cost. This high-tech service provides the following instant information:

stock quotes
market summaries
your brokerage firm's research
analysis of your account and as many as eighty designated additional
    accounts: balances, checks cashed, deposits made, interest earned,
    interest charged for loans, open orders left with your broker, and
    other services
Moody's ratings and comments on various securities
general news and research
latest rates and trends in finance
industry briefs
ability to send electronic mail/messages to your broker/adviser

The cost of these services varies, but all seem to have an annual sign-up fee, or a onetime sign-up fee of $25 to $100. Usage charges for the computer links range between about 10 cents per minute for basic nonprime-time needs to $1.20 per minute for multiservice, prime-time usage.

Dow Jones has the most sophisticated and full range of services, but they're expensive versus other providers. Several brokerage firms are offering computer links at varying levels of service and charges. Their services are designed to capture clients' assets so that trading is best facilitated at their firm, because of easier tracking of same and the general computer linkup.

Good marketing—but also a good service. Some firms that offer this service are Merrill Lynch, Chase Manhattan Bank, Charles Schwab, Fidelity Securities, and Dean Witter. You can even subscribe to services that provide hand-held calculator-sized receiver/transmitter units, so that you can get up-to-the-minute quotes wherever you are, even on the golf course. What's more, you don't need a personal computer in your home for a linkup, just a television set and an adapter. Your firm can supply the equipment, sometimes free if your account is large enough.

Several linkups give multiple quotes at one time—your entire stock portfolio can appear with the click of a button. Other services carry quotes from all exchanges, in some cases even foreign exchanges, and OTC stocks. Also available are bond prices, portfolio analysis, daily valuation, news briefs preprogrammed to reflect only your needs and/or securities, trading strategies, and even software to experiment with a new strategy in a simulated trading environment. These machines and services can perform technical analyses on stocks, research historical data on the markets, do theoretical calculations employing all this data, and display up to 100 quotes at the same time, whether your eyes can handle the strain or not.

Yes, we are talking high tech, resources similar to your broker's office communications system. Now you can send him nasty messages when you feel it justified. Today, brokers are electronically insulted on their quote screens as well as scolded on the telephone. But they do get important messages, too. So if you have a high level of involvement with your investments, this idea may well be worth your review and implementation.

FINANCIAL PLANS

Most people do not have financial plans—but they should. The secret to good financial planning is basic: Do a great deal of work on your own to make the plan preparation and investigation worthwhile. Be thorough. Garbage in, garbage out, financial planners say. But the client still pays the fee.

First of all, ask around for references to determine that your planner is honest and competent. Then find a planner you can categorize as fee-only, commission-only, or a combination of the two. Next, do your own homework. And finally, act on the changes the plan recommends—but not right away. Don't be sold anything. Investigate the recommendations as ably as you can. Look for any bias(es) the planner might be hiding from you. Everybody seems to have a few.

After you have studied your planner's recommendations and agree that changes should be made, do them. Uncoordinated financial wanderings cost big dollars in the long run, and often the short run, too. In today's complex financial world of taxes, investments, estate planning, education expenses, and retirement funding, a lot needs to be considered, and costly errors are sadly the norm.

The immediate benefits of financial plans are not always obvious. Here are a few. Excessive costs for life insurance and lopsided coverage for one spouse versus another are monitored. College educations can be planned for with specific investments. Retirement funding and tax planning can save you money. Estate taxes can be anticipated. Wills are drawn reflecting recent tax changes, new family members, or different family alignments. These areas should be considered, reviewed, and updated on a consistent basis, but too often they are left to chance, error, or ignored altogether.

Questions to ask about financial plans:

1. What licenses in regard to investments do you or your firm hold? Is the planner part of a major FP organization? Does the planner have a license in one or two areas of investment or many? Diversity helps.
2. How long have you and your firm been in business?
3. Do you have references I may check?
4. How do you/your firm anticipate you will be compensated for doing my financial plan?
5. May I see a facsimile of the type of plan you anticipate producing for me?
6. What are the various levels and respective client profiles for each of the plans your firm creates? May I see examples of them?
7. Do you offer follow-up services after I have received my plan? When? At what cost?
8. May I see in advance the forms and questions that I will be required to review and complete in order to research my plan?
9. How long after we have completed the research/data-gathering phase is my plan completed and ready for review?

PROFESSIONAL MONEY MANAGERS

Although I've already discussed this subject in a previous chapter, I want to emphasize the value of a good money manager and tell you how best to employ one.

First of all, you need an adviser/broker who will help you locate a qualified portfolio manager through computer banks that have analyzed several hundred managers' performances over an extended time frame. (One- or two-year results, a few dozen manager searches, and local financial wizards do not qualify as a quality search program.)

Also, consider paying a wrap fee. If you can get good execution and pay one percent or less per year for all the trading in your account, that is a reasonable deal. Substantial accounts of $10 million and more may end up paying 0.6 percent or less per year. But good execution is still a variable, and very important to the overall worth of this equation.

What constitutes a good manager? Consistency. And a return of about 120 percent of whatever the indexes have returned, on average. Such managers exist, but they don't operate around everyone's corner either. You have to hunt for them.

Sadly, a lot of investors choose alternatives to a good manager search. Those same investors could have done better had they employed a well-researched manager to oversee their money. You don't have to be rich to consider using a manager. Many good ones accept minimum-sized accounts of $100,000—at least for now. So collar your financial advisers to help you find one if your asset base qualifies you to consider the search.

PROFESSIONALLY MANAGED COMMODITY FUNDS

These funds are *not* for conservative or faint-hearted investors. The commodity marketplace is historically full of tales of risk and disasters. But it is an area that allows investors the ability to diversify. Some professionally managed commodity funds have sufficiently positive track records by their managers that consideration is at least a reasonable idea, and hardly crazy. By mid-1986, commodity funds had $700 million under management, and 1985's increase was substantial—50 percent more assets under management than the previous year.

The average successful commodity manager has an enviable record, because commodities in general tend to be extreme—they make heroes and take no prisoners. The contracts themselves are highly leveraged investments, and the marketplace is volatile. But the commodity marketplace has many diverse areas to invest in—international currencies, metals, interest rate futures, oil, gasoline, and farm products such as wheat and corn—even the proverbial pork bellioo get hot fuom time to time. So if you want your professional manager to make you money in areas you normally would never be involved in, you've come to the right investment area.

If you can handle the gyrations and the risk, you are ripe for commodities and their rewards. Using the managers will reduce the risk and also increase your potential for gain, for the managers have been investing in these parts for quite some time, or they would not have been chosen for the fund by your brokerage firm, from among the hundreds of active managers, to manage their clients' assets.

In a managed commodity fund, millions are raised in usually $5,000 or $10,000 minimums. The assets are divided up between four to six managers, each with an equal share. So theoretically if one manager gets in trouble and creates big losses, he won't make a tremendous dent in the whole fund.

The positive side: That's where the numbers get very appealing for those with the gambler's mind-set and wallet depth. A good commodity manager can average 40 percent per year in bad markets or good ones. They are less likely to be affected by overall weak commodity markets, for unlike their stock market cousins, they tend to "go short" more than one might expect. Part of the reason is that most of their trades are long term in their minds if they last three days. So being short, or long, is nothing other than a method to make a fast buck, rather than outline a basic tenet of investment philosophy. In and out, short or long, the trades happen like a machine gun firing, and the theory is that the profits, though not individually massive, add up nicely and quickly.

Let's separate the good commodity management funds from the poorer ones. First, upon closer examination, the funds, like their cousins the tax shelter partnerships, have several fees, all labeled differently. But a good fund has cut back or eliminated many fees so that most of the investor's money has a good shot at profits. The incentive to managers is a share of the profits, unlike a mutual fund, which gets paid by a management fee. The profit share percentage runs as low as 15 percent, as high as 40 percent to 50 percent, and typically is 20 percent. The manager receives a piece of net profits, after all other fees have been deducted. The other fees typically are a sales charge (4 percent to 8 percent), management fee (about 6 percent annually), exit/sales fee (1 percent), and commissions that are charged to the fund for executing the trades directed by managers. The commissions may be at the full (maximum) rate or discounted.

Recently, one firm has gone even further in making its commodities fund a good investment. It has waived sales charges, won't let managers charge a management fee, has no exit/sales fee, and has reduced substantially the commissions charged to the fund from standard rates. The manager's incentive is 20 percent of the fund's profits. But the profits can be considered only those that come from trading commodities, for only about 20 percent of the assets are used directly for that—about 80 percent are held as collateral in T-bills, which pay interest. The interest obviously accrues for the fund, but it does not get equated into the manager's profit shares. As long as the managers do a good job, everyone should be happy. Of note, no client may leave the fund during the first year—which means no liquidity. Period. After one year the investor may exit quarterly, when a request is made in advance. Funds such as these are normally closed funds. Investors subscribe, and then they are closed. They are not like mutual funds.

Several past commodity funds have created mediocre results; few have caused noticeable losses, just unnoticeable gains. In 1985 an index of 70 percent of such funds was +15.6 percent. With improved structures and reduced fees, things may change for the better. For those of deep crimson blood, ask your broker the following:

1. What sales charge and fees does your fund have?
2. How large is the fund?
3. How many managers? Will they share the assets equally?
4. What liquidity does your fund offer?
5. What are the track records of your managers and your past funds of this type?
6. What is the minimum invested?

BUT BEFORE YOU INVEST

At this point, you have seen that good, sound investment should be a part of everyone's future, and that there are several intelligent ways to go about it. But before you begin, know your personal financial goals, style, and abilities. If you think you will enjoy the process of investing, then look for someone who can help you make sound, informed decisions. If you feel you won't ever get too involved, find someone who will get involved for you, but do the job in an unbiased manner.

Chapter Thirteen

FINANCIAL PUBLICATIONS: FAVORITES OF THE PROS

> A good analyst is wrong one-third of the time. An average one is wrong half the time. A poor analyst is worse than a coin toss.
>
> —AN INSTITUTIONAL BROKER FRIEND

We're back to trying to beat the Coin-Toss Axiom because once again we're discussing the opinions of Wall Street. The words of a former desk partner on the day he left the business still ring in my ears: "One good thing about leaving this business: I won't have to read any more rotten reports that are dropped on our desk every day." That was ten years ago, and although some of his grumbling was sour grapes, I still find myself agreeing with him most of the time. While my present research department has had some outstanding years of late, they don't have them every year, and others on Wall Street seem eternally lost in Mathemagicland.

I learned early on, as did my former desk partner, that neutral sources were less dangerous than biased ones. I look for publications that aren't trying to sell stocks, but rather information. I read to gain knowledge instead of someone's opinions. I like to win or lose my way, rather than let someone else do it for me. I will review low-key opinions if they come with the report, but I rarely pay them much heed.

The following sources and publications are worthy of review and helpful in the long run. Most brokers use them all. I know of no one who dislikes them, although a few question the bias and accuracy of some of the newspapers and magazines. As a rule, however, brokers don't throw stones at those who foul up in financial reporting, because our own glass houses could stand some improvement.

233

These financial publications have both limited and extended shelf lives as reference sources. Options, commodities, futures, and even tax-related publications can have limited shelf life. Options and commodities/futures expire every thirty to ninety days, and even the symbols for the securities change. It therefore doesn't help much to use a publication on such items over ninety days old. But for stocks and mutual funds, various reports and articles may be relevant a year or more, and thus justify your keeping them in your library.

And speaking of references, as a librarian's son I should point out that most of these sources can be found in your local library. As I've stated, many brokers, especially discount brokers and brokers from small firms, do use the local library for their research in locating their next hot tip.

STANDARD & POOR'S STOCK GUIDE

Standard & Poor's Corp.,
New York, NY
The cost per copy is $7 and per year, $84.

This stock guide, issued monthly, is an excellent shelf reference. It is the broker's bible because it contains a great deal of information

84 **ESI-Far**   Standard & Poor's Corporation

about all securities S & P follows: each stock's ticker symbol, its fifteen years of highs and lows, earnings, dividends, shares outstanding, split information, P/E ratio, financial rating, and a short description of the company's business. It is a must for anyone who needs or wants to follow stocks. The last section of the guide covers mutual funds extremely well. Of special importance is its analysis of how a $10,000 investment performed in each fund over a period of five years, stated in understandable total-accumulated-present-value terms. The year-end January edition is advertised in newspapers around the country and sells well, although many brokers provide copies to their best accounts on a semiregular basis. S & P also issues a bond guide for those who have an above-average interest in bonds.

The following page is from the important, but much overlooked, section on mutual funds. As mentioned earlier, a brief review of the "$10,000 Invested . . . Now Worth" column gives you a quick and accurate reference as to which funds are performing better than others. Front-end sales charges are noted, but back-end fees are not. Check out those details before investing. This section is a superb brief and succinct reference in addition to the securities review.

Common and Preferred Stocks ESI-Far 85

Index	Splits ◆	Dividends Latest Payment			Dividends Total $			MH-$			Financial Position				Capitalization				Earnings $ Per Shr.							Interim Earnings				Index
	Cash Divs. Ea. Yr. Since	Per$	Date	Ex. Div.	So Far 1986	Ind. Rate	Paid 1985	5% Stk	Stk	5% Stk	Cash$ Equiv.	Curr. Assets	Curr. Liab.	Balance Sheet Date	Lg Trm Debt MH-$	Pfd.	Shs. 000 Com.	End	Years 1982	1983	1984	1985	1986	Last 12 Mos.	Period	$ Per Shr. 1985	1986	
1●		5% Stk	12-9-86	11-3	½5% Stk	Stk	5% Stk	0.33	14.0	4.92	9-30-86	2.73	..	+3595	Dc	0.07	d0.33	0.33	0.68		0.39	9 Mo Sep	0.49	0.22	1
2●	1977	A0.40	11-18-86	10-20	0.40	0.40	0.40	6.41	14.7	0.51	3-31-86			1217	Ja	1.71		2.23	3.16	2.41	P1.42	1.29	3 Mo Sep	0.55	0.42	2
3		None Since Public			Nil			0.05	10.6	6.70	8-31-86	0.85	..	1629	Mr		●0.12	0.35	d1.51	Pd0.24	d0.05	3 Mo Aug	d0.18	*0.01	3
4	1976	0.72	4-11-86	3-21	0.72	0.72	0.72	20.6	28.5	9.35	9-30-86			483	Dc	4.32		4.68	1.76	d0.11		0.31	9 Mo Sep	d0.15	0.27	4
5	1984	Q0.14	12-2-86	11-17	0.56	0.56	0.44	57.5	463.	256.	9-30-86	93●		20318	Dc		1.18	*1.56	*1.61		1.94	9 Mo Sep	*1.21	*1.54	5
6●	1975	Q0.15	11-10-86	10-6	0.57	0.60	0.524	0.97	67.3	42.2	9-30-86	38.9		5985	Dc	1.07	0.70	1.17	1.40		1.49	9 Mo Sep	1.21	1.30	6
7	1969	0.18	7-31-86	6-30	0.54	Nil	0.72	0.18	8.94	7.78	6-30-86	1.37		1227	Dc	0.43	0.50	0.30	d0.42		0.76	9 Mo Sep	d0.10	d0.39	7
8●	1957	Q0.09½	1-1-87	12-9	0.31½	0.38	0.263	5.82	121.	61.2	7-31-86	29.5		8444	Dc	1.26	0.91	2.14	*0.16		0.12	9 Mo Sep	0.14	0.10	8
9●	1967	Q0.60	1-1-87	12-9	2.40	2.40	2.40	78.5	497.	226.	9-30-86	399.	174	125785	Dc	●0.58	●0.65	●0.86	0.91	E1.32	1.28	9 Mo Sep	0.61	0.98	9
10								Conv into 20.8 com					60			Dc	b2.99	b3.43	b4.39	b2.41						10
11	1951	Q0.70	12-22-86	12-1	2.74	2.80	2.63	1.95	17.9	22.1	6-30-86	74.7	101	1999	Dc	3.79	4.00	3.40	3.24		3.49	12 Mo Sep	3.55	3.49	11
12	1978	0.11	10-3-85	9-17		0.11	0.11	3.15	20.1	16.4	3-31-85	3.13		1724	Mr	2.85	1.54	d0.04			0.04				12
13	1973	Q0.01	9-26-86	9-8	0.03	0.04	0.036	4.32	83.2	25.8	8-30-86	28.6		*4713	Fb	0.77	1.38	1.24	0.44		0.40	6 Mo Aug	d0.58	d0.62	13
14		None Since Public			Nil			27.6	74.6	39.2	6-27-86	4.97		8077	Dc	1.10	0.83	0.72			1.20	9 Mo Sep	0.29	0.77	14
15	1971	Q0.02½	11-14-86	10-27	0.10	0.10	0.10	2.30	74.8	28.9	9-26-86	43.3		18063	Dc	0.45	0.04	0.15	d0.61		d0.40	9 Mo Sep	d0.05	d0.18	15
16	1980	Q0.05	11-14-86	10-27	0.20	0.20	0.20							5706	Dc	0.45	0.04	0.15	d0.61		d0.39	9 Mo Sep	d0.03	d0.19	16
17		None Since Public			Nil			0.04	0.16	1.11	6-30-86			2774	Dc	d0.28	*0.08	d0.15	d0.14		d0.14	3 Mo Mar	d0.02	d0.02	17
18		None Since Public			Nil			4.66	32.4	31.9	6-30-86	0.74		6111	Mr	0.10	1.02	1.15	0.83		0.29	6 Mo Sep	0.50	d0.04	18
19	1984	Q0.10	10-20-86	9-17	0.39	0.40	d0.354	0.02	36.4	18.6	9-30-86	26.6		4693	Dc	d1.00		d1.27			1.18	9 Mo Sep	0.58	1.01	19
20	1973	0.40	12-26-86	12-8	‡1.78	1.64	†1.86	Net Asset Val $18.49			11-21-86			2221	Dc	¶16.76	¶16.17	¶16.60	¶18.16						20
21	1936	0.10	3-27-85	3-8		Nil	0.10	0.19	20.6	8.20	9-30-86	20.5	51	1981	Dc	0.39	1.40	d1.02		d1.83	9 Mo Sep	d0.05	d0.86	21
22		None Since Public			Nil			0.81	0.85	0.08	6-30-86			2899	Dc	d0.16	d0.20	d0.25	d0.42		d0.44	6 Mo Jun	d0.27	d0.29	22
23		None Since Public			Nil			4.32	38.8	14.7	8-30-86	1.51		5324	Dc	0.08	0.75	0.48	0.52		0.71	9 Mo Sep	0.39	0.53	23
24	1986	Q0.06	12-27	12-11	0.24	0.24		14.3	38.8	14.7	8-30-86	24.5		2316	So	d0.99	0.25	1.37	PH*61	1.61					24
25	1882	Q0.90	12-10-86	11-5	3.60	3.60	3.45	2111	14868	14808	9-30-86	*4668		72215§	Dc	4.82	5.78	6.77	6.46	E6.50	7.79	9 Mo Sep	4.03	5.36	25
26	1976	A0.60	1-5-87	12-4	0.50	0.60	0.40	3.63	82.4	18.1	8-30-86	1.13		3632	Nv	1.85	2.12	2.55	2.39		2.91	9 Mo Aug	1.67	2.19	26
27●	1986	Q0.07	12-12-86	11-21	0.28	0.28	0.28	2.70	80.1	37.2	8-2-86	13.4		4969	Ja	1.60	0.90	0.76	0.20	0.32	6 Mo Jul	d0.38	d0.26	27
28	1975	S0.06	9-3-86	8-14	0.12	0.12	0.11	0.22	75.0	35.8	8-2-86	19.4		2685	Ja	d0.47	d0.32	d0.02	0.85	0.58	3 Mo Sep	0.22	0.13	28
29		0.15	1-18-80	12-13		Nil		3.20	76.9	26.7	6-30-86	48.2		3067	DcＨ*68	Ci1.42	Cs1.62	0.21	P*0.55	0.55					29
30		None Since Public			Nil				2.51	1.42	6-30-86	0.60		2686	Dc	d0.66	d1.11	d0.08	*0.01		d0.21	6 Mo Jun	*0.08	d0.14	30
31●	1966	Q0.04	11-14-86	10-20	0.16	0.16	0.16	7.85	15.0	12.2	9-30-86	51.1		●13198	Ja	0.34	d*0.40	d*0.45	0.45	P0.49	0.50	3 Mo Sep	d0.03	d0.02	31
32	1966	Q0.05	10-3-86	9-16	0.20	0.20	0.50	90.9	463.	264.	9-28-86	138	3436	14295	Dc	1.90	1.51	d0.82	☼d3.17		0.55	9 Mo Sep	d13.25	*0.47	32
33	1961	Q0.90	10-15-86	9-25	3.60	3.60	3.60	Conv into 1.51 shrs common					3436		Dc	b1.55	b1.30	bd3.40				Redeem 10% fr $9.$46			33
34	1978	Q0.05	11-28-86	11-7	0.20	0.20	0.10	Equity per shr $11.70			8-31-86	240		10640	Dc	0.16	1.29	1.49	0.83		0.48	6 Mo Aug	0.59	0.24	34
35		0.060	12-15-83	11-7		Nil		Equity per shr $5.68			3-31-86	426		5272	Dc	d0.38	d0.25	d0.25	d0.72		1.25	9 Mo Sep	d0.53	*d1.06	35
36		None Since Public			Nil			0.03	11.6	6.11	8-2-86	12.9		1602	Dc	d0.41	d*2.44	d*0.01	d0.18		d0.37	9 Mo Jun	*0.13	d0.06	36
37●		g0.10	9-30-81	9-10		Nil		277.	737.	168.	p-30-86	1216		*4348	Dc	2.92	0.91	d0.23	d0.39		d1.57	9 Mo Sep	d0.77	*d0.37	37
38		0.10	2-12-72	12-30		Nil		35.3	113.	33.6	8-31-86		94	4550	Dc	*0.28	*0.30	d*0.30	d1.23		d0.89	9 Mo Sep	d1.11	*0.07	38
39●	1976	Q0.06	1-15-87	12-9	0.23	0.24	0.186	0.42	155.	57.0	6-30-86	43.		26928	Ja	0.32	0.38	0.55	0.83	P1.06	1.06				39
40		None Since Public			Nil			0.70	3.81	8.92	7-13-86	4.43		5996	Dc	0.20	d0.48	d0.33	*0.01		d0.01	9 Mo Sep	*0.06	*0.06	40
41●	1973	Q0.15	1-5-87	12-9	0.45	0.60	0.60	0.12	88.7	22.5	6-30-86	23.0		8599	Dc	0.98	0.97	1.30	0.90		0.68	9 Mo Sep	1.46	0.56	41
42	1983	Q0.07	11-17-86	10-27	0.28	0.28	0.28	Book Value $16.12			6-30-86	493		9490	Dc	Cr2.84	Cr1.94	2.44	2.51	1.73	9 Mo Jul	1.93	2.44	42
43	1983	Q0.22	12-1-86	10-28	0.88	0.88	0.88	5.31	169.	52.1	8-30-86	19.2		5685	Dc	1.84	2.02			E0.95	1.47	9 Mo Jul	*1.13	0.82	43
44●	1971	Q0.08	11-15-86	10-24	Nil		0.32	38.9	439.	211.	6-30-86	866.	*6713	25	Dc		0.69	0.79	1.02	0.74		0.76	36 Wk Sep	0.52	0.54	44
45		2% Stk	7-12-84	6-18		Nil		34.3	92.0	50.7	9-6-86	79.4		p13412	Dc	0.99	0.79	1.02	0.74		0.76	36 Wk Sep	0.52	0.54	45
46		5% Stk	11-7-86	10-6	5% Stk	Stk	5% Stk	34.3	92.0	95.3	7-18-86	34.7		7383	Mr	*0.01	*0.29	0.47	0.07		0.21	28 Wk Sep	d0.18	0.41	46

◆ Stock Splits & Divs By Line Reference Index ¹Adj to 5% '86. ³3-for-1, '84(wi'83). ¹⁰%, '82,'83,'84,5-for-4,'85,'86. ²2-for-1,'83,'85,'86. ¹⁹9-for-1,'85. ¹⁰10% '85(ex'84),'86. ²³3-for-2,'86. ³²3-for-2,'86. ³⁵4-for-3,'85. ¹²½for-2,'82,'83,'85. ¹⁰½-for-4,'82,'83:2-for-1,'84. ³⁷3-for-1,'84. ¹³3-for-2,'83:2-for-1,'83. ⁵5-for-3,'86. ³⁷5-for-1,'85. ²²2-for-1,'83:3-for-2,'83(wi'82),'85. ¹⁹3-for-1,'83:2-for-1,'84. ²³3-for-1,'86. ³³½-for-2,'83:Adj for 2% '84. ¹¹0%, '82 Adj to 5% '86.

Reprinted by permission of Standard and Poor's.

Standard & Poor's Corporation

Fund	Year Formed	Prin. Obj.	Type	See Foot-notes	Total Net Assets (Mil.$) Sept.30,1986	Cash & Equiv (Mil.$)	NAV %Chg '82	'83	'84	'85	Nov 28 '86	Min. Unit	Max Sales Chg %	Inv.Inc 1985	Inv.Inc 1986	Sec.Prof 1985	Sec.Prof 1986	$10,000 Invested 12-31-80 Now Worth	1986 High	1986 Low	NAV Now Per Shr	Offer Price	% Yield From Inv.Inc.
ABT Growth & Inc.Trust	*'70	GI	C	[2]	116.0	3.0	+12.0	+20.6	+0.1	+31.9	−2.4	$1,000	8.5	0.60	0.30	3.52	0.22	14,986	14.53	11.74	11.74	12.83	4.7
ABT Util.Income Fund	'78	IG	C	[3]	124.0	4.0	+16.4	−2.1	+17.3	+21.9	−20.5	$1,000	8.5	1.291	0.68	1.075	0.22	20,185	17.18	11.82	15.58	17.03	7.6
AMEV Capital Fund	'49	GI	C	[4]	97.6	17.0	+26.2	+20.1	+4.9	+30.9	−26.9	$500	8.5	0.245	0.52		1.06	23,824	15.24	12.15	14.04	15.34	1.6
AMEV Growth Fund	'59	G	C		149.3	22.2	+22.0	+21.9	+8.4	+34.8	+22.9	$500	8.5	0.21	0.154		0.59	22,208	18.53	14.11	16.92	18.49	1.1
Acorn	'70	G	C		395.5	33.1	+16.3	+24.0	+3.9	+30.1	−14.6	$1,000	None	0.51	0.50	1.86	1.97	20,843	43.08	36.24	40.89	40.89	1.2
Affiliated	'34	GI	C		3008.0	76.0	+12.3	+25.1	+6.2	+25.6	−25.9	$250	7.25	0.56	0.55	0.81	1.14	25,744	11.93	9.69	10.79	11.63	4.8
Alliance Mtge.Secs.Inc.	'83	—	GB		737.5	43.2						$250	5.5	1.217	0.798		0.205		9.98	9.49	9.79	10.36	11.7
Alliance Technology	'82	G	O	[5]	132.6	n/a						$250	8.5	0.197	0.012				25.20	19.94	23.58	25.77	0.8
AMCAP	'67	G	C		1385.0	268.0						$1,000	8.5	0.19	0.19	0.24	0.65	22,451	10.65	9.46	10.36	11.32	1.7
Amer.Balanced	'32	IS	B		162.0	15.0						$250	8.5	0.64	0.64	0.50	1.10	24,627	12.05	10.87	11.84	12.94	4.9
Amer.Cap.Corporate Bond	'71	IS	BD		118.0	4.0						$500	8.5	0.829	0.813		0.488	22,278	7.62	7.19	7.31	7.99	10.4
Amer.Capital Comstock	'68	G	FL		896.0	116.0						$500	8.5	0.55	0.382	0.275		24,217	16.84	14.61	16.36	17.88	3.1
Amer.Capital Enterprise	'53	G	FL	[7]	577.0	18.0						$500	8.5	0.29	0.267		1.635	16,733	17.50	14.00	14.82	16.20	0.9
Amer.Capital Govt.Secs	*'84	I	GB		8068.0	179.0						None	8.5	1.20	0.833	0.53	0.603		12.06	11.36	11.76	12.61	9.5
Amer.Capital Harbor	'56	ISG	CV,BD		267.0	28.0						$500	6.75	0.84	0.84	0.08	0.63	22,673	15.50	13.26	14.55	15.90	5.3
Amer.Capital Munic.Bond	'76	—	TF	[8]	159.0	7.0						None	4.75	1.43	1.43			22,070	21.76	19.69	21.29	22.35	7.0
Amer.Capital Pace	'69	G	FL	[10]	2133.0	194.0						$500	8.5	0.79	0.65	0.515	0.835	28,078	24.82	21.28	23.22	25.38	3.1
Amer.Capital Venture	*'70	G	L,FL	[11]	335.0	42.0						$500	8.5	0.153	0.52		0.515	21,508	9.66	7.43	7.75	8.47	0.9
Amer.Growth Fund	'58	G	C,CV		64.6	32.3						None	8.5	0.39	0.29		1.09	18,922	9.36	6.91	7.32	8.00	4.6
Amer.Investors Fund	'57	G	C,BD		67.4	24.0						$400	None	0.14	0.30	0.84		7,620	13.86	12.16	13.45	14.70	1.9
Amer.Leaders	'68	ISG	C		115.6	31.0						$500	None	0.52	0.38	0.84		25,922	13.37	10.94	13.37	14.61	3.9
Amer.Mutual	'49	—	C	[12]	1992.0	665.0						$250	8.5	0.72	0.74	0.70	0.86	25,237	19.81	16.29	19.42	21.22	3.4
Amer. Natl Growth	*'70	G	C	[13]	90.3	n/a						$20	8.5	0.36	0.416		0.305	21,097	5.56	4.47	4.69	5.13	7.0
Analytic Option Equity	'78	GI	O		82.6	n/a						$5,000	None	0.50	0.50		0.618	18,967	5.52	4.38	5.52	5.56	8.9
Axe-Houghton Income	'39	—	BD		46.2	2.0						$1,000	None	0.50	0.66			23,789	5.73	5.17	5.56	5.56	9.0
Axe-Houghton B.	'38	B	B		182.5	32.5						$1,000	None	0.66	0.06		0.70	23,384	13.37	10.94	13.37	13.37	4.9
Axe-Houghton Stock	'32	G	C		92.0	4.2						$1,000	None		0.06		0.04	19,042	10.85	8.68	10.21	10.21	
Babson(D.L.) Growth	'59	G	C	[13]	236.2	2.0						$500	None	0.625	0.353	1.629		16,689	15.01	12.47	13.92	13.92	4.5
Babson(D.L.)Bond Trust	'44	IS	FL	[14]	65.5	20.0						$500	None	0.163	0.12			21,458	1.72	1.61	1.68	1.68	9.7
Benham GNMA Income	*'85	I	GB		255.6	n/a						$1,000	None	1.44	0.542				10.50	9.99	10.48	10.48	9.0
Bond Fund of Amer.	*'74	—	BD		598.0	36.6						$1,000	8.5		1.20		1.56	23,712	15.02	13.88	14.60	15.96	
Boston Co.Fd.Cap.Apprec.	'47	G	C	[15]	422.4	13.3						$1,000	None	0.74	1.171		3.04	22,068	35.85	29.52	35.63	35.63	2.1
Bull & Bear Cap.Growth	'59	G	C	[16]	63.0	5.0						$1,000	8.5	0.13	0.20		1.69	14,687	17.00	14.19	15.05	15.05	0.9
Bullock Balanced Shares	'32	RS	B	[17]	78.9	13.5						$1,000	8.5	0.72	0.52	0.30	0.53	27,019	16.40	13.10	15.21	16.62	4.3
Bullock Dividend Shares	'32	IG	C	[18]	344.8	32.5						$1,000	8.5	0.13	0.525	0.35		25,285	4.14	3.23	3.59	3.92	3.3
Bullock Growth Shares	'32	G	C	[19]	159.0	5.2						$1,000	8.5	0.22	0.10		2.84	25,828	11.79	7.61	7.97	8.71	2.5
Bullock High Inc.Shs.	*'80	—	BD	[20]	203.8	1.7						$1,000	7.25	1.518	1.171			19,461	11.05	10.04	10.04	10.82	14.0
Bullock Monthly Inc Shs.	'74	—	BD		45.2	2.8						$1,000	8.5	1.26	0.99			23,265	12.93	11.96	12.55	13.72	9.2
Bullock Tax-Free Shares.	*'77	—	TF		110.8	3.1						$100	4.75	0.867	0.717		0.84	20,597	11.30	10.41	11.30	11.86	7.3
Cardinal Fund	'75	GI	C		84.9	0.0						$1,000	8.5	0.34	0.37	0.84		26,323	16.63	13.12	15.05	16.45	2.1
Century Shares Trust	'28	GI	C		150.0	6.0						$500	None	0.54	0.24	0.91		28,061	21.55	17.43	19.40	19.40	2.8
Charter Fund	'67	GI	C		79.0	21.0						$2,000	None	0.18	0.17		0.51	19,371	11.05	6.74	8.23	8.64	2.1

Uniform Footnote Explanations—See end of alphabet.   Stock Splits & Divs. (figures adjusted): [1]Was Amer.Birthright Trust. [2]20% stk.divis in 82,86. Was Tax-Man Fd.Util.Shs. [3]Was St.Paul Capital. [4]Was St.Paul Growth. [5]Was Amer.Gen'l Bond. [6]Was Amer.Gen'l Comstock. [7]Was Amer.Gen'l Enterprise. [8]Was Amer.Gen'l Harbor. [9]Min.of 80%rated "A". [10]Was Amer.Gen'l Munic Bd. [11]Was Amer.Gen'l Pace. 2-for-1 split Jan.83. [12]Was Amer.Gen'l Venture. 2-for-1 split Dec.'83. [13]10-for-1 split,Jun'86. [14]Was Babson(D.L.)Invest. [15]Was Babson(D.L.)Income Trust. [16]Was Capital Shares. [17]Was Nation-Wide Secs. [18]Was Dividend Share. [19]Was Bullock Fund. 2-for-1 split,Feb.86. [20]Was High Income Shares. [29]Was Monthly Inc Shs. [21]3-for-1 split Mar.'84.

STANDARD & POOR'S STOCK REPORTS

Standard & Poor's Corp.
New York, NY
   It is an expensive service (NYSE is $589 per year; the AMEX/OTC is $508 per year), but it is another must for all brokers and serious investors.

These reports are a mainstay of every brokerage firm's branch office. If your broker can't provide you with an S & P sheet on a security that S & P follows, fire him. These reports should be available to clients on a regular basis.

   The reports consist of a summary paragraph, details of all relevant information on a company, and charts outlining the stock's movement over several years. For example, they report on quarterly and annual earnings, stock splits of the distant past, book values, and data going back ten years. The reports also list a summary of all securities issued by a company—common stock, preferreds, warrants, etc.—and provide brief summaries of the terms and details of unusually complex securities. And finally, they provide corporate headquarters data, officers, addresses, phone numbers, and transfer agents.

   The following *S & P Stock Reports'* analysis obviously provides a lot of data on securities. Although several lesser-known OTC securities are not in the *Reports,* those that are have long financial histories. By using the notations at the bottom of the page, for example, you can research the number and form of all splits in a security for the past fifteen years. The second half of the page primarily covers the financial doings of the company: dividends, earnings, and major aspects of each company's capitalization, such as short- and long-term debts, current cash position, etc. There is a lot to be learned from a short review of each "line."

   In fact, the *S & P Reports* are the all-purpose bible in most branch offices. The charts aren't as detailed in time frame as *Value Line*'s (our next publication), but the data on pages 238 and 239 provide a long-term historical review in ample detail. The initial summary, though brief, is a good introduction to what Wall Street is thinking about a security. Again, many small OTC stocks are not reviewed, even in the OTC section (a separate set of volumes) of the reports. Current news is well detailed, and the breakdown of sales generation is quite helpful, especially for diversified concerns. The corporate

Exxon Corp. 846F

NYSE Symbol XON Options on CBOE (Jan-Apr-Jul-Oct) In S&P 500

Price	Range	P-E Ratio	Dividend	Yield	S&P Ranking	Beta
Aug. 1'86 $60\frac{1}{2}$	1986 $61\frac{5}{8}$-$48\frac{3}{8}$	8	3.60	6.0%	A	0.74

Summary

Over recent years XON has had ongoing programs to phase out inefficient capacity, upgrade retained facilities, and strengthen its resource base. It also has been generous with its shareholders by raising dividends and buying back shares. Now, in the current low oil price environment, XON has become very aggressive in cutting personnel and capital spending; moves which could be designed to make room for a major acquisition of petroleum assets should the current buyers' market provide the opportunity.

Current Outlook

Earnings for 1986 are estimated to decline to about \$6.00 a share from 1985's \$6.46. A further decline to about \$5.40 a share is estimated for 1987.

Dividends, however, are expected to continue at a minimum of \$0.90 quarterly.

Revenues and profits for 1986 are projected to decline, reflecting much lower average crude oil prices and charges related to XON's reorganization and employee separation program. The withdrawal of over \$1 billion in excess pension funds will not add to 1986 earnings. Prospective lower average oil and gas prices will likely keep pressure on 1987 earnings.

[1]Gross Oper. Rev. (Billion \$)

Quarter:	1986	1985	1984	1983
Mar.	21.7	22.9	24.5	23.4
Jun.	---	22.7	24.0	22.6
Sep.	---	22.1	23.2	23.1
Dec.	---	23.9	24.1	24.4
	---	91.6	95.9	93.4

Revenues for the 1986 first half declined 13%, year to year. Net income gained 36%, to \$3.90 a share from \$2.70. The gain reflected the absence of a \$0.71 a share special charge in the 1985 second quarter and much improved refining and marketing profits.

Capital Share Earnings (\$)

Quarter:	1986	1985	1984	1983
Mar.	2.35	1.71	1.75	1.22
Jun.	1.55	0.99	1.63	1.25
Sep.	E1.00	1.33	1.58	1.41
Dec.	E1.10	2.43	1.81	1.90
	E6.00	6.46	6.77	5.78

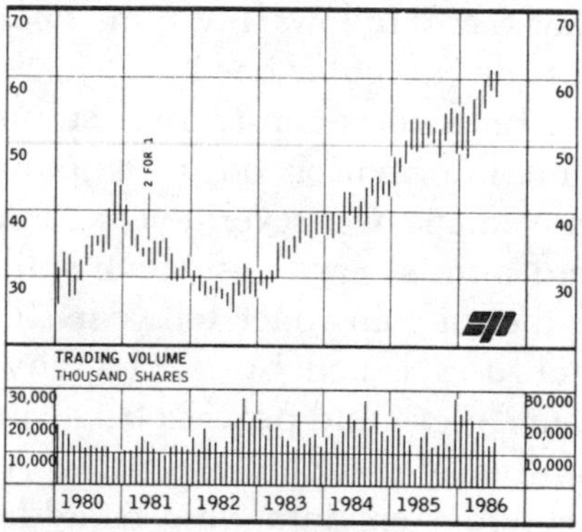

Important Developments

Mar. '86—XON announced a streamlining program that would eliminate certain operations overseas and at its New York headquarters. The news came less than one week after XON said it was reducing its 1986 capital and exploration spending budget 26% from 1985's \$10.8 billion. Speculation was that all these steps were being taken to conserve cash in order to acquire sizable reserves in the current buyers' market for oil properties that is expected to last for several years. Due to its size and high level of perceived public accountability, XON probably would be more inclined to buy parcels of reserves rather than a major oil company. But an acquisition under friendly circumstances cannot be ruled out. XON is one of the few major oil companies that has not leveraged its balance sheet with debt.

Next earnings report due in late October.

Per Share Data (\$)

Yr. End Dec. 31	1985	1984	1983	1982	1981	1980	1979	1978	1977	1976
Book Value	**39.80**	36.85	34.80	32.84	32.84	29.41	25.70	22.80	21.81	20.61
Earnings	**6.46**	6.77	5.78	4.82	6.44	6.49	4.87	3.10	2.71	2.95
Dividends	**3.45**	3.35	3.10	3.00	3.00	2.70	1.95	1.65	1.50	$1.36\frac{3}{8}$
Payout Ratio	**52%**	47%	53%	62%	47%	41%	40%	53%	55%	46%
Prices—High	**$55\frac{7}{8}$**	$45\frac{1}{2}$	$39\frac{3}{4}$	$32\frac{1}{4}$	41	$44\frac{1}{2}$	$30\frac{5}{8}$	$26\frac{7}{8}$	$27\frac{7}{8}$	$28\frac{1}{2}$
Low	**$44\frac{1}{8}$**	$36\frac{1}{8}$	$28\frac{1}{2}$	$24\frac{7}{8}$	$29\frac{1}{2}$	26	$24\frac{1}{2}$	$21\frac{1}{2}$	$22\frac{1}{2}$	$21\frac{3}{8}$
P/E Ratio—	**9-7**	7-5	7-5	7-5	6-5	7-4	6-5	9-7	10-8	10-7

Data as orig. reptd. Adj. for stk. div(s). of 100% Jun. 1981, 100% Jul. 1976. **1.** Incl. excise taxes. E-Estimated.

Standard NYSE Stock Reports
Vol. 53/No. 153/Sec. 9

August 8, 1986
Copyright © 1986 Standard & Poor's Corp. All Rights Reserved
Standard & Poor's Corp.
25 Broadway, NY, NY 10004

816F

Exxon Corporation

Income Data (Million $)

Year Ended Dec. 31	Revs.	Oper. Inc.	% Oper. Inc. of Revs.	Cap. Exp.	Depr.	Int. Exp.	Net Bef. Taxes	Eff. Tax Rate	[2]Net Inc.	% Net Inc. of Revs.
1985	86,673	14,397	16.6%	8,844	4,274	998	[1] 9,797	47.9%	[2]4,870	5.6%
1984	90,854	13,865	15.3%	7,842	4,073	668	[1]10,807	46.9%	5,528	6.1%
1983	88,561	12,896	14.6%	7,124	3,528	1,020	[1] 9,907	48.2%	4,978	5.6%
1982	97,173	10,378	10.7%	9,040	3,333	877	[1] 7,875	45.4%	[2]4,186	4.3%
1981	108,108	11,177	10.3%	9,003	2,948	1,015	[1] 9,912	42.5%	5,567	5.2%
1980	103,143	12,269	11.9%	6,465	2,282	772	[1]11,273	48.2%	5,650	5.5%
1979	79,107	14,256	18.0%	5,351	2,027	494	[1]12,886	65.6%	4,295	5.4%
1978	60,335	9,921	16.4%	4,187	1,678	427	[1] 8,622	66.8%	[2]2,763	4.6%
1977	54,126	9,963	18.4%	3,596	2,155	453	[1] 8,151	69.1%	2,423	4.5%
1976	48,631	9,123	18.8%	4,098	1,872	490	[1] 7,945	65.3%	2,641	5.4%

Balance Sheet Data (Million $)

Dec. 31	Cash	Current Assets	Current Liab.	Ratio	Total Assets	Ret. on Assets	Long Term Debt	Common Equity	Total Cap.	% LT Debt of Cap.	Ret. on Equity
1985	2,474	17,355	19,089	0.9	69,160	7.6%	4,820	29,096	46,340	10.4%	17.4%
1984	3,290	17,239	15,265	1.1	63,278	9.1%	5,105	28,851	44,166	11.6%	19.7%
1983	4,096	18,596	15,039	1.2	62,963	8.0%	4,669	29,443	44,337	10.5%	17.4%
1982	3,449	19,793	16,465	1.2	62,289	6.7%	4,556	28,440	42,858	10.6%	14.7%
1981	3,884	23,848	17,744	1.3	62,931	9.3%	5,153	28,517	43,002	12.0%	20.6%
1980	4,926	23,459	16,884	1.4	56,577	10.7%	4,717	25,413	37,662	12.5%	23.7%
1979	4,508	20,478	15,883	1.3	49,490	9.5%	4,258	22,552	32,088	13.3%	20.2%
1978	4,756	16,369	12,041	1.4	41,531	6.9%	3,749	20,229	28,295	13.3%	14.0%
1977	4,684	15,332	10,713	1.4	38,453	6.5%	3,870	19,513	26,864	14.4%	12.8%
1976	5,074	15,052	10,521	1.4	36,331	7.6%	3,697	18,470	25,092	14.7%	14.9%

Data as orig. reptd. 1. Incl. equity in earns. of nonconsol. subs. 2. Reflects accounting change.

Business Summary

Exxon Corp. is the world's leading petroleum enterprise.

Oper. Profits	1985	1984
U.S. expl. & prod.	35%	35%
U.S. ref. & mkt.	4%	3%
Foreign expl. & prod.	46%	49%
Foreign ref. & mkt.	10%	4%
International marine	−1%	−1%
U.S. chemical	2%	4%
Foreign chemical	2%	4%
Coal & other	2%	2%

In 1985 net crude oil and natural gas liquids production averaged 1,701,000 barrels a day, natural gas production available for sale 5.7 billion cubic feet a day, refinery crude oil runs 2,903,000 b/d, and petroleum product sales 4,082,000 b/d.

Net proved reserves at the 1985 year-end stood at 7,568 million barrels of crude and natural gas liquids and 46,802 billion cubic feet of natural gas.

In February, 1986 XON paid $2.1 billion in alleged

oil price overcharges on its East Texas Hawkins Field (one-half of which it expected to recover from tax refunds and another of the field's owners). The $0.71 a share charge in the 1985 second quarter related to this liability.

Dividend Data

Dividends have been paid since 1882. A dividend reinvestment plan is available.

Amt. of Divd. $	Date Decl.	Ex-divd. Date	Stock of Record	Payment Date
0.90	Oct. 30	Nov. 5	Nov. 12	Dec. 10'85
0.90	Jan. 29	Feb. 4	Feb. 10	Mar. 10'86
0.90	Apr. 30	May 7	May 13	Jun. 10'86
0.90	Jul. 30	Aug. 7	Aug. 13	Sep. 10'86

Next dividend meeting: late Oct. '86.

Capitalization

Long Term Debt: $4,818,000,000 (3/31/86).

Minority Interest: $1,382,000,000.

Capital Stock: 722,200,000 shs. (no par).
Institutions hold about 34%.
Shareholders of record: 776,172.

Office—1251 Ave. of the Americas, NYC 10020-1198. Tel—(212) 333-1000. Chrmn & CEO—C. C. Garvin, Jr. Pres—L. G. Rawl. VP-Secy—E. R. Cattarulla. VP-Treas—E. A. Robinson. Shareholder Contact—R. C. Darcey. Dirs—W. A. Andres, J. F. Bennett, R. W. Bromery, J. G. Clarke, C. C. Garvin, Jr., J. Hay, W. R. Howell, Sir H. Laing, P. E. Lippincott, D. S. MacNaughton, M. L. A. MacVicar, D. K. McIvor, M. E. J. O'Loughlin, M. Peterson, B. Phillips, L. G. Rawl, L. R. Raymond, C. R. Sitter, O. Wolff von Amerongen. Transfer Agent—Morgan Guaranty Trust Co., NYC. Incorporated in New Jersey in 1882.

Information has been obtained from sources believed to be reliable, but its accuracy and completeness are not guaranteed.   Earl L. Lester, CFA

Reprinted by permission of Standard and Poor's.

address and phone number at the end are helpful when ordering annual reports or offering comments, compliments, or complaints.

VALUE LINE INVESTMENT SURVEY

Value Line, Inc.
New York, NY
Cost per year is $395.

Value Line is a service similar to *S & P Stock Reports*. It covers a great deal of financial information on one page, which includes a chart with supporting financial data from the past fifteen years. It provides twenty-two series of financial and operating statistics. What sets *Value Line* apart from S & P is that it projects detailed estimates on these statistics several years into the future. It also offers ratings as to "timeliness" for purchase and "investment safety," on a ranking system of one to five. A new segment of the overall survey is published weekly, and individual stock reports are updated quarterly.

I like *Value Line* because it statistically places itself on the record for estimating a variety of valuable financial topics, long into the future, on a wide variety (1,700) of stocks. Their analyses are precise and clear-cut.

A weakness of *Value Line*'s is that it does not follow all companies on the NYSE, AMEX, and especially those on the OTC. But it is a concise, superb service with an above-average review of stocks.

Value Line covers a lot on one page. Its charts and data have the longest historical review and the longest-running estimates for the future (two to four years). In terms of recommendations, its summary is more specific than S & P's because it rates each security followed numerically. It is also more opinionated about a security's worth to an investor, and the summaries tend to direct your thinking rather than provide information as the *S & P Reports* do. *Value Line* is an excellent one-page review.

Financial Publications: Favorites of the Pros 241

EXXON CORP. NYSE-XON | RECENT PRICE **61** | P/E RATIO **9.0** (Trailing: 7.4 / Median: 8.5) | RELATIVE P/E RATIO **0.60** | DIV'D YLD **6.1%** | VALUE LINE **410**

High →	20.6	22.3	25.8	24.9	23.5	28.4	27.9	26.8	30.6	44.4	41.0	32.3	39.8	45.5	55.9	61.6
Low →	16.8	17.0	21.0	13.7	16.3	21.3	22.4	21.5	24.4	26.0	29.5	24.9	28.5	36.1	44.5	48.4

Insider Decisions 1985
	D	J	F	M	A	M	J	J	A	S	O	N	D	J	F
to Buy	4	0	1	1	2	3	2	5	0	3	0	5	1	4	4	1
to Sell	3	1	1	3	1	1	0	1	0	1	0	0	1	0

5.0 x "Cash Flow" p sh
Target Price Range 64

Options Trade On CBO

2-for-1 split
2-for-1 split

1988 | 1989 | 1990 | 1991
July 11, 1986 Value Line

TIMELINESS 3 Average
(Relative Price Performance Next 12 Mos.)

SAFETY 1 Highest
(Scale: 1 Highest to 5 Lowest)

BETA .80 (1.00 = Market)

1989-91 PROJECTIONS
	Price	Gain	Ann'l Total Return
High	80	(+30%)	12%
Low	60	(Nil)	6%

© Value Line, Inc. 89-91E

Institutional Decisions
	1Q'85	2Q'85	3Q'85	4Q'85	1Q'86
to Buy	144	126	146	153	179
to Sell	219	241	220	215	235
Hdg's(000)	244286	240782	235378	234263	234186

Percent 3.0 shares 2.0 traded 1.0

Relative Price Strength

1970	1971	1972	1973	1974	1975	1976	1977	1978	1979	1980	1981	1982	1983	1984	1985	1986	1987		© Value Line, Inc.	89-91E
18.50	20.85	22.64	28.73	47.02	50.13	54.27	60.40	68.00	90.14	119.36	124.50	112.21	104.87	116.03	118.57	108.55	108.55	Sales per sh	114.30
2.63	2.90	2.89	4.00	4.93	4.50	4.56	4.44	5.01	7.20	9.19	9.81	8.65	10.05	12.26	13.25	12.95	12.80	"Cash Flow" per sh	13.80
1.48	1.69	1.71	2.73	3.51	2.80	2.95	2.71	3.10	4.87	6.50	6.44	4.82	5.78	6.77	7.43	6.75	6.50	Earnings per sh (A)	7.00
.94	.95	.95	1.06	1.25	1.25	1.36	1.50	1.65	1.95	2.70	3.00	3.00	3.10	3.35	3.45	3.60	3.60	Div'ds Decl'd per sh (B)	4.00
2.00	2.02	2.21	2.50	3.25	3.98	4.57	*4.01	4.72	6.10	7.48	10.37	10.44	8.42	10.02	12.10	9.15	9.00	Cap'l Spending per sh	10.00
12.24	12.93	13.68	15.32	17.58	19.02	20.61	21.77	22.80	25.70	29.41	32.84	32.84	34.80	36.85	39.80	42.90	45.55	Book Value per sh (C)	49.00
894.92	896.91	897.06	895.47	894.58	894.8	896.18	896.18	887.23	877.64	864.16	868.37	866.01	846.10	783.00	731.00	710.00	700.00	Common Shs Outst'g (D)	700.00
10.4	11.0	11.4	8.5	5.2	7.4	8.5	9.3	7.7	5.5	5.3	5.2	5.9	6.0	6.1	6.9	Bold figures are		Avg Ann'l P/E Ratio	10.0
.75	.70	.78	.84	.73	.99	1.09	1.22	1.05	.80	.70	.63	.65	.51	.57	.56	Value Line estimates		Relative P/E Ratio	.85
6.1%	5.1%	4.9%	4.6%	6.9%	6.0%	5.5%	6.0%	7.0%	7.3%	7.9%	8.9%	10.5%	8.9%	8.1%	6.8%			Avg Ann'l Div'd Yield	5.7%

CAPITAL STRUCTURE as of 12/31/85

Total Debt areas mill. Due in 6 Yrs $1300 mill.
LT Debt 16.3% 17.3% 16.4% 18.0% 11.9% 10.9% 10.7% 14.6% 15.3% 16.6% 16.0% 16.0% Operating Margin 17.0%

LT Debt $4820 mill. **LT Interest** $500 mill.
1448.4 1558.3 1677.9 2027.1 2282.3 2947.9 3333.5 3527.8 4073.0 4274.0 4200 4400 Depreciation ($mill) 4700

Incl. $543 mill. capitalized leases.
2641.0 2423.0 2763.0 4295.2 5650.0 5567.5 4155.9 4978.0 5528.0 5415.0 4900 4550 Net Profit ($mill) 4960
(LT interest earned: 12.9x; total interest 65.3% 69.1% 66.8% 65.6% 48.2% 42.5% 45.6% 48.2% 46.9% 47.4% 44.0% 46.0% Income Tax Rate (E) 48.0%
coverage: 11.8x)
5.4% 4.5% 4.6% 5.4% 5.5% 5.2% 4.3% 5.6% 6.1% 6.3% 6.5% 6.0% Net Profit Margin 6.2%

(14% of Cap'l)
4530.6 4618.5 4328.1 4595.0 6574.3 6104.9 3328.0 3556.8 1974.0 d1734 300 300 Working Cap'l ($mill) 300

Leases, Uncapitalized Annual rentals $437 mill.
3696.8 3870.0 3749.2 4258.0 4717.1 5153.4 4555.6 4668.9 5105.0 4820.0 7000 7000 Long-Term Debt ($mill) 7000

Pension Surplus: $1203 mill.
18470 19513 20229 22552 25413 28517 28440 29443 28851 29096 30450 31900 Net Worth ($mill) 34300
12.6% 11.0% 12.2% 16.7% 19.5% 17.3% 13.4% 15.3% 17.1% 17.3% 14.0% 12.5% % Earned Total Cap'l 13.0%

Pfd Stock None
14.3% 12.4% 13.7% 19.1% 22.2% 19.5% 14.6% 16.9% 19.2% 18.6% 16.0% 14.5% % Earned Net Worth 14.5%

Common Stock 731,000,000 shs. (86% of Cap'l)
7.7% 5.5% 6.4% 11.4% 13.0% 10.4% 5.5% 7.8% 9.7% 9.7% 7.5% 6.5% % Retained to Comm Eq 6.0%
46% 55% 53% 40% 42% 47% 63% 54% 50% 48% 53% 55% % All Div'ds to Net Prof 57%

CURRENT POSITION 1983 1984 12/31/85
(SMILL.)
Cash Assets	4096.1	3290.0	2474.0
Receivables	7900.3	7366.0	7527.0
Inventory(LIFO)	4970.8	4702.0	4796.0
Other	1628.3	1881.0	2558.0
Current Assets	18595.5	17239.0	17355.0
Accts Payable	11000.2	10845.0	13359.0
Debt Due	867.3	1277.0	3089.0
Other	3171.2	3143.0	2641.0
Current Liab.	15038.7	15265.0	19089.0

ANNUAL RATES Past Past Est'd '83-'85
of change (per sh)	10 Yrs	5 Yrs	to '89-'91
Sales	10.5%	4.0%	1.0%
"Cash Flow"	10.0%	10.5%	5.5%
Earnings	8.5%	8.5%	5.0%
Dividends	11.0%	9.5%	4.0%
Book Value	8.0%	7.5%	6.5%

Cal-endar QUARTERLY SALES ($ mill.) Full Year
	Mar. 31	June 30	Sept. 30	Dec. 31	Year
1983	23401	21303	21796	22061	88561
1984	23361	22488	21854	23151	90854
1985	21717	21299	20774	22883	86673
1986	20468	18000	18000	19032	75500
1987	19000	18500	18500	20000	76000

Cal-endar EARNINGS PER SHARE (A) Full
	Mar. 31	June 30	Sept. 30	Dec. 31	Year
1983	1.22	1.25	1.42	1.89	5.78
1984	1.75	1.63	1.58	1.81	6.77
1985	1.71	1.70	1.51	2.47	7.43
1986	2.52	1.50	1.30	1.43	6.75
1987	1.50	1.60	1.60	1.80	6.50

Cal-endar QUARTERLY DIVIDENDS PAID (B) Full
	Mar. 31	June 30	Sept. 30	Dec. 31	Year
1982	.75	.75	.75	.75	3.00
1983	.75	.75	.80	.80	3.10
1984	.80	.85	.85	.85	3.35
1985	.85	.85	.85	.90	3.45
1986	.90	.90			

BUSINESS: Exxon Corporation is the world's largest integrated oil company. Net daily crude & liquid supplies in '85: 1.9 mill. bbls. U.S. reserves: 2.7 bill. bbls. crude & liquids; 17.9 trill. cu. ft. gas. Est'd pretax present value of U.S. reserves: $22 billion. Daily refinery runs, 2.9 mill. bbls.; product sales, 4.1 mill. bbls. Owns Reliance Electric, 70% of Imperial Oil. Exxon Enterprises acts as venture capital arm. Operating earnings: U.S., 50%; foreign, 50%. Wage costs: 6.2% of sales. '85 depreciation rate: 5.8%. Employs 146,000; has 785,062 stockholders. Insiders own less than 1% of stock. Chairman: G.C. Garvin, Jr. Inc.; NJ. Address: 1251 Avenue of the Americas, New York, NY 10020. Tel.: 212-333-1000.

Exxon will probably turn in a surprisingly decent year despite the oil price decline. Significantly offsetting the anticipated drop in exploration and production earnings has been the dramatically improved contribution from refining and marketing operations. Earnings advanced almost $600 million over 1985 in the March quarter as product prices fell more slowly than input costs and the dollar weakened to the further benefit of results abroad where Exxon does almost three-fourths of its product sales. The June quarter domestically should prove even better, we think. We do not anticipate severe margin erosion over the rest of the year since we expect downstream participants will refrain in this industry environment from price-cutting grabs at market share. Exxon is also continuing to flourish in chemicals, and we expect its tax rate will also be lower this year by several points. We have raised our original estimates by $1.80 a share. (Note that we have restored 17¢ a share to March results, the net of nonrecurring charges and gains, and we exclude a sizable gain likely in June on the sale of some Danish operations.) **Exxon is obviously not optimistic about** an energy price recovery soon, however. And it's worth remembering, given current downstream success, that oil companies make their biggest and most dependable money at the wellhead, not the gas pump. Exxon has significantly been reorganizing operating structures recently; and 6,000 workers on the U.S. dollar payroll will be leaving soon as part of the effort to lower costs. More employee departures overseas and in non-energy areas are also likely. Such moves, while indicating the inefficiencies built into large companies during boom times, imply to us by their severity that Exxon sees little reason to expect better times and $25 oil over the next several years. We agree, and think. . .

Exxon shares are unlikely to beat the averages over the coming year, although they'll do better than most oil stocks as a quality holding in the group. In fact, they have posted another new yearly high in the last three months. The dividend is secure even under more adverse energy prices, sustained by Exxon's strong cash flow. The share buyback program is winding down, however, thus removing one of the stock's supports. W.E. Higgins

(A) Based on ave. shs. outst'g. Qtrs. and year may not equal due to diff. no. of shs. Next egs. report due late July. Excl. non-recur. gain (chg.); In '85, (93¢); In '86,(17¢). (B) Next div'd meeting about July 23. Goes ex about Aug. 5. Approx. div'd. dates: Mar. 10, June 10, Sept. 10, Dec. 10. (C) Includes deferred charges. In '85: $1232 mill. $1.64/sh. (D) In mill., adjusted for stock splits and div'ds. (E) Lower tax rate due to change in accounting for Aramco, 1980. Div'd reinvst. plan available.

Company's Financial Strength	A++
Stock's Price Stability	95
Price Growth Persistence	20
Earnings Predictability	70

Factual material is obtained from sources believed to be reliable but the statistics and comments published herein cannot be guaranteed as to accuracy or completeness.

Reprinted by permission of Value Line Investment Survey.

DAILY GRAPHS

Wm. O'Neil & Co.
Los Angeles, CA

Issued weekly. Cost per year: NYSE issue and 50 OTC stocks is $325 per year. AMEX issue and 150 OTC stocks is $290 per year. Subscribing to both editions costs $580 per year.

If you like charts, you'll love *Daily Graphs*. Just about every technical charting broker (technician) I know uses these charts to guess where his favorite stock will be moving next.

Daily Graphs comes in two versions: The NYSE issue follows 1,600 stocks, and the AMEX follows 1,024. These charts provide detailed tracking of the past twelve months' movement of a stock with a very short statement as to the operating fundamentals of the company. Some of the studies include a relative ranking of stock performance by industry, bank and mutual fund ownership statistics, various ratios, trading volume statistics, and 100-day moving average analyses. Charts of various indexes and economic indicators for the past ten years, relative strength statistics on the top 100 stocks, short interest positions, and quote symbols for companies are updated weekly.

This service is for technical analysis. It has some value as a reference tool if received periodically. It is an excellent review of the past year but gives no information before this period and no estimates other than earnings forecasts for the present and upcoming operating years.

Daily Graphs is a chartist's dream. Pages 243 to 245 are examples of the detailed overview offered and updated weekly. The breakdown of various subjects is long and detailed. Little is left open after reviewing *Daily Graphs*'s weekly publication. Page 245 details the individual security review. All recent necessary financial data are provided in one graph. There is little need in most chartists' minds for analyzing past one year when trying to anticipate short-term trading moves—a good reason to use *Daily Graphs*. They even provide a review of "key trades," major blocks (either sells or buys) that have recently taken place. Unless you like charting or are very much into trading equities, much of the information may be too detailed or superfluous. But if trading is your game, this level of charting is a must.

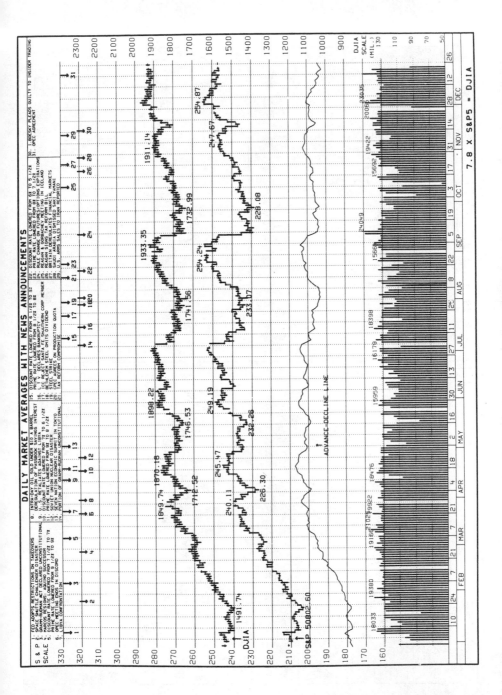

DAILY MARKET AVERAGES WITH NEWS ANNOUNCEMENTS

7.8 X S&P5 = DJIA

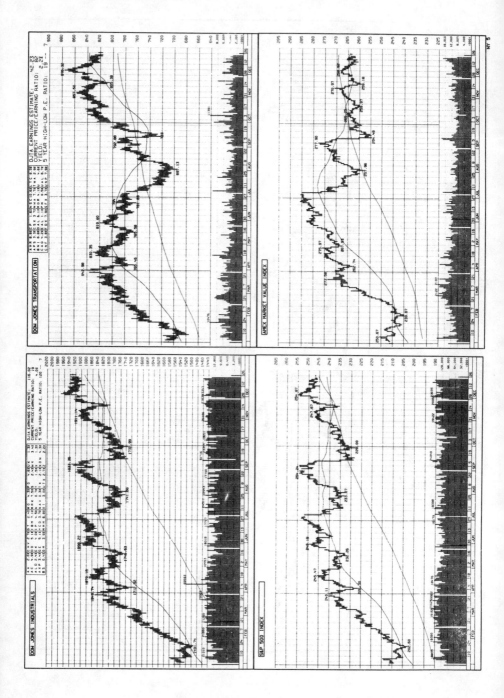

DOW JONES TRANSPORTATION

DJTA EARNINGS ESTIMATE: 42.23
CURRENT PRICE/EARNING RATIO: 2.82
YIELD:
5 YEAR HIGH-LOW P.E. RATIO: 19--- 7

DOW JONES INDUSTRIALS

DJIA EARNINGS ESTIMATE: 16.60
CURRENT PRICE/EARNING RATIO: 31
YIELD:
5 YEAR HIGH-LOW P.E. RATIO: 120---

AMEX MARKET VALUE INDEX

S&P 500 INDEX

NY 5

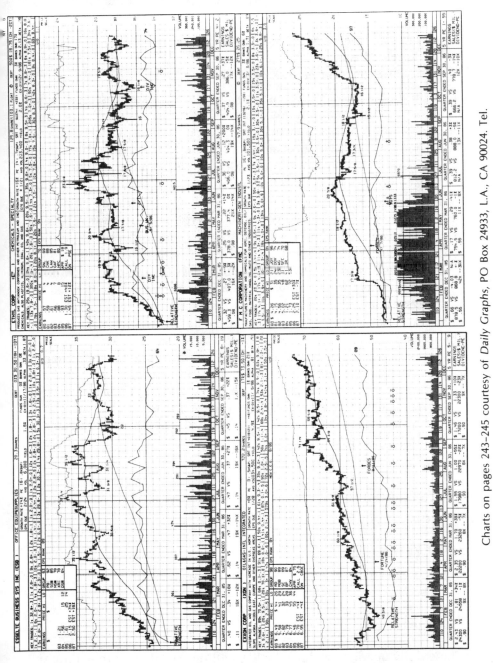

Charts on pages 243–245 courtesy of *Daily Graphs*, PO Box 24933, L.A., CA 90024. Tel. (213) 820-7011.

245

DAILY GRAPHS STOCK OPTION GUIDE
Daily Graphs, Wm. O'Neil & Co.
Los Angeles, CA
Issued weekly. Cost per year is $145.

This publication is a first cousin to *Daily Graphs'* stock issue and includes all the information you need to chart and follow the trading of stock options, which gyrate in price even more rapidly than their underlying stocks. Most brokers who trade options review this guide. And revere it. It offers computer-selected strategies for buying and writing options, additional information on the most widely held and actively traded options, and a review of all options traded on all exchanges. It also includes many of the general index reviews of stocks from *Daily Graphs.* It is of use somewhat as a shelf reference if periodically received and is a must for active option traders.

Daily Graphs Stock Option Guide (opposite) is for the option trading junkie, much as the *Daily Racing Form* is a must if you're headed to the races. The mere fact that it updates the confusing and fast-changing symbols of each option traded makes the publication worthy of its price to active options traders, whether they are brokers or investors. Its weekly update and thorough attention to detail make this guide a bargain-price investment. But remember, many brokers think options have great entertainment value—but not too much investment worth—when the final tallies come in.

WALL STREET JOURNAL
Dow Jones & Co., Chicopee, MA

INVESTOR'S DAILY
Investor's Daily Co., Los Angeles, CA

NEW YORK TIMES
New York Times Co., New York, NY

The *Journal* costs $114 per year (5 days per week), *Investor's Daily* is $84 per year (5 days per week), and *The New York Times* is $234 per year (7 days per week).

These daily newspapers have little shelf life, but if you are willing to risk divorce over your squirreling habits, throw them into a closet, then years later go back, test your memory, and see how misleading some headlines were and how poor so many forecasts turned out to be.

DAILY GRAPHS STOCK OPTION GUIDE

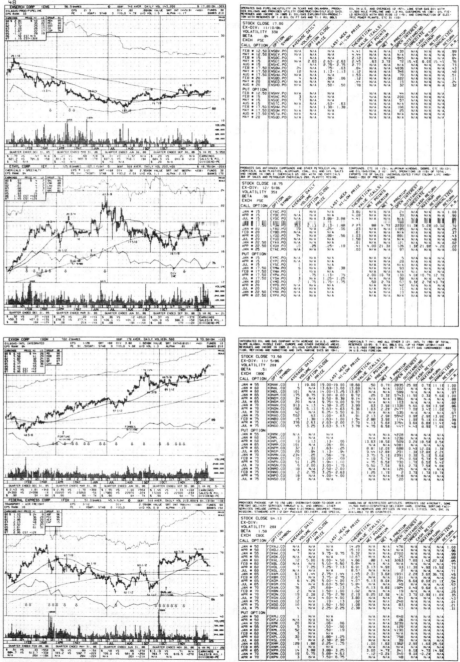

Charts courtesy of *Daily Graphs*, PO Box 24933, L.A., CA. 90024. Tel (213) 820-7011.

While the *Wall Street Journal* enjoys the status of being the nation's largest-circulation newspaper, the *Investor's Daily* is the new kid on the block attempting to gain a market—a difficult task. The *Journal* is a good paper with the weaknesses prone to all newspapers. A major problem occurs, however, when they point their readers in an investment direction via their reporting, because frequently people do lose a lot of money. On the flipside, they profit at times too. Neither scenario—losing or making money—is likely to occur as a result of reading the *Boston Globe* or the *Christian Science Monitor*.

The *Investor's Daily* is most respected by brokers for its wealth of statistical information provided daily. However, not every investor needs daily statistics, so the *Journal* is read for more broad-based financial coverage, albeit at times imperfect.

The *New York Times* Financial Section is the best of the full-service papers. I love the *Times*. For overall value, I rate it number one. Its Sunday financial section is worth the price of the entire paper. Either way, reading these papers can help a lot more than hurt when following your investments and the economy in general.

BARRON'S

Dow Jones & Co.,
Chicopee, MA

Cost per year is $82.

Barron's covers most all of the major securities, even international ones, and the major indexes and financial barometers. It also has an excellent section on statistics.

Barron's has a refreshing irreverence for Wall Street that permeates its pages. You have the sense that it doesn't really trust what is going on in downtown New York. Its feature articles discuss in detail Wall Street's good and bad research, strange practices in the business, and corporations' misleading or awkward quarterly and annual reports. As a result, it is generally acknowledged that *Barron's* moves the market on Monday by what it says on Saturday.

I've lost money on the typical *Barron's* article that has found dirt under a company's rug. The news might actually have been known to half of all shareholders, but after the critical *Barron's* article hits Saturday newsstands, what was previously dust turns into radioactive mud. On a Bloody Monday investors (and institutions) head for the exits at the opening bell. The "chosen" stock is killed in a day, although most recover somewhat over the next three months. Every broker I know has a *Barron's* Bloody Monday story to tell. It's a mark of your longevity in the business as to how many you can tell over one beer. Nevertheless, when *Barron's* is good, it's very good—a worthwhile investment for serious investors.

THE FINANCIAL MAGAZINES

Forbes	*Money*
Business Week	*Changing Times*
Fortune	*Sylvia Porter's Personal Finance*

Financial magazines are popular with brokers and investors alike. I like those, such as the five above, that question and search for the inequalities, ineptitudes, and imbalances of various investments, styles, and trends. *Forbes* is especially good at this. Many articles have saved me and my clients money. For example, articles such as "Where Are the Customers' Yachts" (*Forbes*), which discusses (among other things) how no one can rate a tax shelter or private placement because there is no uniform way to analyze a rate of return, make me respect the value of these publications for investors. And this particular article confirmed my distrust in shelters and gave me ammunition in case my company ever wanted to know why I wasn't selling any to qualified clients. Nobody ever did question me, but it was nice to know I wasn't lost in the desert, thanks to *Forbes*'s reporting. Such articles would have saved everyone even more money if they had been printed sooner rather than later. But better late than never. If you want to become more deeply involved with your investments and keep your broker on his toes, read the financial magazine(s) of your choice.

MUTUAL FUND ADVISORY SERVICES

Lipper Analytical Services, Inc., Westfield, NJ
Wiesenberger Investment Companies Service, New York, NY
Lipper's service is quite expensive and according to their sales representative is available only to financial organizations and not individuals. Your broker should have copies in his office, however, or there is always the library.

Wiesenberger's cost per year is $295 for the full subscription, and $100 per year for its quarterly fund analyses.

If you want detailed analyses of virtually every mutual fund available in the United States today, the above services are superb. Their reports are issued quarterly, they cover all forms of funds, categorize the funds as to their type (balanced, growth, income, etc.), and report returns against each other over identical time frames of one year, five years, and ten years. Indexes of each major type of fund are compared to the major general stock and bond indexes—S & P, Dow Jones, etc. And again, these services are neutral.

One weakness, though, is that their reports fail to consider commissions. This is understandable because of the enormous differences in fees, depending upon the size of purchase, and/or selling agent, but in too many cases sales fees and withdrawal charges are considerable. Nevertheless, a thorough and close review of these reports, and a less accepting attitude toward your financial adviser's/ broker's sales brochures may likely save you a lot of money. If your needs are less complicated, remember the faithful *Standard & Poor's Stock Guide's* back section on mutual funds for $7.00 per monthly issue.

NEWSLETTERS: THE MISSING AND WEAK LINKS

Financial newsletters have always been with us—but so have circuses. Most of them are glorified mass-mail sales organizations, and they are selling themselves, some in excess of a hundred thousand subscriptions a year. Others are happy to have a thousand subscriber/followers. Today there are more than 1,200 newsletters, with one million long-term subscribers. Their sales, like fads, have a tendency to rise and fall, depending on their marketing success and guesses. Some letters shoot up to great heights—*The Wall Street Journal* started as a newsletter.

As I mentioned when discussing gurus, most newsletters rely on the trusting nature, gullibility, and bad memories of investors who hope someone has the Answer. I've never found a letter that did, and I can best summarize the brokers in my office who used the letters in past years as letter junkies. They shot up one letter like a drug until it eventually put holes in the brokers' (and their clients') wallets— and then dropped that subscription only to eventually sign on with some other newsletter. As with all addictions, the cycle began again.

My rich Uncle Froyd (rich from his salary), of infamous Penn Central fame, has subscribed to a bunch of newsletters over many years. As a result he has found a new and more convoluted way of carving up his portfolio than any other client or broker I've ever known. He enjoyed the huge run-up in gold, but like the tide of gold newsletters, he became cocky and bought even more at the top when it was around $800 an ounce (because it was going higher) and then rode his investment into the ground. Occasionally it moves up slightly to give him added hope. He still thinks that gold will hit $3,000 an ounce and that the U.S. government, because of mismanagement, will go bust.

Uncle Froyd's commentaries on future events, based in part on his subscriptions to newsletters, were a vivid part of my childhood. I was able to picture neighbors racing around with wheelbarrows full of dollar bills trying to buy a loaf of bread in a society gone mad. And I remember when I was a rookie broker in 1974 and Uncle Froyd guaranteed chaos would occur before the end of the decade. I'd be in the soup lines before I turned thirty. Fortunately, I've lasted longer than his newsletters and aged better than his portfolio of silver, gold, diamonds, oil, and uranium. If the newsletter authors who sent Uncle Froyd so much mail really knew what they were preaching and predicting with such incredible confidence, they would be so rich that they wouldn't need to write newsletters.

Some newsletters deserve a review because they follow areas that few standard sources care to research, such as embryonic companies, penny stocks, and foreign issues. If you are fascinated with these areas and feel they hold investment promise, consider the newsletter a form of specialized entertainment. But don't bet the ranch on their ideas.

Prices vary almost as much as the quality of the product. Investor beware.

FOR THE GENERAL INVESTOR SHORT ON TIME

In the preceding commentaries you've been given a tour of the range of financial publications. For those investors who want to branch out and specialize, many of these publications can be useful—even crucial to read. But many investors don't have the time or inclination to read them all, and for those general investors, I'd suggest they do as follows. For a newspaper, read my favorite—*The New York Times*. Its business section will more than suffice because it has excellent coverage and is to the point. By all means buy or ask your broker for a *Standard & Poor's Stock Guide,* at least on an annual basis, perhaps every six months. For a magazine that looks for the dirt that flies around the Street, that covers a multitude of financial topics, is statistically proficient without being overwhelming, and has a healthy dose of skepticism in its writings on Wall Street, buy *Forbes.* In spite of what they said about oil prices in March 1982. And remember to bring your own skepticism to bear on everything you read.

Chapter Fourteen

DEALING WITH YOUR BROKER

> A broker is someone who invests other people's money until it's all gone.
>
> —WOODY ALLEN

Woody Allen's definition of a broker may be applicable to your broker, but it is unfair to consider them all financial vacuum cleaners. I've often asked myself how I would handle my investments if I ever retired or left the brokerage business. Now that I have left the business, my answer is twofold. I'd use the least biased consultant I could find, and a darn good broker at a major firm.

WHERE DO I GET A BROKER—WALL STREET OR ITS COMPETITORS?

You *can* get good service from a competent broker, so the search for one can be worth the time spent. Choose a broker with a lot of backup—a full-service environment. You'll pay more in certain areas, but you will more than save that money in other ways. And often you can receive discounted commission rates merely by asking. Besides, commissions reduce your net gains or add to your net losses, so despite the tax law changes they are still an indirect tax-deductible expense.

Remember, too, not to rely on any single financial adviser at all times—be it a broker, banker, planner, lawyer, or accountant. Today, I feel a fee-based planner is the best bet for advice. When looking for your broker, though, seek out one who can consistently provide you with the know-how to recognize what is good and who offers those solid alternative investments. He has an incentive. If you're happy, he'll continue to receive your business and some referral business as well.

ARE YOU A BIG OR SMALL FISH?

First, it is important to judge the attention your account needs and warrants. Combining your assets, income, areas of investment interest, and portfolio size will give you a "worth" to your broker in terms of the time he spends with you and the income he makes from trades. For example, if you get lots of attention on a $15,000 portfolio, it could mean the broker is a rookie, a loser, or he's churning your account. On the other hand, if your account is large ($100,000 or more) or just above average ($50,000 or more), and you are receiving little attention, it could mean you are being overlooked or handled too conservatively. I am amazed how many large clients perceive themselves as small (partly due to a broker's orchestration) and how many small clients think they are John D. Rockefeller. It is important that you know what you are fairly entitled to—and then receive it.

If you are a client with a $100,000 portfolio, you deserve one or two thorough consultations and several recommendations, not just the product of the month. If you hold stock, you should receive the firm's research reports on your securities and offers for free insurance and income tax analysis. Your broker should return your phone call within twenty-four hours—if not the same day. If you have expressed an interest in trading securities, prompt action within a trading day is required.

Clients with $25,000 or smaller portfolios cannot reasonably expect a successful broker to call back every time within ten minutes. Or review a fifteen-stock portfolio unless the broker and client foresee a larger portfolio down the road. I was not an active stock-trading broker, so my clients rarely needed immediate service, and if they did, I had an assistant who could handle it. But I did try to reach every client who called within twenty-four hours or less. If the client desired the service and did the type of business that warranted its usage, I would also provide a free computer linkup, which, among other things, offered checking account analysis, portfolio evaluation, my firm's research, Standard & Poor information, and quotes.

Basically, holders of good accounts ($100,000 or more) or active smaller accounts should locate a broker who will consistently provide service in a straightforward manner, and should communicate their needs to the broker at the outset. The parallel to "the rich get richer and the poor get poorer" is that rich clients get better service from brokers and poor clients get poorer service. But even a smaller client can make up for his size through loyalty and proof that as he grows financially he will give his broker more business. A good broker recognizes this possibility and provides excellent service before a client's size may warrant it.

HOW TO HAVE A SUCCESSFUL BROKER-CLIENT RELATIONSHIP

There are several aspects to having a good relationship with your broker. The first is choosing a broker whom you like and trust. This is the foundation on which your relationship will be built, so make your selection carefully. The second aspect is knowing how your broker can help you. What are his areas of expertise and his firm's general services? The third aspect is knowing your own investment personality and philosophy. Accurately. You and your broker can't make any sound decisions unless you both know how you feel about risk and if you can handle its inherent unpredictability. The fourth aspect to having a good broker-client relationship is knowing what you the investor can do to make your relationship more rewarding, knowing what your responsibilities are as a knowledgeable client. And finally, you must know how to evaluate your current broker's performance. Let's look at each of these more closely.

FINDING A COMPETENT BROKER

Interview several potential brokers and avoid the Man of the Day. For if you call or visit a brokerage firm without a particular broker in mind to interview, the firm has someone for you—the Man of the Day. He is not the answer to your day, believe me. He is the three-piece-suit equivalent of the luck of the draw. Usually he is a rookie, although anybody in the office may fill in this spot, depending on the manager's system.

What often comes hand-in-hand (or prospectus-in-hand) with the Man of the Day is the Product of the Month. In the last two weeks, he has read five or six different summaries of this product and watched two videotapes. He may not know much about anything else, but he does know this product, and he will probably try to sell it to you. So ask the manager for a referral or ask friends for the name of their broker—if he is making them money.

When looking for a broker also keep in mind your worth to a broker as well as his worth to you. You can't expect to get a millionaire's level of service if you have $20,000. Don't try to change your broker's stripes, either. Just try to find out what they are or if he might later be wearing them permanently behind bars. Here's what to ask your potential broker in your initial interview.

1. What types of investments does he like to handle, and why?
2. What type of people are his clients, or are they primarily corporations?
3. How long has he been in the business?
4. What are his areas of specialization? If you know anything about these areas, ask deeper questions and find out what he knows.
5. Ask him what type of hours he keeps.
6. Ask what business areas he does not deal in at all or does not like to deal in, and why.
7. Ask questions about his firm—interest charges on margin accounts, money market and cash management sweep accounts, free services, strengths he feels are evident, and weaknesses.
8. Ask to see brochures from his firm on his recommendations. Take them home and read them and see if you like the style of presentation, for some firms are different from others.
9. Ask for an example of the monthly statement you will be receiving, and ask to have it explained to you.
10. Find out who will cover your calls when he is out. Does he have a full-time assistant or a competent desk partner?

Don't prolong your first interview with a broker with details unless you know you want to deal with him and he feels the same way. If you are conservative and he likes to trade options, even if your interview goes smoothly, you both are wasting your time.

WAYS YOUR BROKER CAN HELP YOU

Once you have found a broker you want to work with, do take full advantage of the services he offers you. In addition to investment advice, most brokers also provide the following services:

Explanations and Recommendations in Writing

Over the years I've come to believe that brokers should put their investment recommendations to clients in writing. Not always, but often. Brokers don't like to do this because it takes extra time and organization—and they would prefer to sell you over the phone. But the written word is helpful in several ways:

1. It eliminates confusion about what your broker told you.
2. It reduces fast-talking, quick-selling broker abuses as the sale slows down via the mails.
3. It gives you a handy file reference about your investments.
4. It forces the broker to better understand his own product recommendation (it is harder to write about something than to talk about it—believe me!).
5. It subtly weeds out the rookie brokers, because letter-writing requires good secretarial backup, something only senior brokers have in sufficient quantity and quality.

Access to the Firm's Backup Systems

A full-service broker is given a lot of support by his firm. If your broker uses his firm's backup, he can soon become knowledgeable in many investment areas. For example, a full-service firm has a lot of brochures on file. Many are selling tools, but some are surprisingly informative and downplay sales for the sake of a clear explanation. I've always believed that good investments needn't be sold, merely explained. They sell themselves. It's the junk that needs to be pushed. Today most brokerage firms can supply a brochure on any investment product they sell. If they can't, go elsewhere.

Free Services and Analyses

I am amazed at how few investors use these services—no doubt because they fear they're going to be sold something. However, you are indirectly paying for these services when you make transactions, so feel entitled to use them. Many are excellent. Two services from my former firm stand out in my mind. The first is an analysis of your tax liability for the present calendar year. The service is as complete and accurate as the client's information. Many accountants use the same computer service and charge $100 or more for the identical review.

I used the tax analysis myself, because the tax laws have been so complex and ever-changing that it's best to analyze all the angles using a computer. The service allows for variables, adding and subtracting levels of expense/write-offs, IRA deductions, etc. The plus for the broker is that it shows the client in real dollar terms the benefits of several forms of potential investment programs, especially tax-advantaged ones. Also, it is accurate and doesn't rely on any false assumptions.

The second free service is insurance analysis. Take in your old policies and their latest bills, and several firms can tell you what your cash values, dividend yields, and level of overall benefits are. The sales incentive is that they will also tell you if they can provide the same level of insurance for less, or more insurance for the same premiums. Apples to apples. You may even choose to invest some of your long-buried cash value that you are entitled to borrow on (often at a 5 percent interest charge), which may be growing at only 3 percent. You may not have even known the cash value existed, let alone how large its value was. Internal brokerage studies have shown that as a result of comparing old policies issued years ago to the newer, more competitive policies, in about 80 percent of their analyses they saved clients about 50 percent of what they were spending on premiums. Several insurance companies also provide this service.

Another service offered by many firms is a free minifinancial planning analysis. While the end result may be too basic, at least it can start the client in the direction of a more comprehensive plan. Some plans start as low as $100 and are well worth the price.

Competent Assistant and Secretary

A good broker is only as efficient as his secretary. My clients tolerated my absence (for example, when writing this book), because they felt well covered by my secretary. She was excellent and eliminated the bookkeeping problems and paper headaches that plague all brokerage firms. So in addition to evaluating your broker, gauge his secretary's efficiency before signing up for a long-term relationship—and hope the latter is well paid enough to stay on.

The Computer Support of His Firm

You can make or save a lot of money if your broker has instant access to accurate information. For example, I could push a button and discover all the articles that were reported in the *Journal* or on the ticker about a given stock during that day, or even all articles published in the past three months—all labeled as to time (day and hour) and source. I could then "raise " the article and either read excerpts to my client or print it and send it to him. I could also push a button and get my firm's research report on a stock held by clients, push another button and find which clients owned the stock and how many shares, and then push a final button and get envelopes addressed to mail that report to all my shareholders that same day. Access to so much information helps educate the broker as well as his client.

An Analysis of Past Limited Partnerships and Private Programs

Can your broker provide an analysis of the past limited partnerships he has sold or the private programs his firm has dealt in? These types of investments often get swept under the rug, partly because there is no universal method for reporting progress—or lack of it—and partly because results are usually so awful that the broker and his firm hope the client will forget about them. Their rationale is: Let's not remind anyone about all the dogs we've sold, especially in understandable numbers that allow people to judge for themselves.

Some firms attempt to follow up all past and present programs in these areas. But even these follow-up programs can often be less than accurate. Nevertheless, something is better than nothing, unless you keep buying dogs because the "review" process impressed you too much.

KNOW YOUR INVESTMENT PERSONALITY

Few investors really understand their own investment personalities—which is perhaps why so many end up with the wrong broker and inappropriate investments. They tell their brokers they are risk takers and can tolerate an occasional dip in their assets when the market dives. But when it happens they fall apart.

Before you begin working with a broker, sit down and have a talk with yourself and with your spouse if you are investing the family's assets. Here are some questions to ask yourself:

Would you label your investment personality as conservative, or are you a risk taker?

What investments have you made in the past?
Do you know whether those investments were risky or conservative?
What investment direction have you given your past brokers?
Have you asked your broker for the worst-case scenario?
How have you reacted to market-generated losses in the past?
How many arguments have you had with a broker or your spouse
over your investments?

Remembering the number of sleepless nights and the arguments
that you've had over your investments should give you an idea
about how much risk you can tolerate. After all, life is too short to
have an ulcer from Wall Street, although people get them all the
time by investing in the wrong areas for their personalities.

When you analyze the tables and charts at the end of this book,
you will gain an appreciation for lower-risk and simpler investments
such as those I talked about in "The Right Stuff." They perform
quite well against volatile investments fraught with unpredictability. If you want to live in fear and scare yourself, try driving a race
car or flying a plane. I've advised more than a few clients along the
way not to invest in a risky venture. I knew they weren't bona fide
risk takers, and I didn't want the responsibility—or the angry telephone calls later—if the venture failed. For those clients who are risk
takers, I always tell them the worst-case scenario for their investments. I don't expect it to happen, but if it does, they were
forewarned. When, after you think you've found a good broker and
you've had several investment talks with him, ask him to rate you
honestly as to your ability to ride out possible storms. You both need
to know where you stand.

HOW TO BE A SUCCESSFUL INVESTOR

Over the years I've found that successful investors have several traits
and habits in common. Lazy investors usually get eaten up by the
sharks on the Street because they didn't adopt even the most basic
strategies to protect themselves. Here are several suggestions for your
role as investor once you've chosen your broker carefully:

1. Always do your homework before you purchase an investment.
   Even if you hate reading brochures and statements, do it anyway. It will alert your broker that you will be following his per-

formance and therefore keep him on his toes. Being a lazy investor is like wearing an orange bathing suit in shark-infested waters.

2. Don't be sold an investment; buy one knowledgeably. Ask questions. Know each investment's pros and cons. All investments have some weaknesses. Discover them and then judge which ones you can live with.

3. Ask your broker to identify all assumptions. Too often they are the primary selling aids, no more, no less. The problem is that when the assumption is flat wrong the investment is a goner. Period. Brokers and lay people often lose sight of that. Get your broker to identify assumptions and explain their rationale and then go home and decide which assumptions you are willing to live with—even if you and your broker eventually disagree. It is better to lose your money on your own informed decision than to turn it over to someone and have him lose it for you. (See chapter 11 for a discussion of assumptions.)

4. Identify all fees that you will be charged. Ask how much your investment is worth after day one.

5. Avoid a broker who trades for maximum pay. A broker can work hard and give careful investment advice, or he can treat his clients as replaceable every four or five years. Brokers get paid on the basis of the business they created in the past month. Toward month's end if it isn't going well, some brokers "push" things they wouldn't normally suggest.

6. Be wary of margin accounts. Fully margined, your account instantly doubles in size for purchasing securities—and for creating twice as many commissions. In fairness, your equity is leveraged, and good ideas from your broker can return a far greater profit on deposited funds. But if his advice is wrong, your equity is negatively affected twice as much, you owe interest charges to the firm for the loan, and those charges are no longer easily deductible. Finally, there are "the forced exits." If performance is so bad that your initial equity becomes too small versus the debt you incurred when you margined (borrowed), you will receive notice to sell securities or come up with cash—quick. That situation is called a "margin call"—as well as bad news.

7. Don't sign papers that allow your broker discretionary trading privileges. If you don't want to be bothered with last-minute

calls, perhaps your account should be in the hands of a good money manager.

8. Don't be a pawn in a sales contest. Many firms throw sales contests that offer prizes ranging from Rolex wristwatches to fully paid vacations for two to Rio. I've won trips to Rio, London, Copenhagen, Switzerland, Paris, Scandinavia, Hawaii, Mexico, Puerto Rico, Greece, Alaska, and to several major U.S. resorts, as well as Carribean cruises. All first-class. Your broker might be marketing a particular product because he wants to win a contest. Fortunately, most contests, like those that I've won, have no restrictions and require only an increase in business. A few, however, do require the broker to sell certain products exclusively, and it is these contests that can influence a broker's recommendations. Few clients know these trips are being offered. Similarly, though less direct, contests are offered by brokerage firms to pension fund managers enticing them to execute their larger transactions through a particular firm.

   One broker I know is obsessed with winning contests. As a result, he tells his clients to buy whatever he needs to sell to win. He's won Rolexes, cars, afghans, trips—you name it. He stores trophies and trinkets the way I store *Barron's* and *Wall Street Journals*. You should know if the product you are buying is part of a restricted contest. About the only way to know, however, is to ask.

9. Recognize seductive selling methods, such as the financial seminar, where brokers, in the role of teacher, offer education and usually some extra free service. But the broker is only as good as the product he sells—helped by a slide show provided by the firm. These shows come with scripts that many brokers practically memorize.

   I once gave seminars in oil programs. I believed the government and my firm knew where oil prices were going—certainly the slides I used were impressive, but they fooled me and many of my clients. I hadn't yet learned to question my sources, and none of my seminar clients knew to do so either.

10. Keep all correspondence, prospectuses, and brochures related to your investments in a file for later review.

11. Do not spread your account too thin among too many brokers. You are better off in the long run dealing with a broker who knows all of your financial situation (and values your business

because your account is larger) rather than having several brokers who consider your account a "small fish."

12. Don't get bogged down with complex strategies unless you are
quite wealthy and your other financial consultants agree with
this plan. Complicated plans may make your broker/adviser
rich and you poor. Simple and logical investing is usually the
best investing.

13. Place a high value on the liquidity of your investments. Investing in something is one thing, marrying it is another. Being unable to sell something can be disastrous.

14. Don't assume that a famous-name investment is a good one.
Check them out. Several of the big names are famous for past
results and advertise them, but more recent results are less spectacular.

15. Consult neutral sources for investment information in addition
to the sales advice given by your broker.

If you combine the above guidelines with a sound knowledge of
your own investment personality, you will be prepared to deal with
a competent broker, and well armed to play Wall Street's investment game.

HOW TO EVALUATE YOUR CURRENT BROKER'S PERFORMANCE

Finding a good broker isn't impossible, but your homework doesn't
stop there. Periodically, you should also assess your working relationship and his ongoing performance. A good broker should provide the following:

1. growth and profits from your investments
2. good ideas and clear explanations
3. time to think about his recommendations
4. understandable statements and prompt bookkeeping
5. swift correction of errors
6. important support and serviccs

These factors nurture a healthy broker-client relationship. Some
are more important than others—like number one. If you lose
money year after year, superb bookeeping isn't going to make you
feel better. If your broker isn't keeping up on tax changes, your in-

vestment needs, or returning your phone calls promptly, he may be bored with his job or you. Either way you lose.

Learn to Recognize Your Exit Cues

You also need to be able to recognize some of the danger signs that mean get out now, while you still have a portfolio. If commissions total up to 10 percent of your account value, you may be being churned. Ten percent is a high rate of turnover for standard trading accounts, unless you are dealing with commodities or options. If your broker wants to put you into entirely different investments, listen, but be careful he's not playing a Jekyll-and-Hyde routine on your portfolio. Experimentation is OK, but limit it to small doses until you are sure that at least one of you knows what he is doing. If your statement reflects the product of the month twelve times a year, your broker may be caught in the end-of-the-month syndrome of creating business. Have a plan set with reasonable parameters, and stick to them. And finally, if your broker's lack of discipline or sales prowess begins to complicate your life, find another broker who will listen to your needs and abide by them.

FIFTY WAYS TO LEAVE YOUR BROKER

Paul Simon had the right idea in more ways than one—but you don't need fifty to leave your broker. A few will do. I had one client tell me that he stayed with his former broker for years because he didn't know how to fire him; it all seemed too complicated. It isn't.

One way to leave your broker is to write a brief, civil note saying that you are making a change and will no longer be using his services.

Another way is to call him and tell him you have decided to leave because of a change in investment philosophy, or your cousin has a broker who has done fantastically and yours hasn't, or that you want to go entirely into cash and find a cave. He's heard all the reasons, believe me, and he won't argue.

Leaving a Broker You Never Want to Speak to Again

On the other hand, if your broker has made disastrous investments for you, you might not want to write a "brief, civil note" or even talk to him. But you definitely want to leave him. Another method is to find a new broker. First he will review your portfolio and suggest ways to improve its performance. Then he will give you a form to sign that allows his bookkeeping department in New York to contact your former broker's firm's bookkeeping department in New York and say that you are making a change. Presto, it's done. You don't have to talk to your former broker and make lengthy explanations as to why you are leaving him. If he calls, you don't have to answer his call—just as he didn't answer yours.

This process happens much more frequently than most investors realize. It may take as long as two to four weeks to transfer all positions from one firm to another, but when you sign the transfer form your new firm should consider your account instantly there for trading and margin purposes. After all, they want your new business. Your old broker then receives a notice from his wire room that "account #123456789 is being transferred to XYZ firm." Short and sweet. He and his manager may not do a jig, but unless you are a giant account they will shrug it off as one of the bumps along the road.

Finally, if you have no stock positions or cash in the account, simply never call your old broker again. Use a new broker and hope the old one never phones you. About half the time this works, because the broker has already expected you to leave and knows that you've decided to permanently tune him out. So if you don't like your broker, and your reasons are valid, make sure you leave him. Otherwise you may not have much left to entice a worthy replacement to take on your account.

WINNING IS ALWAYS MORE FUN

I hope somewhere in the beginning or middle of this book, and certainly by the end, that you began to realize two things: that you shouldn't be losing so much money in your investments; and that your money could be making you more than you thought. A new client came to me recently with what she thought were extremely high expectations for her $200,000 account. "Please, just don't lose us any money," she said. "We've been losing money from bad investment advice for the last ten years. This is all we have left for our retirement in five years." For the next two hours we discussed various investments and talked about several alternatives. Suddenly she looked at me and said, "You mean we're actually going to make money?" She could hardly believe it.

You should be making money too. And you should be making it

on Wall Street. In spite of its shortcomings, Wall Street can be the best place for your money. It is true that finding an informed, thorough, honest, and intelligent broker is not easy. And risky investments are just that—not guaranteed to be perfect in all ways. But the end result of sound and growing investments is well worth the effort of the hunt. Besides, if you don't search for a good broker, it is likely that a mediocre broker—or even worse, the competition— is going to find you.

When you do find a good broker, treat him like a favorite in-law— with wariness and respect—and expect a long-term relationship that makes you both money. Welcome to Wall Street. It's an exciting place to be when your team is winning the game.

Appendix

Appendix

CHARTS: A QUARTER CENTURY REVIEWED

> Nobody in your business has a sense of history. You guys
> worry about today, and sometimes tomorrow, but you
> really ought to learn more about yesterday.
> —A CLIENT WHO IS ALSO A PROFESSOR OF HISTORY

At the outset of this book you learned that I've always had a thing
about numbers. By eleven, I was keeping stats on everyone's batting
and pitching prowess for its historical significance. In the past two
dozen years the address has changed from Prospect Road to Wall
Street, and I've substituted percentages and quotes for balls and
strikes. But my curiosity is still the same, and so is the situation. No
one else is doing the stats.

Frankly, baseball has the right idea. They keep statistics on everything—you can compare games to games, players to players, errors
to errors, in the present and the past. Apples to apples—with the exception of Roger Maris's undeserved asterisk for his well-earned
home run record. But Wall Street is way behind baseball. Therefore,
the Street and its investors have a basic problem: How can they
properly compare and invest today for tomorrow if they don't have
a comprehensive central source of information that tells what has
taken place in the past? Is it possible Wall Street wants it that way?

The following tables are a step toward making those stats available. They are a revolution in accuracy for those who want to invest—intelligently, after doing some homework. So what is this
chapter about? Well, for starters, have you ever wondered how various investments have really performed over the years? And have you
also wished you could accurately compare one investment to another—say gold to the Dow Jones, or T-bills to Baa Bonds? Well, I

have. And so have my clients and colleagues, but there just wasn't any efficient or quick way to look it up and get the answers. There wasn't even an indirect way to look it up because no single source had all this information in one place. I knew the information was out there, in bits and pieces, here and there, yet putting it together seemed like wishful thinking. Still, the same questions about "yesterday" kept coming up—my history professor client was right. So I decided to get some stats together on another competitive endeavor, investing.

My curiosity with numbers led me on a research odyssey that lasted over two years. My assistant and I plowed through pile after pile of *Federal Reserve Bulletins*, U.S. Department of Commerce surveys, financial weeklies, *Economic Reports of the President,* International Monetary Fund reports, Federal Tax Policy reports, and gained access to massive computer data banks of major universities in the Boston area. Most of our work was painstaking and tedious number-crunching.

We had set out with several basic questions and expected to come up with basic and predictable answers. No way. Our research uncovered many exciting and often astonishing answers and shattered some long-held investment myths. Here are some surprising facts my tables reveal:

Despite the Swiss Franc's reputation as a prime hedge against inflation in the United States, in all five-year intervals of comparison over a quarter century, Inflation outperformed the Swiss Franc.

The New One-Family House Price Index was only an average performer.

The best of all extremely safe investment vehicles for return, safety, and acceptable levels of liquidity was the 3-year U.S. Treasury bond.

The Dow Jones Thirty Industrials Average was the next to worst of all competitors over twenty-five years. However, when you included the dividends excluded by the Average (yet paid by the stocks) the same Dow Jones Thirty Industrials was a top performer.

In two of the three most recent five-year intervals, U.S. Government Bonds (10-year maturity) beat the Growth Mutual Fund Index.

The best and most consistent investment in terms of total returns over the past twenty-five years was the Baa Bond Index.

In spite of its recent volatility, Crude Oil has been a good performer over the past twenty-five years.

A comparison of two dozen entirely different forms of investments shows that the most volatile in the past two decades was Gold.

A comparison of the Table of Savings Deposits to the Inflation Tables over blocks of five, ten, fifteen, twenty, and twenty-five years, shows that Inflation outpaced the banks' mainstay in all cases.

The Disposable Personal Income Index of U.S. workers' salaries performed quite well over twenty-five years. It proved that capitalism works well for the workers.

An investment of $1,000 in 1961 made in the Dow Jones Thirty Industrials (with dividends included) rose over 720 percent. However, an investment in the same Dow Jones, with (1) dividends excluded, and (2) adjusted for inflation, *lost* $309—a difference of 750 percent in return over twenty-five years, or, put another way, a 30 percent annual difference in return. Yet both comparisons were made from the same famous index—the Dow Jones Industrials.

And this is just the beginning. The following pages of tables, charts, and summaries are a statistical information breakthrough. They represent the first true "apples-to-apples" comparisons of just about any financial investment medium (and their respective index or table) that matters to investors.

For comparison purposes, I even offer comparison tables for financial icons such as the Prime Rate, treating them as though they could have been invested in over the years. For example, if you had invested $1,000 in the prime rate (as your bank does by making loans), you would have tallied a sum of $7,447.76 after twenty-five years. That's a lot more than the $3,076.79 that an investor received from a bank Savings Deposit over the same time frame . . . and banks usually make loans at the prime rate plus 1 percent to 10 percent.

By now you may already have flipped through the tables and charts and said, "Can I really understand all that?" The answer is yes! They may look complicated, but they're not. Here's what this section does for you:

—First of all, my statistics reflect the annual compound return of over two dozen investments over the past twenty-five years in a table

format. A hypothetical investment of $1,000 in each is then ana-
lyzed in separate five-year intervals—going back a quarter century.
Then the same $1,000 investment is analyzed for *longer* time
frames—five years, ten years, fifteen years, twenty years, and
twenty-five years.

—Next, the returns are then compared by placing a given investment with three other investments—over the above five different
time frames. All in chart form. For the sake of consistency, one "investment" always included in the four-way comparison is the Inflation Index Table. Thus, we can always see how our other
investments did against inflation.

—Then, in nonmathematical terms, I highlight the most critical
factors regarding these investments and their relationships over the
past quarter century.

These four-part chart comparisons cover many bases. Examples of
the comparisons are:

	Inflation
S & P Stock Yield versus:	Corporate Bond Averages
	Savings Deposits
	Inflation
Silver versus:	T-bills
	Gold
	Inflation
Baa Bonds versus:	T-bills
	Aaa bonds
	Inflation
Lipper Growth Mutual Fund	3-Year Treasury Bonds
Index versus:	Dow Jones Industrials
	(dividends included)

There are a total of twenty-four charts comparing apples to
apples, four subjects at a time. In these comparison charts I have
grouped interest-sensitive items together and capital gain investments together. But occasionally I crossed the two major types for
fun—and knowledge. I suggest you do the same. Compare what you

are most interested in to other Indexes and financial icons you want to know more about. Someday, doing these comparisons may save you a lot of money.

Let's take an example: What if you want to know how Silver did compared to the conservative T-bill over the past twenty-five years? Now you'll know: It beat the T-bill by exactly 1.5 percent per year. But the ride, as noted in the charts and tables, may not have been worth the annual average margin of victory. It's up to you to decide what to invest in—given an investment's return in the past, and the way it achieved its return (with or without wild fluctuations in value—my good old Ulcer Factor).

Most investors have a favorite investment, so they will also have their favorite combinations of comparisons. If I haven't analyzed your particular combination, you can easily analyze the tables and charts of your choice on your own.

Finally, because you should plan your investments based on the thinking that taxes change, recessions come and go, stocks pay certain average levels of dividends, and inflation ebbs and flows, I have included an addendum of additional miscellaneous charts, such as average stock yields, changes in income tax brackets, and lengths of recessions, all of which are interesting in themselves.

JUST TELL ME THE FACTS

This appendix is a chartist's, broker's, research analyst's, and yes, an investor's dream. It will help you ward off the advice of gurus who have faulty figures and bad memories. Or save you from your own rusty memory. These numbers won't change. They are not assumptions; they are not somebody's guess. They are facts. They are investment history at your fingertips.

Use these tables. Play with them. If you feel we are headed for inflationary times, look up when inflation was rampant in the past twenty-five years. Then look to see which investments did well and which did poorly during the corresponding time frame. History doesn't always repeat itself, but at least this reference will be less biased than a sales brochure's table showing you statistics from "selected" years. These tables and charts are your best defense against a confusing sales pitch or a "surefire" investment that gives you that uneasy feeling. These tables sink or swim on their own merits—which is the way all investments should be analyzed.

APPENDIX CONTENTS

(The following Tables reflect statistics based on average annual rate of return, excluding the Dow Jones, the S & P 500, and the Lipper Growth Mutual Fund Index, which reflect Jan. 1–Dec. 31 change in return.)

Table A.1 / INFLATION
(calculated from CPI*)

Year	Inflation	Compound growth of $1,000, in five-year periods	Compound rate of growth
1985	3.57%	1981–85	
1984	4.26%		5.46%
1983	3.40%	. . . $1,304.60	
1982	5.99%		
1981	10.24%		
1980	13.46%	1976–80	
1979	11.47%		8.91%
1978	7.60%	. . . $1,532.22	
1977	6.45%		
1976	5.77%		
1975	9.14%	1971–75	
1974	10.97%		6.75%
1973	6.23%	. . . $1,386.19	
1972	3.30%		
1971	4.30%		
1970	5.92%	1966–70	
1969	5.37%		4.24%
1968	4.20%	. . . $1,230.67	
1967	2.88%		
1966	2.86%		
1965	1.72%	1961–65	
1964	1.31%		1.27%
1963	1.21%	. . . $1,065.33	
1962	1.12%		
1961	1.01%		

	How the value of $1,000 increased over			
5 years	10 years	15 years	20 years	25 years
1981–85 $1,304.60 (5.46%)†				
	1976–85 $1,998.93 (7.17%)			
		1971–85 $2,770.89 (7.03%)		
			1966–85 $3,410.04 (6.33%)	
				1961–85 $3,632.81 (5.30%)

*Source: U.S. Department of Commerce, Business Statistics and Survey of Current Business.

† Compound inflation rate for that period.

INFLATION

Fortunately, Inflation has not been a runaway performer. It worries us—it did especially during the bad times of the 1970s—but as a hypothetical investment versus our other competitors it was a consistent low-end performer. Of note, in all periods reviewed, it always beat one well-known investment—the Savings account. Therefore, one can surmise that money held in a Savings account probably won't keep up with Inflation, if history is a good guide.

CHART A.1
Inflation Versus Savings, Silver, and Dow Jones With Dividends

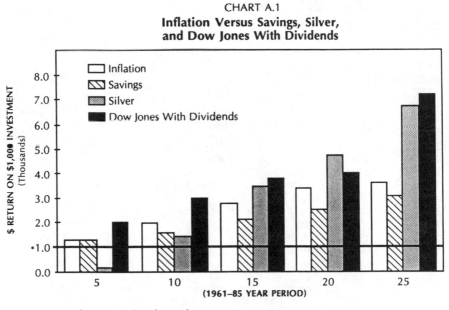

*Initial investment: $1.0 thousand.

Table A.2 / DISPOSABLE PERSONAL INCOME
(per capita, in current $)

Year	Income*	Income growth	Compound growth of a $1,000 income over five-year periods	Compound rate of growth
1985	$11,727	3.97%	1981–85	
1984	11,279	9.09%		6.84%
1983	10,339	6.24%	. . . $1,392.40	
1982	9,732	5.24%		
1981	9,247	9.80%		
1980	8,422	9.63%	1976–80	
1979	7,682	10.25%		9.74%
1978	6,968	11.27%	. . . $1,591.70	
1977	6,262	9.02%		
1976	5,744	8.56%		
1975	5,291	8.98%	1971–75	
1974	4,855	8.35%		8.68%
1973	4,481	12.03%	. . . $1,516.51	
1972	4,000	6.95%		
1971	3,740	7.19%		
1970	3,489	7.72%	1966–70	
1969	3,239	6.65%		6.85%
1968	3,037	7.39%	. . . $1,392.86	
1967	2,828	5.72%		
1966	2,675	6.79%		
1965	2,505	6.51%	1961–66	
1964	2,352	7.06%		4.76%
1963	2,197	3.49%	. . . $1,261.59	
1962	2,123	4.38%		
1961	2,034	2.42%		

How a $1,000 income grew over				
5 years	10 years	15 years	20 years	25 years
1981–85 $1,392.40 (6.84%)†				
	1976–85 $2,216.29 (8.28%)			
		1971–85 $3,361.02 (8.42%)		
			1966–85 $4,681.45 (8.02%)	
				1961–85 $5,906.07 (7.36%)

*Source: *Economic Report of the President*, 1986.

† Compound income growth rate for that period.

DISPOSABLE PERSONAL INCOME, U.S. PER CAPITA

I analyzed this subject as a hypothetical investment so that you might appreciate the capitalistic system. It works. The average worker's salary almost always seemed to outpace Inflation. As an "investment" this Table never did poorly or superbly, but it at least never embarrassed itself versus its competitors. It performed logically by maintaining a fair rate of increase over many years, a positive reflection on the structure of our economy itself.

CHART A.2

Disposable Personal Income Growth Versus Inflation, T-Bills (3-Month), and Savings

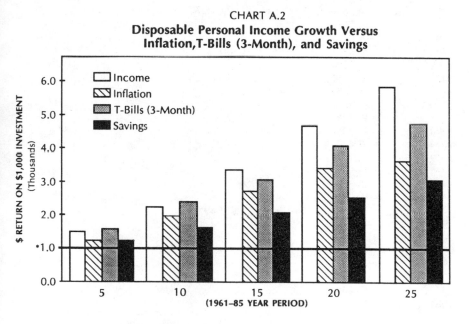

*Initial investment: $1.0 thousand.

Table A.3 / DOW JONES THIRTY INDUSTRIALS AVERAGE
TOTAL RETURN
(appreciation plus dividend yield)*

Year	Yield*	Compound return on a five-year $1,000 investment	Compound rate of return
1985	31.67%	1981–85	
1984	1.24%		15.06%
1983	24.76%	... $2,016.72	
1982	24.77%		
1981	−2.81%		
1980	20.57%	1976–80	
1979	10.27%		8.04%
1978	2.88%	... $1,472.25	
1977	−11.76%		
1976	21.98%		
1975	42.71%	1971–75	
1974	−21.45%		4.84%
1973	−12.43%	... $1,266.84	
1972	17.77%		
1971	9.58%		
1970	8.58%	1966–70	
1969	−10.95%		0.97%
1968	7.59%	... $1,049.58	
1967	18.53%		
1966	−14.88%		
1965	13.83%	1961–65	
1964	18.14%		12.78%
1963	20.07%	... $1,824.60	
1962	−7.24%		
1961	21.82%		

	How a $1,000 investment performed over			
5 years	10 years	15 years	20 years	25 years
1981–85 $2,016.72 (15.06%)†				
	1976–85 $2,969.12 (11.50%)			
		1971–85 $3,761.40 (9.23%)		
			1966–85 $3,947.89 (7.11%)	
				1961–85 $7,203.32 (8.22%)

*Combined from Dow Jones Industrials Index growth and Dow Jones Industrials dividend yield tables.

† Compound rate of return for that period.

DOW JONES THIRTY INDUSTRIALS TOTAL RETURN, WITH DIVIDENDS

This Table, which *includes* dividends that are paid by the stocks within the average, is the fairest way to judge the market's performance (although the Dow Jones is normally quoted *without* dividend performance). People who buy stock usually get a dividend. To forget about this means our most quoted stock average's performance is presented in a consistently misleading manner. It is always an understatement as to what is actually happening.

One criticism of heeding the Dow Jones is that it is an average reflecting only the bluest "blue chips," not a true reflection of the stocks you and I commonly purchase. As long as investors are aware of this fact, the Dow Jones is worth monitoring—but keep in mind those excluded dividends. In my example here they were not excluded, but note that in the chart where they were, its overall performance is dramatically affected—for the worse.

You can bet that competitors offering dissimilar financial products will quote the averages—either the Dow or S & P—*without the dividends.* Their defense is that that is the way they are normally reported. That's true. But it also makes their product look better through making the competition look worse. Remember that dividends are part of your overall return. Use this chart for making the fairest comparisons to other investments.

Overall the Dow Jones With Dividends was a fine performer and noticeably the best in the last five years reviewed. In only one five-year interval did it do worse than the mean performer, reflecting the bad stock market years of 1966–70. An investor could do much worse, but remember, with this investment the ride won't always be smooth.

CHART A.3
Dow Jones Industrials Average With Dividends Versus Inflation, T-Bills (3-Month), and T-Bonds (10-Year)

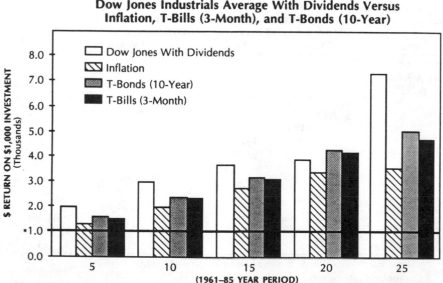

*Initial investment: $1.0 thousand.

Table A.4 / DOW JONES THIRTY INDUSTRIALS AVERAGE
(year-end closing prices; without dividends)

Year	Index* value	Index growth	Compound return on a five-year $1,000 investment	Compound rate of return
1985	1546.67	27.66%	1981–85	
1984	1211.57	−3.76%		9.92%
1983	1258.84	20.29%	. . . $1,604.40	
1982	1046.54	19.60%		
1981	875.00	−9.23%		
1980	963.99	14.93%	1976–80	
1979	838.74	4.19%		2.49%
1978	805.01	−3.15%	. . . $1,130.81	
1977	831.17	−17.27%		
1976	1004.65	17.86%		
1975	852.41	38.32%	1971–75	
1974	616.24	−27.57%		0.32%
1973	850.86	−16.58%	. . . $1,016.11	
1972	1020.02	14.58%		
1971	890.20	6.11%		
1970	838.92	4.82%	1966–70	
1969	800.36	−15.19%		−2.85%
1968	943.75	4.27%	. . . $865.58	
1967	905.11	15.20%		
1966	785.69	−18.94%		
1965	969.26	10.88%	1961–65	
1964	874.13	14.57%		9.49%
1963	762.95	17.00%	. . . $1,573.67	
1962	652.10	−10.81%		
1961	731.14	18.71%		

How a $1,000 investment performed over				
5 years	10 years	15 years	20 years	25 years
1981–85 $1,604.40 (9.92%)†				
	1976–85 $1,814.27 (6.14%)			
		1971–85 $1,843.49 (4.16%)		
			1966–85 $1,595.70 (2.36%)	
				1961–85 $2,511.10 (3.75%)

*Source: Barron's National Business and Financial Weekly.

† Compound rate of return for that period.

DOW JONES THIRTY INDUSTRIALS AVERAGE, WITHOUT DIVIDENDS

As noted in the preceding analysis, this is the way you follow the Dow Jones Industrials index daily—as it is reported in the media without dividends. By such an exclusion, the overall performance is almost halved, and the twenty-five-year review ranks the Dow Jones as a next-to-last performer. This Table even managed to be outdone in quarter-century performance by a much-used alternative—the Savings Deposit. Adding insult to injury, after reviewing the Addendum Table of the Dow Jones Corrected for Inflation, Without Dividends (pages 334–335) and the Dow, instead of $1,000 turning into $7,200, it actually turns into $691. Thus, one analysis can create a picture ten times more advantageous than another, even though we are discussing the same animal, the Dow Jones Industrial Average, the most quoted index of them all.

CHART A.4

Dow Jones Thirty Industrials Average Without Dividends Versus Inflation, Dow Jones With Dividends, and T-Bills (3-Month)

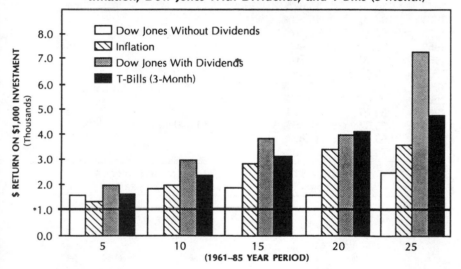

*Initial investment: $1.0 thousand.

Table A.5 / S & P 500 COMPOSITE INDEX
(closing prices, without dividends)

Year	Index* value	Index growth	Compound return on a five-year $1,000 investment	Compound rate of return
1985	211.30	26.38%	1981–85	
1984	167.20	1.39%		9.24%
1983	164.90	17.28%	. . . $1,555.96	
1982	140.60	14.68%		
1981	122.60	−9.72%		
1980	135.80	25.86%	1976–80	
1979	107.90	12.27%		8.53%
1978	96.11	1.06%	. . . $1,505.71	
1977	95.10	−11.53%		
1976	107.50	19.19%		
1975	90.19	31.55%	1971–75	
1974	68.56	−29.72%		−0.43%
1973	97.55	−17.40%	. . . $978.73	
1972	118.10	15.67%		
1971	102.10	10.80%		
1970	92.15	0.10%	1966–70	
1969	92.06	−11.40%		−0.06%
1968	103.90	7.70%	. . . $996.76	
1967	96.47	20.09%		
1966	80.33	−13.11%		
1965	92.45	9.09%	1961–65	
1964	84.75	12.97%		9.73%
1963	75.02	18.89%	. . . $1,590.95	
1962	63.10	−11.81%		
1961	71.55	23.13%		

How a $1,000 investment performed over				
5 years	10 years	15 years	20 years	25 years
1981–85 $1,555.96 (9.24%)†				
	1976–85 $2,342.83 (8.89%)			
		1971–85 $2,293.00 (5.69%)		
			1966–85 $2,285.56 (4.22%)	
				1961–85 $3,636.21 (5.30%)

*Source: Standard & Poor's Corp., *Security Price Index Record*, 1986.

† Compound rate of return for that period.

S & P 500 COMPOSITE INDEX, WITHOUT DIVIDENDS

This is another Table presented as you see it daily, and it, too, unfairly assumes that no dividends were paid on the stocks owned. The S & P's return is substantially higher than the Dow's in all five-year intervals but one, the most recent five years—but even then the Dow won by only a hair. Overall the S & P was a mediocre performer, unless its dividends are included (much like the Dow Jones). Yet it still managed to beat the Savings Deposit in all of the five-year analyses.

CHART A.5
S & P 500 Composite Index Without Dividends Versus Inflation, Corporate Bond Average, and Dow Jones Without Dividends

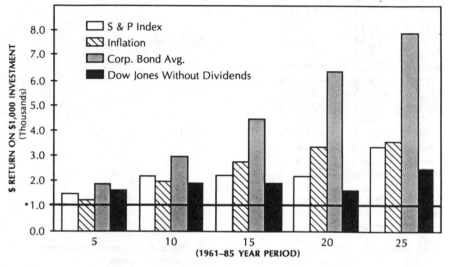

*Initial investment: $1.0 thousand.

285

Table A.6 / LIPPER GROWTH MUTUAL FUND INDEX
(year-end closing prices, dividends included)

Year	Index* value	Index growth	Compound return on a five-year $1,000 investment	Compound rate of return
1985	278.98	30.38%	1981–85	
1984	213.98	−2.79%		11.28%
1983	220.13	22.27%	. . . $1,706.63	
1982	180.04	20.24%		
1981	149.73	−8.41%		
1980	163.47	37.27%		
1979	119.09	27.36%		
1978	93.51	11.11%	1976–80	
1977	84.16	−3.75%		16.88%
1976	87.44	16.68%	. . . $2,181.52	
1975	74.94	32.03%		
1974	56.76	−30.06%		
1973	81.16	−27.01%		
1972	111.20	14.72%	1971–75	
1971	96.93	23.24%		−0.96%
1970	78.65	−9.11%		
1969	86.53	−13.47%	. . . $952.91	
1968	100.00	n.a.		
1967	n.a.	n.a.		
1966	n.a.	n.a.		
1965	n.a.	n.a.		
1964	n.a.	n.a.		
1963	n.a.	n.a.		
1962	n.a.	n.a.		
1961	n.a.	n.a.		

	How a $1,000 investment performed over	
5 years	10 years	15 years
1981–85 $1,706.63 (11.28%)†		
	1976–85 $3,723.04 (14.05%)	
		1971–85 $3,547.73 (8.81%)

*Source: Lipper Analytical Services, Inc.

† Compound rate of return for that period.

LIPPER GROWTH MUTUAL FUND INDEX

This Table must be examined closely. Remember that dividends are included in this index, so it should be compared to similar Tables—such as the Dow Jones With Dividends. Remember, too, that sales charges have been totally ignored and recall how this affected results in the mutual fund chapter. Another important point is that my analysis covers only seventeen years (from 1969 on); therefore no twenty-year or twenty-five-year analysis could be done.

Notice that this Table was number 1 for the past decade but tied for ninth in the past five years. As far back as we can judge (fifteen years), the Lipper Index was an average performer—ranking twelfth out of twenty-four. This acceptable, and sometimes exciting, performance was profitable but also gave you a jolting ride along the way. After studying the Table, go after the best funds and review all the fees involved.

CHART A.6
Lipper Growth Mutual Fund Index Versus Inflation,
T-Bonds (3-Year), and Dow Jones With Dividends

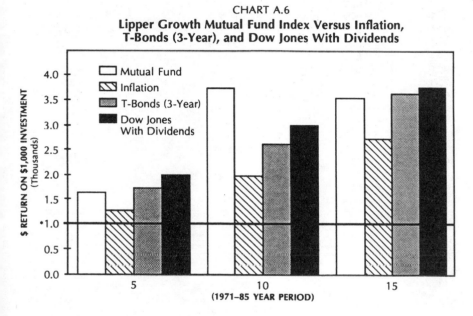

*Initial Investment: $1.0 thousand.

287

Table A.7 / MOODY'S CORPORATE BOND AVERAGE
(average annual yield)

Year	Yield*	Compound return on a five-year $1,000 investment	Compound rate of return
1985	12.05%	1981–85	
1984	13.49%		13.66%
1983	12.78%	. . . $1,896.69	
1982	14.94%		
1981	15.06%		
1980	12.75%	1976–80	
1979	10.12%		9.87%
1978	9.07%	. . . $1,600.68	
1977	8.43%		
1976	9.01%		
1975	9.57%	1971–75	
1974	9.03%		8.39%
1973	7.80%	. . . $1,496.14	
1972	7.63%		
1971	7.94%		
1970	8.51%	1966–70	
1969	7.36%		6.70%
1968	6.51%	. . . $1,383.13	
1967	5.82%		
1966	5.34%		
1965	4.64%	1961–65	
1964	4.57%		4.60%
1963	4.50%	. . . $1,252.04	
1962	4.62%		
1961	4.66%		

5 years	How a $1,000 investment performed over 10 years	15 years	20 years	25 years
1981–85 $1,896.69 (13.66%)†				
	1976–85 $3,035.99 (11.75%)			
		1971–85 $4,542.27 (10.62%)		
			1966–85 $6,282.56 (9.62%)	
				1961–85 $7,865.99 (8.60%)

*Source: U.S. Department of Commerce, Business Statistics and Survey of Current Business.

† Compound rate of return for that period.

MOODY'S CORPORATE BOND AVERAGE

The annual yields from the Table netted out a solid performer. Consider this investment primarily for the long term, if you are willing to accept owning quality-grade, diversified, taxable bonds. Lately, the yields have been down, but other alternatives, such as CDs and Treasury issues, are down, too. The history of this Table shows consistent and sizable returns, and it beat the majority of its competitors. I rate this one a winner. (This Table assumes bonds in this average are held until maturity.)

CHART A.7
**Moody's Corporate Bond Average Yield Versus
Inflation, S & P 500 Yield, and Savings**

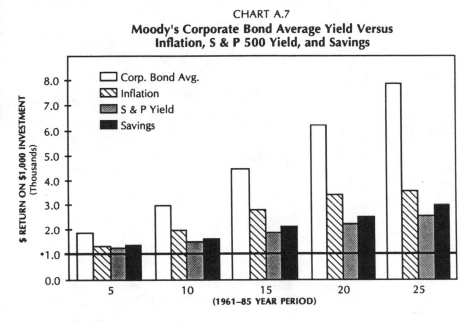

*Initial investment: $1.0 thousand.

Table A.8 / MOODY'S Aaa CORPORATE BOND YIELD
(average annual yield)

Year	Yield*	Compound return on a five-year $1,000 investment	Compound rate of return
1985	11.37%	1981–85	
1984	12.71%		12.81%
1983	12.04%	. . . $1,827.09	
1982	13.79%		
1981	14.17%		
1980	11.94%	1976–80	
1979	9.63%		9.34%
1978	8.73%	. . . $1,562.85	
1977	8.02%		
1976	8.43%		
1975	8.83%	1971–75	
1974	8.57%		7.89%
1973	7.44%	. . . $1,461.58	
1972	7.21%		
1971	7.39%		
1970	8.04%	1966–70	
1969	7.03%		6.37%
1968	6.18%	. . . $1,361.92	
1967	5.51%		
1966	5.13%		
1965	4.49%	1961–65	
1964	4.40%		4.37%
1963	4.26%	. . . $1,238.21	
1962	4.33%		
1961	4.35%		

How a $1,000 investment performed over				
5 years	10 years	15 years	20 years	25 years
1981–85 $1,827.09 (12.81%)†				
	1976–85 $2,855.47 (11.06%)			
		1971–85 $4,173.51 (9.99%)		
			1966–85 $5,684.00 (9.08%)	
				1961–85 $7,037.99 (8.12%)

*Source: U.S. Department of Commerce, *Business Statistics* and *Survey of Current Business.*

† Compound rate of return for that period.

290

MOODY'S CORPORATE BOND YIELD, Aaa

You'll appreciate bonds more after studying these Tables. These gilt-edged, Aaa Bonds are theoretically safe, but keep in mind that what is great today may be downgraded, and scary, in 1989. It doesn't happen frequently, but it can happen. (Even GM and AT&T get downgraded once in a while.) At least the yields are always better than the banks', and results are better than 80 percent of the alternatives.

Be aware of one assumption that isn't always borne out in the real world. This Table assumes that bonds do not fluctuate in price. Given that the bond market can go up or down, this is not always the case. However, it *is* a fair assumption if you consider that, unlike other investments, bonds do mature at some point at the same price they were originally issued at—par—and thus there is no gain or loss if you hold them until maturity. For comparison purposes I expect the bond buyer to do just that—hold till maturity. That is not as easy with long-term maturities of fifteen or more years, but possible, so buy bonds with this in mind.

This Table of Aaa Bonds was consistent, appearing in the top third versus its competitors no matter what the time frame, always beating conservative alternatives like Savings Deposits, and handily beating a major benchmark—Inflation—by a sizable margin.

CHART A.8
Moody's Aaa Corporate Bonds Versus Inflation, T-Bills (3-Month), and T-Bonds (3-Year)

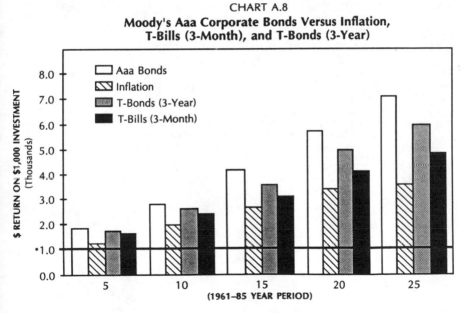

*Initial investment: $1.0 thousand.

291

Table A.9 / MOODY'S Baa CORPORATE BOND YIELD
(average annual yield)

Year	Yield*	Compound return on a five-year $1,000 investment	Compound rate of return
1985	12.72%	1981–85	
1984	14.19%		14.51%
1983	13.55%	. . . $1,969.22	
1982	16.11%		
1981	16.04%		
1980	13.67%	1976–80	
1979	10.69%		10.50%
1978	9.49%	. . . $1,647.56	
1977	8.97%		
1976	9.75%		
1975	10.61%	1971–75	
1974	9.50%		9.01%
1973	8.24%	. . . $1,539.19	
1972	8.15%		
1971	8.56%		
1970	9.10%	1966–70	
1969	7.81%		7.14%
1968	6.94%	. . . $1,411.96	
1967	6.23%		
1966	5.67%		
1965	4.87%	1961–65	
1964	4.83%		4.93%
1963	4.86%	. . . $1,272.15	
1962	5.02%		
1961	5.08%		

	How a $1,000 investment performed over			
5 years	10 years	15 years	20 years	25 years
1981–85 $1,969.22 (14.51%)†				
	1976–85 $3,244.39 (12.49%)			
		1971–85 $4,993.75 (11.32%)		
			1966–85 $7,050.98 (10.26%)	
				1961–85 $8,969.91 (9.17%)

*Source: U.S. Department of Commerce, *Business Statistics* and *Survey of Current Business.*

† Compound rate of return for that period.

292

MOODY'S CORPORATE BOND YIELD, Baa

This is the "champ" in my eyes—much to my surprise. A review of this Table (keeping in mind our discussion on Aaa Bonds and their ability in real life to change price) shows what happens when an investment consistently noses out its competition by 1 percent or 2 percent. After a while, that seemingly minor differential turns into major returns, and a pleasant surprise, say, at retirement.

If you buy investments such as Baa Bonds intelligently (fair fees on purchase, etc.), hold them until maturity, and avoid lemons that go down in rating in future years (there will always be a few), you'll easily attain your financial goals without ulcers. This is an investment that provides an approximate return of 10 percent to 12 percent per year without significant risk, heavy hidden fees, or wild gyrations of the principal. It beats the competition over both medium and long term. You may be bored with it, but you'll be happy and smart.

Notice that the Baa Bond Table is the epitome of consistency and performance. It was third or better in all five-year intervals—first for our twenty-five-year analysis, second for the twenty-year, third for the fifteen-year, second for ten years, and second again for the most recent five-year span.

Incredible. What the investor needs now is an intelligently researched, hedged as well as possible Baa Bond mutual fund/unit trust—with a fair fee structure. I'd buy it pronto.

CHART A.9
Moody's Baa Corporate Bonds Versus Inflation, T-Bills (3-Month), and Aaa Corporate Bonds

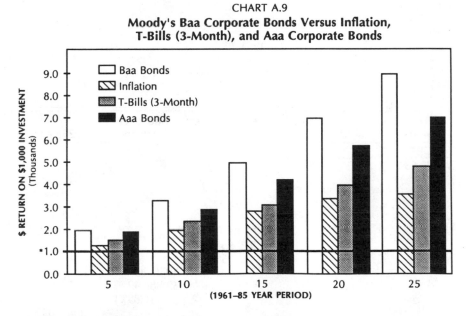

*Initial investment: $1.0 thousand.

293

Table A.10 / MUNICIPAL BOND YIELD
(high-grade S & P fifteen bonds; average annual yield)

Year	Yield*	Compound return on a five-year $1,000 investment	Compound rate of return
1985	9.18%	1981–85	
1984	10.10%		10.31%
1983	9.51%	. . . $1,633.63	
1982	11.57%		
1981	11.23%		
1980	8.51%	1976–80	
1979	6.39%		6.57%
1978	5.90%	. . . $1,374.28	
1977	5.56%		
1976	6.49%		
1975	6.89%	1971–75	
1974	6.09%		5.82%
1973	5.18%	. . . $1,327.16	
1972	5.27%		
1971	5.70%		
1970	6.51%	1966–70	
1969	5.81%		4.92%
1968	4.51%	. . . $1,271.47	
1967	3.98%		
1966	3.82%		
1965	3.27%	1961–65	
1964	3.22%		3.27%
1963	3.23%	. . . $1,174.66	
1962	3.18%		
1961	3.46%		

	How a $1,000 investment performed over			
5 years	10 years	15 years	20 years	25 years
1981–85				
$1,633.63				
(10.31%)†				
	1976–85			
	$2,245.06			
	(8.42%)			
		1971–85		
		$2,979.56		
		(7.55%)		
			1966–85	
			$3,788.42	
			(6.89%)	
				1961–85
				$4,450.11
				(6.15%)

*Source: U.S. Department of Commerce, *Business Statistics* and *Survey of Current Business.*

† Compound rate of return for that period.

S & P MUNICIPAL BOND YIELD, FIFTEEN HIGH-GRADE

This Table is unique for a very important reason: Whatever its overall returns, they are entirely tax-free. No other Table I've presented can make that statement. Therefore, even with the new tax-law changes and your lower bracket, this investment should be taken seriously. The returns are pure, after-tax returns.

This Table was a consistently mediocre performer and often a below-average performer. But when the 28 percent to 33 percent tax-bracket investor takes the tax-free return into account, it becomes an above-average performer, usually at the level of the top third. If you want a simplified investment program of not seeking tax-advantaged income and/or tax shelters of the newer, income-oriented variety, consider buying high-grade municipals (as are reflected here) and forget about outwitting the system or the tax man. But make sure your bracket justifies this move before you jump.

CHART A.10

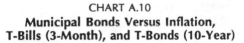

Municipal Bonds Versus Inflation, T-Bills (3-Month), and T-Bonds (10-Year)

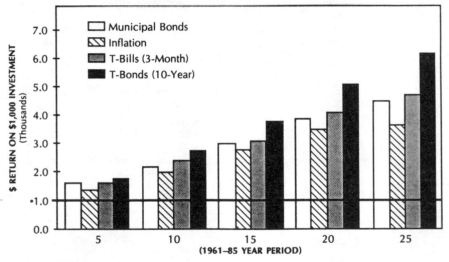

*Initial investment: $1.0 thousand.

Table A.11 / FHA MORTGAGES
(secondary market; average annual yield)

Year	Yield*	Compound return on a five-year $1,000 investment	Compound rate of return
1985	12.24%	1981–85	
1984	13.82%		14.15%
1983	13.11%	... $1,937.82	
1982	15.30%		
1981	16.31%		
1980	13.44%	1976–80	
1979	10.98%		10.33%
1978	9.75%	... $1,634.68	
1977	8.72%		
1976	8.82%		
1975	9.20%	1971–75	
1974	9.55%		8.43%
1973	8.19%	... $1,498.88	
1972	7.53%		
1971	7.70%		
1970	9.03%	1966–70	
1969	8.29%		7.49%
1968	7.19%	... $1,435.18	
1967	6.56%		
1966	6.42%		
1965	5.47%	1961–65	
1964	5.45%		5.55%
1963	5.46%	... $1,309.93	
1962	5.60%		
1961	5.76%		

	How a $1,000 investment performed over			
5 years	10 years	15 years	20 years	25 years
1981–85 $1,937.82 (14.15%)†				
	1976–85 $3,167.72 (12.22%)			
		1971–85 $4,748.04 (10.94%)		
			1966–85 $6,814.29 (10.07%)	
				1961–85 $8,926.26 (9.15%)

*Source: U.S. Department of Commerce, *Business Conditions Digest* and *Handbook of Cyclical Indicators* (annual data approximated).

† Compound rate of return for that period.

FHA MORTGAGES

This is a hypothetical investment, but a major benchmark that most of us live with daily. A primary reason for my investigation was to find out how reasonable or fairly priced mortgages were. Also, there are mortgage pools available that invest exclusively in mortgages, and they are worth looking at as an investment.

There is no doubt that an FHA Mortgage in comparison to competitors is a standout. Statistically it is number 2, behind Baa Bonds over the past quarter century. This is a very consistent Table, never ranking worse than third. In fact, it was the number-3 performer in every five-year interval except for the twenty-five-year higher ranking. Ironically, the houses that the mortgages are secured with performed (within their Table) much worse than the FHA Mortgages.

CHART A.11
**FHA Mortgages Versus Inflation,
Corporate Bond Average, and Prime Rate**

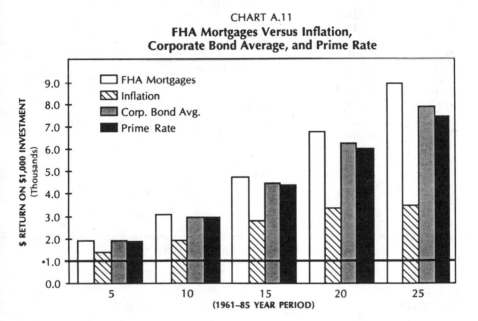

*Initial investment: $1.0 thousand.

Table A.12 / PRIME RATE
(average annual yield)

Year	Yield*	Compound return on a five-year $1,000 investment	Compound rate of return
1985	9.93%	1981–85	
1984	12.04%		13.25%
1983	10.79%	. . . $1,863.08	
1982	14.86%		
1981	18.87%		
1980	15.27%	1976–80	
1979	12.67%		10.08%
1978	9.06%	. . . $1,616.50	
1977	6.82%		
1976	6.84%		
1975	7.86%	1971–75	
1974	10.80%		7.51%
1973	8.02%	. . . $1,436.16	
1972	5.25%		
1971	5.70%		
1970	7.91%	1966–70	
1969	7.95%		6.67%
1968	6.28%	. . . $1,381.24	
1967	5.63%		
1966	5.62%		
1965	4.54%	1961–65	
1964	4.50%		4.51%
1963	4.50%	. . . $1,246.66	
1962	4.50%		
1961	4.50%		

	How a $1,000 investment performed over			
5 years	10 years	15 years	20 years	25 years
1981–85 $1,863.08 (13.25%)†				
	1976–85 $3,011.67 (11.66%)			
		1971–85 $4,325.23 (10.26%)		
			1966–85 $5,974.18 (9.35%)	
				1961–85 $7,447.76 (8.36%)

*Source: U.S. Department of Commerce, *Business Conditions Digest* and *Handbook of Cyclical Indicators*.

† Compound rate of return for that period.

PRIME RATE

This is another hypothetical investment—unless you are a bank. If you were a bank and could receive the returns provided by this Table by pricing your product 1 percent to 4 percent (or more) above this annual return, you would probably have a marble lobby too.

The Prime Rate Table was a standout. It was consistently in the top 20 percent. If we add a few percentage points to the Prime's statistics, you have the number-1 performer in each and every five-year block. Granted, the banks incur some risk with their loans (we've already mentioned foreign loans), but they make them by choice, and they usually do add those extra points. Banks have overhead expenses, but they also have exorbitant credit card rates, too. A Credit Card Rate Table would have blown up my Tables and left everyone behind. The moral here is that banks charge ample rates in relation to their investment competitors—and no matter how low the Prime goes, it is still outpacing most alternatives.

CHART A.12
Prime Rate Versus Inflation,
T-Bills (3-Month), and Corporate Bond Average

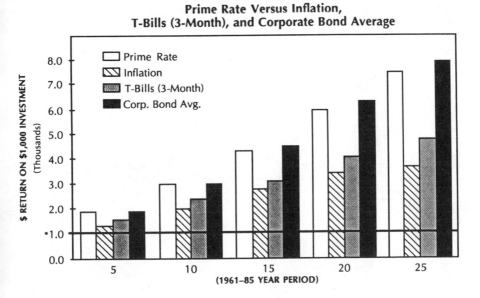

*Initial investment: $1.0 thousand.

Table A.13 / T-BONDS, 10-YEAR MATURITY
(average annual yield)

Year	Yield*	Compound return on a five-year $1,000 investment	Compound rate of return
1985	10.62%	1981–85	
1984	12.44%		12.21%
1983	11.10%	... $1,778.73	
1982	13.00%		
1981	13.91%		
1980	11.46%	1976–80	
1979	9.44%		8.86%
1978	8.41%	... $1,528.63	
1977	7.42%		
1976	7.61%		
1975	7.99%	1971–75	
1974	7.56%		6.95%
1973	6.84%	... $1,399.25	
1972	6.21%		
1971	6.16%		
1970	7.35%	1966–70	
1969	6.67%		5.93%
1968	5.65%	... $1,333.68	
1967	5.07%		
1966	4.92%		
1965	4.28%	1961–65	
1964	4.19%		4.06%
1963	4.00%	... $1,220.16	
1962	3.95%		
1961	3.88%		

| | How a $1,000 investment performed over | | | |
5 years	10 years	15 years	20 years	25 years
1981–85 $1,778.73 (12.21%)†				
	1976–85 $2,719.01 (10.52%)			
		1971–85 $3,804.57 (9.32%)		
			1966–85 $5,074.07 (8.46%)	
				1961–85 $6,191.18 (7.56%)

*Source: *Economic Report of the President,* 1986.

† Compound rate of return for that period.

U.S. TREASURY BONDS, 10-YEAR MATURITY

This Table is for those who want safety, respectable rates of interest, and can accept a ten-year wait to be sure their principal won't disappear—ever. For despite the fact that the U.S. Government 10-Year Maturity was below that of Baa Bonds and Aaa Bonds, it doesn't have as long a maturity date as either of those choices, is more safely backed with 100 percent government protection, and it lost to them by relatively minor amounts, usually about .5 percent, as in the case of Aaa Bonds. This Table was always an above-average performer and improved in the past decade. In summary, Uncle Sam is offering a fair deal. Take him up on it if you can wait ten years. You'll probably feel more comfortable, and throughout most of those ten years your bond won't be sporting a discounted value, and surely not at maturity.

CHART A.13
10-Year T-Bonds Versus Inflation, T-Bonds (3-Year), and Aaa Corporate Bonds

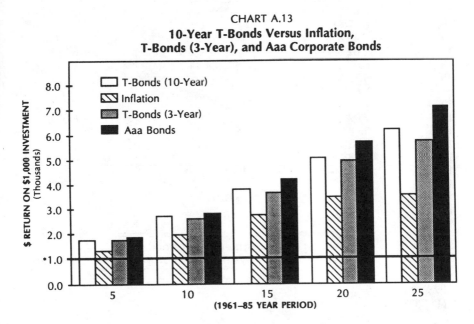

*Initial investment: $1.0 thousand.

Table A.14 / T-BONDS, 3-YEAR MATURITY
(average annual yield)

Year	Yield*	Compound return on a five-year $1,000 investment	Compound rate of return
1985	9.64%	1981–85	
1984	11.89%		11.85%
1983	10.45%	. . . $1,750.95	
1982	12.92%		
1981	14.44%		
1980	11.55%	1976–80	
1979	9.71%		8.59%
1978	8.29%	. . . $1,509.65	
1977	6.69%		
1976	6.77%		
1975	7.49%	1971–75	
1974	7.82%		6.72%
1973	6.95%	. . . $1,384.44	
1972	5.72%		
1971	5.65%		
1970	7.29%	1966–70	
1969	7.02%		6.05%
1968	5.68%	. . . $1,341.13	
1967	5.03%		
1966	5.23%		
1965	4.22%	1961–65	
1964	4.03%		3.79%
1963	3.67%	. . . $1,204.16	
1962	3.47%		
1961	3.54%		

	How a $1,000 investment performed over			
5 years	10 years	15 years	20 years	25 years
1981–85 $1,750.95 (11.85%)†				
	1976–85 $2,643.33 (10.21%)			
		1971–85 $3,659.54 (9.03%)		
			1966–85 $4,907.91 (8.28%)	
				1961–85 $5,909.93 (7.37%)

*Source: *Economic Report of the President,* 1986.

† Compound rate of return for that period.

U.S. TREASURY BONDS, 3 YEAR MATURITY

This Table was a "sleeper" investment in many ways. To start with, these bonds consistently lost out to the 10-year U.S. Government Bond, but only by a small amount, usually .25 percent. For the level of liquidity offered in three years versus ten years, most people would gladly surrender .25 percent. Also, the rate is backed by the U.S. government (a statement applicable to any U.S. government issue I have analyzed), which is the ultimate badge of safety. In addition, the backing in these bonds extends to any and all amounts owned by the investor. Banks can claim government backing only to $100,000 per depositor. (FDIC deposits are insured according to the "rights and capacities" in which the deposits are held or owned.)

Depending on the level of assets you have, you may want to spread your $100,000 blocks at several banks, or buy at one place with great safety, by shopping for Uncle Sam's product. I'm ignoring the possibility that the CD quotes of banks are sometimes more competitive than those of Uncle Sam's respective rates in 1-year, 3-year, and 10-year paper. But assume nothing and shop for the best deal, keeping in mind safety as well as yield.

The 3-Year U.S. Government Bond Table overall did well, especially in the last decade. The worst of its five-year-interval performances was about average, with the rest ranging slightly above average to the upper third of all competitors. This Table profiles a very safe, reasonably liquid, and fair-yielding investment.

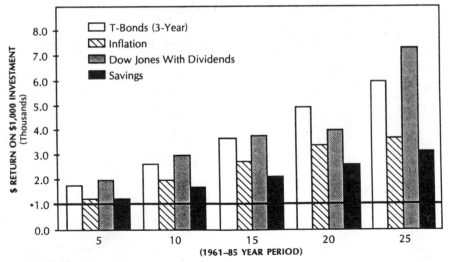

CHART A.14
3-Year T-Bonds Versus Inflation,
Dow Jones With Dividends, and Savings

*Initial investment: $1.0 thousand.

303

Table A.15 / T-BONDS, 1-YEAR MATURITY
(average annual yield)

Year	Yield*	Compound return on a five-year $1,000 investment	Compound rate of return
1985	7.81%	1981–85	
1984	9.91%		10.15%
1983	8.86%	. . . $1,621.27	
1982	11.09%		
1981	13.14%		
1980	10.89%	1976–80	
1979	9.75%		7.90%
1978	7.74%	. . . $1,462.60	
1977	5.71%		
1976	5.52%		
1975	6.30%	1971–75	
1974	7.71%		6.09%
1973	7.01%	. . . $1,343.61	
1972	4.77%		
1971	4.67%		
1970	6.49%	1966–70	
1969	6.79%		5.70%
1968	5.46%	. . . $1,319.45	
1967	4.71%		
1966	5.07%		
1965	4.06%	1961–65	
1964	3.74%		3.38%
1963	3.30%	. . . $1,180.99	
1962	3.01%		
1961	2.81%		

	How a $1,000 investment performed over			
5 years	10 years	15 years	20 years	25 years
1981–85				
$1,621.27				
(10.15%)†				
	1976–85			
	$2,371.27			
	(9.02%)			
		1971–85		
		$3,186.06		
		(8.03%)		
			1966–85	
			$4,203.85	
			(7.44%)	
				1961–85
				$4,964.69
				(6.62%)

*Source: Board of Governors of the Federal Reserve System, *Federal Reserve Bulletin*.
† Compound rate of return for that period.

U.S. TREASURY BONDS, 1-YEAR MATURITY

I was surprised at the minimal additional yield 1-Year U.S. Bonds provided versus the 3-Month Treasury Bill. With the exception of the fifteen-year analysis, the spread between the two was always less than .2 percent. So, considering that there are T-bills and good U.S. government money market funds available, I wouldn't recommend a 1-Year U.S. Government Bond—unless you need to park money for just one year—no more, no less.

As for its ranking versus other competitors in this analysis, the 1-Year U.S. Government Bond landed a slightly below-average rating but was at least consistent in its rankings and did not give anyone a roller coaster ride.

CHART A.15
1-Year T-Bonds Versus Inflation, T-Bills (3-Month), and Savings

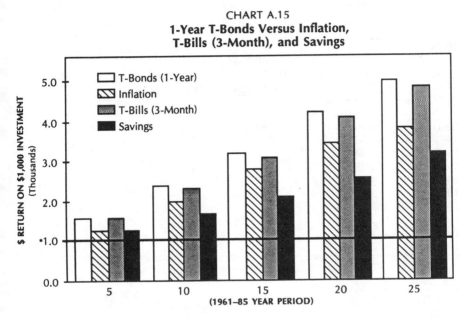

*Initial investment: $1.0 thousand.

Table A.16 / T-BILLS, 3-MONTH MATURITY
(secondary market; average annual yield)

Year	Yield*	Compound return on a five-year $1,000 investment	Compound rate of return
1985	7.48%	1981–85	
1984	9.52%		10.03%
1983	8.61%	. . . $1,612.52	
1982	10.61%		
1981	14.03%		
1980	11.43%	1976–80	
1979	10.07%		7.76%
1978	7.19%	. . . $1,452.90	
1977	5.27%		
1976	4.98%		
1975	5.80%	1971–75	
1974	7.84%		5.80%
1973	7.03%	. . . $1,325.88	
1972	4.07%		
1971	4.33%		
1970	6.39%	1966–70	
1969	6.67%		5.50%
1968	5.34%	. . . $1,307.22	
1967	4.29%		
1966	4.85%		
1965	3.95%	1961–65	
1964	3.54%		3.15%
1963	3.16%	. . . $1,167.99	
1962	2.77%		
1961	2.36%		

	How a $1,000 investment performed over			
5 years	10 years	15 years	20 years	25 years
1981–85				
$1,612.52				
(10.03%)†				
	1976–85			
	$2,342.83			
	(8.89%)			
		1971–85		
		$3,106.32		
		(7.85%)		
			1966–85	
			$4,060.64	
			(7.26%)	
				1961–85
				$4,742.80
				(6.42%)

*Source: Board of Governors of the Federal Reserve System, *Federal Reserve Bulletin*.
† Compound rate of return for that period.

U.S. TREASURY BILLS, 3-MONTH MATURITY

The famous T-Bill is the epitome of safety in a short-term investment. Short-term rates are almost always less competitive than long-term rates, and this has been true for T-Bills. Over twenty-five years, the Table was a bottom-third performer but makes a decent showing nonetheless given its safety and liquidity. In the past decade, T-Bills have improved to average. They also proved to be a level-headed investment. Of note, T-Bills always outperformed two famous competitors—Inflation and the Savings Deposit. And don't forget that all U.S. government issues are free from state tax on interest income. Other than municipal bonds issued by your state, no other competitor can say that.

CHART A.16
3-Month T-Bills Versus Inflation, Savings, and Corporate Bond Average

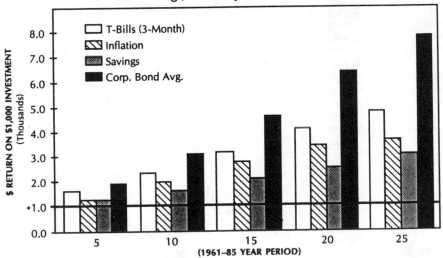

*Initial investment: $1.0 thousand.

307

Table A.17 / CERTIFICATES OF DEPOSIT, 6-MONTH MATURITY
(secondary market; average annual yield)

Year	Yield*	Compound return on a five-year $1,000 investment	Compound rate of return
1985	8.25%	1981–85	
1984	10.68%		11.28%
1983	9.27%	. . . $1,706.15	
1982	12.57%		
1981	15.77%		
1980	12.99%		
1979	11.44%	1976–80	
1978	8.61%		8.88%
1977	5.92%	. . . $1,530.09	
1976	5.63%		
1975	6.89%		
1974	9.98%		
1973	8.31%	1971–75	
1972	5.02%		7.07%
1971	5.21%	. . . $1,406.85	
1970	7.66%		
1969	7.91%		
1968	6.00%		
1967	5.22%	1966–70	
1966	5.63%		6.48%
1965	4.43%	. . . $1,368.70	
1964	n.a.		
1963	n.a.		
1962	n.a.		
1961	n.a.		

	How a $1,000 investment performed over		
5 years	10 years	15 years	20 years
1981–85			
$1,706.15			
(11.28%)†			
	1976–85		
	$2,610.56		
	(10.07%)		
		1971–85	
		$3,672.66	
		(9.06%)	
			1966–85
			$5,026.77
			(8.41%)

*Source: Federal Reserve Bank of Boston.
† Compound rate of return for that period.

CERTIFICATES OF DEPOSIT, 6-MONTH MATURITY

This investment is a close cousin to the 3-Month T-Bill and handily beat it. Because the margin was slightly in excess of 1 percent in all five-year intervals, you should consider investing in 6-Month CDs as long as you can accept the extended maturity date and keep the investment to $100,000 per insured banking institution. There were no statistics for a full twenty-five-year analysis for this Table, so we can compare only the past twenty years. The Table was consistently either ninth or tenth versus all competitors in every five-year interval. Thus it proved a slightly above-average competitor, providing safety, liquidity, a fair rate of return—and no sleepless nights.

CHART A.17
**6-Month Certificates of Deposit Versus
Inflation, T-Bonds (10-Year), and T-Bills (3-Month)**

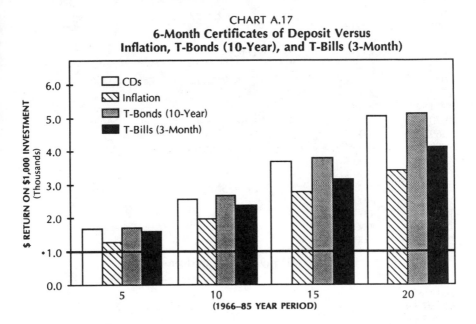

*Initial investment: $1.0 thousand.

Table A.18 / SAVINGS DEPOSITS

Year	Yield*	Compound return on a five-year $1,000 investment	Compound rate of return
1985	5.50%	1981–85	
1984	5.50%		5.35%
1983	5.25%	. . . $1,297.69	
1982	5.25%		
1981	5.25%		
1980	5.25%	1976–80	
1979	5.00%		5.05%
1978	5.00%	. . . $1,279.32	
1977	5.00%		
1976	5.00%		
1975	5.00%	1971–75	
1974	5.00%		4.70%
1973	4.50%	. . . $1,258.14	
1972	4.50%		
1971	4.50%		
1970	4.50%	1966–70	
1969	4.00%		4.10%
1968	4.00%	. . . $1,222.50	
1967	4.00%		
1966	4.00%		
1965	4.00%	1961–65	
1964	4.00%		3.80%
1963	4.00%	. . . $1,204.95	
1962	4.00%		
1961	3.00%		

	How a $1,000 investment performed over			
5 years	10 years	15 years	20 years	25 years
1981–85 $1,297.69 (5.35%)†				
	1976–85 $1,660.16 (5.20%)			
		1971–85 $2,088.71 (5.03%)		
			1966–85 $2,553.45 (4.80%)	
				1961–85 $3,076.79 (4.60%)

*Source: Board of Governors of the Federal Reserve System, *Federal Reserve Bulletin.*
† Compound rate of return for that period.

SAVINGS DEPOSITS

I was curious about this index because so many people have used it, especially before the advent of money market funds. A Savings Deposit is safe, up to the government insurance level of $100,000 per account at each institution—and that is about as far as its appeal goes. It was consistent in its poor performance and relatively consistent in its low return. It was third or fourth from the bottom in all five-year intervals, with the exception of the most recent five years when it was sixth from last. In fact, it never got out of the bottom 25 percent. Most revealing of all, Savings Deposits *never beat Inflation* in any five-year interval of the past quarter century. If we can use that statement as a guide, whenever you see a passbook savings account rate, you can count on the rate of inflation exceeding that rate, on average, over the next five years. It almost makes you want Savings Deposit rates to go down. Sad but true.

CHART A.18
Savings Versus Inflation,
T-Bills (3-Month), and Aaa Corporate Bonds

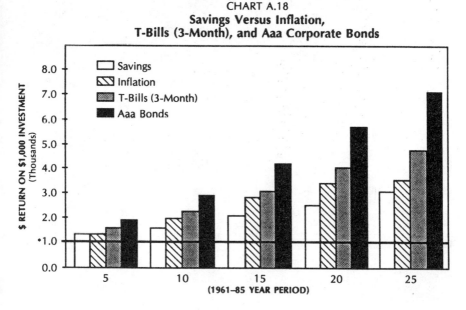

*Initial investment: $1.0 thousand.

Table A.19 / SILVER
(New York, $/ounce; average annual price)

Year	Price* [$/ounce]	Price growth	Compound return on a five-year $1,000 investment	Compound rate of return
1985	6.142	−24.55%	1981–85	
1984	8.140	−28.84%		−21.52%
1983	11.440	43.97%	. . . $297.75	
1982	7.947	−24.44%		
1981	10.518	−49.02%		
1980	20.632	85.97%	1976–80	
1979	11.094	105.41%		36.10%
1978	5.401	16.83%	. . . $4,669.00	
1977	4.623	6.20%		
1976	4.353	−1.49%		
1975	4.419	−6.14%	1971–75	
1974	4.708	84.05%		20.07%
1973	2.558	51.81%	. . . $2,495.27	
1972	1.685	8.99%		
1971	1.546	−12.70%		
1970	1.771	−1.12%	1966–70	
1969	1.791	−16.50%		6.50%
1968	2.145	38.39%	. . . $1,369.77	
1967	1.550	19.88%		
1966	1.293	0.00%		
1965	1.293	0.00%	1961–65	
1964	1.293	1.09%		7.18%
1963	1.279	17.88%	. . . $1,414.49	
1962	1.085	17.42%		
1961	0.924	1.09%		

How a $1,000 investment performed over				
5 years	10 years	15 years	20 years	25 years
1981–85 $297.75 (−21.52%)†				
	1976–85 $1,390.22 (3.35%)			
		1971–85 $3,468.97 (8.65%)		
			1966–85 $4,751.67 (8.10%)	
				1961–85 $6,721.18 (7.92%)

*Source: U.S. Department of Commerce, *Business Statistics* and *Survey of Current Business.*

† Compound rate of return for that period.

312

SILVER, NEW YORK MERCANTILE RATE, PER OUNCE

I call this analysis the "Air-Bag Table." You need one to follow the paths of re-turns—or the lack of them. For three of the five-year periods, Silver performed slightly above average—with lackluster returns versus many competitors. Then the last decade came along (and the Hunt brothers, who tried to "corner the market") and everything went haywire. In that ten-year interval, Silver crashed to next-to-last. It then did even worse and fell to dead last with an awful return of *minus* 21.52 percent average annual rate in the latest five years. Such a wild, poor performance is almost impossible to describe.

Sooner or later, Silver will be a very nice buy. I say that because in the volatile issues we analyzed, we noted distinct levels of elasticity. When you pulled either up or down on a volatile subject, it had a tendency to return to where you started pulling—usually within a five-year time frame. "What goes up comes down" certainly applies to the volatile performers. Silver may not allow you to age well, but at $3 to $5 per ounce it could put a Ferrari in your driveway—if, of course, the marketplace cooperates and you know when to sell.

CHART A.19
**Silver Growth Versus Inflation,
T-Bills (3-Month), and Gold**

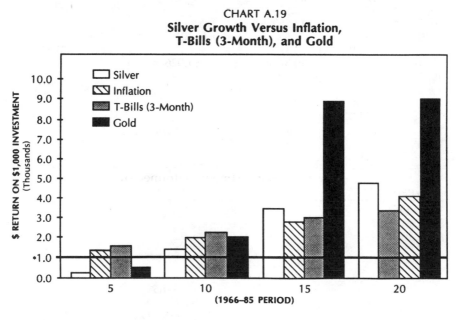

*Initial investment: $1.0 thousand.

Table A.20 / GOLD
(London, $/ounce; average annual price)

Year	Price* [$/ounce]	Price growth	Compound return on a five-year $1,000 investment	Compound rate of return
1985	317.18	−11.98%	1981–85	
1984	360.36	−14.70%		−12.20%
1983	422.47	12.42%	. . . $521.80	
1982	375.80	−18.26%		
1981	459.75	−24.37%		
1980	607.87	98.22%	1976–80	
1979	306.67	58.70%		30.43%
1978	193.24	30.82%	. . . $3,775.07	
1977	147.72	18.35%		
1976	124.82	−22.49%		
1975	161.03	1.12%	1971–75	
1974	159.25	63.62%		34.98%
1973	97.33	67.35%	. . . $4,480.55	
1972	58.16	42.51%		
1971	40.81	13.55%		
1970	35.94	−12.53%	1966–70	
1969	41.09	6.37%		0.53%
1968	38.63	10.37%	. . . $1,026.90	
1967	35.00	0.00%		
1966	35.00	0.00%		
1965	35.00	0.00%		
1964	35.00	n.a.		
1963	n.a.	n.a.		
1962	n.a.	n.a.		
1961	n.a.	n.a.		

	How a $1,000 investment performed over		
5 years	10 years	15 years	20 years
1981–85 $521.80 (−12.20%)†			
	1976–85 $1,969.82 (7.01%)		
		1971–85 $8,825.90 (15.62%)	
			1966–85 $9,063.34 (11.65%)

*Source: International Monetary Fund, Bureau of Statistics, *International Financial Statistics*, 1986.

† Compound rate of return for that period.

GOLD, LONDON SPOT PRICE, PER OUNCE

The infamous inflation hedge (and recommendation of the Armageddon Soothsayers such as Howard Ruff) is a wild study. First of all, until President Nixon changed things almost two decades ago, the price of gold was fixed ($35 per ounce) versus U.S. currencies. This artificial price fixing has hindered our twenty-five-year analysis of Gold and limited this Table to the past twenty years, or four five-year intervals.

Gold is unique. It was ranked number 1 in two five-year studies over twenty years, a remarkable feat. In the other two five-year intervals it was in the bottom 20 percent, and in the last five years it ranked second from last, beating only the terrible performance of Silver. Gold averaged a *minus* 12.20 percent per year over the past five years.

A volatile investment, when Gold was good it was phenomenal, and when it was bad it was the pits. If you don't like ulcers and don't expect higher inflation, leave a Gold investment to those of more crimson blood.

And keep in mind another point that sets Silver and Gold apart from other "real" investments in our analysis. They do not pay interest or dividends, and you can't rent them out like a house. So if you need cash flow from your investments (no matter how small), or if you don't want an investment whose only return occurs through rising prices (rather than from a combination of income and gains), you should look elsewhere. Commodity investments, such as Gold and Silver, are definitely a different breed.

CHART A.20
Gold Growth Versus Inflation,
T-Bills (3-Month), and Dow Jones With Dividends

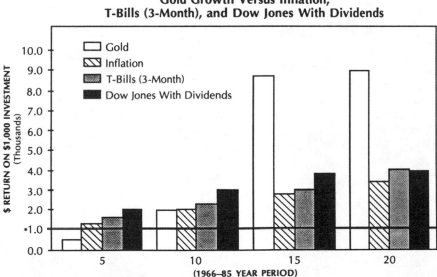

□ Gold
◧ Inflation
▨ T-Bills (3-Month)
■ Dow Jones With Dividends

$ RETURN ON $1,000 INVESTMENT (Thousands)

(1966–85 YEAR PERIOD)

*Initial investment: $1.0 thousand.

315

Table A.21 / CRUDE PETROLEUM PRICE INDEX
(producer, 1967 = 100; average annual price)

Year	Index* value	Index growth	Compound return on a five-year $1,000 investment	Compound rate of return
1985	619.30	−7.64%	1981–85	
1984	670.50	−1.60%		2.17%
1983	681.40	−7.09%	. . . $1,113.05	
1982	733.40	−8.72%		
1981	803.50	44.41%		
1980	556.40	47.78%	1976–80	
1979	376.50	25.46%		17.76%
1978	300.10	9.45%	. . . $2,264.68	
1977	274.20	8.12%		
1976	253.60	3.22%		
1975	245.70	16.01%	1971–75	
1974	211.80	68.10%		18.29%
1973	126.00	10.72%	. . . $2,315.84	
1972	113.80	0.53%		
1971	113.20	6.69%		
1970	106.10	0.86%	1966–70	
1969	105.20	4.37%		1.56%
1968	100.80	0.80%	. . . $1,080.49	
1967	100.00	1.11%		
1966	98.90	0.71%		
1965	98.20	−0.10%	1961–65	
1964	98.30	−0.41%		−0.08%
1963	98.70	−0.40%	. . . $995.89	
1962	99.10	0.20%		
1961	98.90	0.30%		

	How a $1,000 investment performed over			
5 years	10 years	15 years	20 years	25 years
1981–85 $1,113.05 (2.17%)†				
	1976–85 $2,520.70 (9.69%)			
		1971–85 $5,837.54 (12.48%)		
			1966–85 $6,307.42 (9.65%)	
				1961–85 $6,281.46 (7.63%)

*Source: U.S. Department of Commerce, Business Statistics and Survey of Current Business.

† Compound rate of return for that period.

316

CRUDE PETROLEUM PRICE INDEX, PRODUCER PRICE

Crude Oil is a commodity too, and it doesn't pay dividends. But it performed rather sanely over the past twenty-five years. Except for the most recent five-year interval, the Crude Oil Table was always above average, and in two five-year intervals it was a true standout—ranking second and fourth respectively. While its ride was not volatile when compared to Silver and Gold, it fluctuated enough to make me hesitate in considering it a good investment. Unless Crude Oil drops substantially (like Silver and Gold), I would not be inclined to invest in it.

On the other hand, Crude Petroleum might be a buy sooner rather than later at the $10 to $12 per barrel price range, for it certainly had a drop to those levels. But remember: These Tables are researched facts, the projections are still guesses.

CHART A.21
Crude Petroleum Index Versus Inflation, Silver, and Dow Jones With Dividends

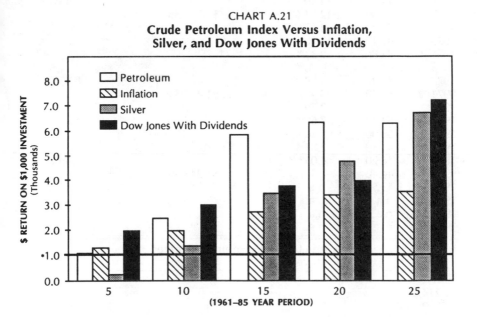

*Initial investment: $1.0 thousand.

317

Table A.22 / NEW ONE-FAMILY HOUSE PRICE INDEX
(1977 = 100; average annual price)

Year	Index* value	Index growth	Compound return on a five-year $1,000 investment	Compound rate of return
1985	176.40	2.62%	1981–85	
1984	171.90	3.87%		3.97%
1983	165.50	2.48%	. . . $1,214.89	
1982	161.50	2.60%		
1981	157.40	8.40%		
1980	145.20	11.01%		
1979	130.80	14.24%	1976–80	
1978	114.50	14.50%		12.19%
1977	100.00	12.74%	. . . $1,777.35	
1976	88.70	8.57%		
1975	81.70	10.70%		
1974	73.80	9.33%	1971–75	
1973	67.50	8.70%		
1972	62.10	6.52%		8.12%
1971	58.30	5.42%	. . . $1,477.31	
1970	55.30	2.79%		
1969	53.80	7.60%		
1968	50.00	5.26%		
1967	47.50	2.81%	1966–70	
1966	46.20	4.05%		4.49%
1965	44.40	2.07%	. . . $1,245.39	
1964	43.50	n.a.		
1963	n.a.	n.a.		
1962	n.a.	n.a.		
1961	n.a.	n.a.		

How a $1,000 investment performed over			
5 years	10 years	15 years	20 years
1981–85 $1,214.89 (3.97%)†			
	1976–85 $2,159.29 (8.00%)		
		1971–85 $3,189.94 (8.04%)	
			1966–85 $3,972.70 (7.14%)

*Source: U.S. Department of Commerce, Bureau of the Census.
† Compound rate of return for that period.

NEW ONE-FAMILY HOUSE PRICE INDEX

Prior to our research, I thought this Table would be a top performer. It wasn't. Although statistics weren't available for a full quarter-century review, housing was analyzed for twenty years, and never once in four five-year intervals did this Table finish above average. It was consistently below average, and in the past five years it got even worse, placing fifth from last.

As a resident of the Boston area, which has had an amazing increase in housing prices, I was surprised at the mediocre-to-poor results of the Housing Index. But the survey reflected the national mean index of New One-Family Houses, and not every region of the country is doing as well as Boston. The "rust belt" and oil-producing states are seeing sharp declines in housing prices. In the 1970s California's housing prices were skyrocketing, but they aren't today. So when looking at the map, and then my Table, you realize that housing can be hot or cold, depending on the region, although the average for all will show slightly below-average returns.

A few final points about housing. Unlike Gold, Silver, and Crude Oil, it can produce income through rentals or simply provide a roof over your head. It's hard to place a value on a roof, but the dual benefits of appreciation and shelter shouldn't be lost in a sea of statistics. In this regard, Housing is similar to the Dow Jones Thirty Industrials Without Dividends in its ability to give a false impression about overall net return. As a result, I feel the Housing Table deserves a higher ranking. The saying that the best investment you can make is to "buy a house and put a roof over your head" still stands. This index may not be number 1, but it still counts that way in most people's lives.

CHART A.22
House Price Index Growth Versus Inflation, Savings, and Dow Jones With Dividends

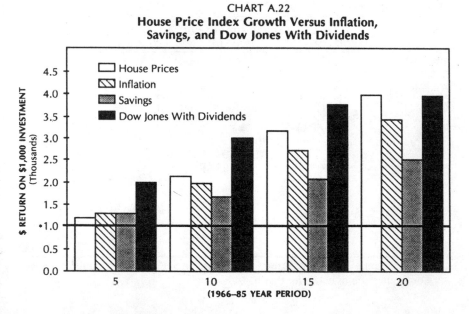

*Initial investment: $1.0 thousand.

Table A.23 / SWISS FRANC
(average annual price)

Year	Price* (dollar/franc)	Price growth	Compound return on a five-year $1,000 investment	Compound rate of return
1985	0.40732	−4.28%	1981–85	
1984	0.42553	−10.61%		−7.36%
1983	0.47605	−3.23%	... $682.33	
1982	0.49196	−3.21%		
1981	0.50829	−14.86%		
1980	0.59698	−0.70%	1976–80	
1979	0.60121	6.82%		9.03%
1978	0.56284	34.93%	... $1,541.00	
1977	0.41714	4.25%		
1976	0.40013	3.28%		
1975	0.38743	15.01%	1971–75	
1974	0.33688	6.27%		10.80%
1973	0.31700	21.02%	... $1,669.98	
1972	0.26193	7.65%		
1971	0.24331	4.88%		
1970	0.23199	0.06%	1966–70	
1969	0.23186	0.07%		0.08%
1968	0.23169	0.28%	... $1,004.00	
1967	0.23104	−0.04%		
1966	0.23114	0.03%		
1965	0.23106	−0.20%	1961–65	
1964	0.23152	0.06%		−0.04%
1963	0.23139	0.06%	... $998.00	
1962	0.23124	−0.12%		
1961	0.23151	0.00%		

	How a $1,000 investment performed over			
5 years	10 years	15 years	20 years	25 years
1981–85 $682.23 (−7.36%)†				
	1976–85 $1,051.48 (0.50%)			
		1971–85 $1,755.94 (3.82%)		
			1966–85 $1,762.97 (2.88%)	
				1961–85 $1,759.44 (2.29%)

*Source: Board of Governors of the Federal Reserve System, *Federal Reserve Bulletin.*
† Compound rate of return for that period.

SWISS FRANC

Those people who preach doom and gloom and expect the U.S. government's mounting debts to eventually cause its own currency's collapse prefer the "ultimate safe currency"—the Swiss Franc. They believe that Switzerland's neutrality will keep its currency healthy.

Over the past twenty-five years, however, the Swiss Franc was the worst performer in my survey—and Uncle Sam's debt has been mushrooming over much of that time. It is possible that a massive rise of the Swiss Franc is imminent, but after all, a quarter century should be ample time to prove yourself a winner.

In fairness, the U.S. Dollar was not fantastic either, and statistics were available for only the past fifteen years. But when compared head-on in the three five-year intervals when comparisons were possible, the Swiss Franc lost two out of three and was trounced in the most recent five-year period. Neither currency was a great investment as a commodity, and they were more than capable of being volatile. Nevertheless, I'll take my chances with having to cart around a wheelbarrow of U.S. Dollars to buy a loaf of bread in 1992, and as a hedge I'll choose not to run to a neutral source, such as the Swiss Franc. It is capable of providing only a mediocre-to-poor return (as a supposed hedge), a result I can duplicate without such complicated investment strategies. Pass on this one. The numbers just aren't there.

CHART A.23
Swiss Franc Versus Inflation, T-Bills (3-Month), and Dow Jones With Dividends

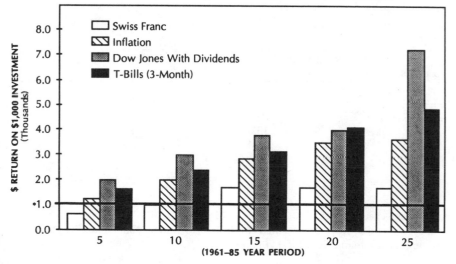

*Initial investment: $1.0 thousand.

Table A.24 / U.S. DOLLAR INDEX

Year	Index* value	Index growth	Compound return on a five-year $1,000 investment	Compound rate of return
1985	143.01	3.49%	1981–85	
1984	138.19	10.25%		10.35%
1983	125.34	7.52%	. . . $1,636.34	
1982	116.57	13.24%		
1981	102.94	17.79%		
1980	87.39	−0.79%		
1979	88.09	−4.65%		
1978	92.39	−10.57%	1976–80	
1977	103.31	−2.14%		−2.33%
1976	105.57	7.35%	. . . $888.72	
1975	98.34	−3.03%		
1974	101.41	2.29%		
1973	99.14	−9.10%		
1972	109.07	−7.42%		
1971	117.81	−2.69%	1971–75	
1970	121.07	−1.08%		−4.07%
1969	122.39	0.27%	. . . $812.29	
1968	122.06	1.76%		
1967	119.95	n.a.		
1966	n.a.	n.a.		
1965	n.a.	n.a.		
1964	n.a.	n.a.		
1963	n.a.	n.a.		
1962	n.a.	.n.a.		
1961	n.a.	n.a.		

5 years	How a $1,000 investment performed over 10 years	15 years
1981–85 $1,636.34 (10.35%)†		
	1976–85 $1,454.26 (3.82%)	
		1971–85 $1,181.27 (1.12%)

(Average against other G-10 countries, 1973 = 100)
*Source: Board of Governors of the Federal Reserve System, *Federal Reserve Bulletin.*
† Compound rate of return for that period.

U.S. DOLLAR

I'd like to be patriotic and say buy U.S. Dollars, but the numbers aren't awesome with this Table, either. And you are involved with it in almost every investment you make. So unless you are a multinational company interested in your foreign trade statistics, you want to see the good ol' Dollar Index rise.

Over the fifteen years of available statistics, the returns were mediocre. In the fifteen-year study the U.S. Dollar was dead last. But as noted earlier, in two of the three five-year comparisons, the Dollar beat the Swiss Franc. In the most recent five-year interval, the U.S. Dollar was an above-average performer, unusual for a currency.

So it's nice that the Dollar hasn't been too embarrassing over the years. Although its returns aren't inspiring enough to consider going out of our way to double up on this investment through the currency futures marketplace, it is important to realize that everyone is invested in it already. The Table's numbers simply don't make Uncle Sam's "standard" a standout. Maybe in our hearts, but not in our wallets.

CHART A.24
U.S. Dollar Versus Inflation, Swiss Franc, and Gold

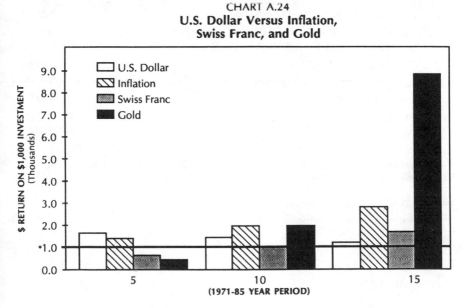

*Initial investment: $1.0 thousand.

THE TWENTY-FIVE-YEAR RANKINGS:
Average Annual Returns, 1961–1985*

1.	Moody's Corporate Bond Yield, Baa	9.17%
2.	FHA Mortgages	9.15%
3.	Moody's Corporate Bond Average	8.60%
4.	Prime Rate	8.36%
5.	Dow Jones Thirty Industrials, With Dividends	8.22%
6.	Moody's Corporate Bond Yield, Aaa	8.12%
7.	Silver	7.92%
8.	Crude Petroleum Price Index, Producer Price	7.63%
9.	U.S. Treasury Bonds, 10-Year Maturity	7.56%
10.	U.S. Treasury Bonds, 3-Year Maturity	7.37%
11.	Disposable Personal Income, U.S. per Capita	7.36%
12.	U.S. Treasury Bonds, 1-Year Maturity	6.62%
13.	U.S. Treasury Bonds, 3-Month Maturity	6.42%
14.	S & P Municipal Bond Yield, 15 High-Grade	6.15%
15.	Inflation†	5.30%
15.	S & P 500 Composite Index, Without Dividends†	5.30%
17.	Savings Deposits	4.60%
18.	Dow Jones Thirty Industrials, Without Dividends	3.75%
19.	Swiss Franc	2.29%

* These rankings do not include the following, which did not have data available for the entire time period studied:

Lipper Growth Mutual Fund Index
Certificates of Deposit, 6-Month Maturity
Gold
New One-Family House Price Index
U.S. Dollar

† Note equal rate.

THE TWENTY-YEAR RANKINGS:
Average Annual Return, 1966–85*

1.	Gold	11.65%
2.	Moody's Corporate Bond Yield, Baa	10.26%
3.	FHA Mortgages	10.07%
4.	Crude Petroleum Price Index, Producer Price	9.65%
5.	Moody's Corporate Bond Average	9.62%
6.	Prime Rate	9.35%
7.	Moody's Corporate Bond Yield, Aaa	9.08%
8.	U.S. Treasury Bonds, 10-Year Maturity	8.46%
9.	Certificates of Deposit, 6-Month Maturity	8.41%
10.	U.S. Treasury Bonds, 3-Year Maturity	8.28%
11.	Silver	8.10%
12.	Disposable Personal Income, U.S. per Capita	8.02%
13.	U.S. Treasury Bonds, 1-Year Maturity	7.44%
14.	U.S. Treasury Bills, 3-Month Maturity	7.26%
15.	New One-Family House Price Index	7.14%
16.	Dow Jones Thirty Industrials, With Dividends	7.11%
17.	S & P Municipal Bond Yield, 15 High-Grade	6.89%
18.	Inflation	6.33%
19.	Savings Deposits	4.80%
20.	S & P 500 Composite Index, Without Dividends	4.22%
21.	Swiss Franc	2.88%
22.	Dow Jones Thirty Industrials, Without Dividends	2.36%

* These rankings do not include the following, which did not have data available for the entire time period studied:

Lipper Growth Mutual Fund Index
U.S. Dollar

THE FIFTEEN-YEAR RANKINGS:
Average Annual Return, 1971–85

1. Gold	15.62%
2. Crude Petroleum Price Index, Producer Price	12.48%
3. Moody's Corporate Bond Yield, Baa	11.32%
4. FHA Mortgage	10.94%
5. Moody's Corporate Bond Average	10.62%
6. Prime Rate	10.26%
7. Moody's Corporate Bond Yield, Aaa	9.99%
8. U.S. Treasury Bonds, 10-Year Maturity	9.32%
9. Dow Jones Thirty Industrials, With Dividends	9.23%
10. Certificates of Deposit, 6-Month Maturity	9.06%
11. U.S. Treasury Bonds, 3-Year Maturity	9.03%
12. Lipper Growth Mutual Fund Index	8.81%
13. Silver	8.65%
14. Disposable Personal Income, U.S. per Capita	8.42%
15. New One-Family House Price Index	8.04%
16. U.S. Treasury Bonds, 1-Year Maturity	8.03%
17. U.S. Treasury Bills, 3-Month Maturity	7.85%
18. S & P Municipal Bond Yield, 15 High-Grade	7.55%
19. Inflation	7.03%
20. S & P 500 Composite Index, Without Dividends	5.69%
21. Savings Deposits	5.03%
22. Dow Jones Thirty Industrials, Without Dividends	4.16%
23. Swiss Franc	3.82%
24. U.S. Dollar	1.12%

THE TEN-YEAR RANKINGS:
Average Annual Return, 1976–85

1. Lipper Growth Mutual Fund Index   14.05%
2. Moody's Corporate Bond Yield, Baa   12.49%
3. FHA Mortgage   12.22%
4. Moody's Corporate Bond Average   11.75%
5. Prime Rate   11.66%
6. Dow Jones Thirty Industrials, With Dividends   11.50%
7. Moody's Corporate Bond Yield, Aaa   11.06%
8. U.S. Treasury Bonds, 10-Year Maturity   10.52%
9. U.S. Treasury Bonds, 3-Year Maturity   10.21%
10. Certificates of Deposit, 6-Month Maturity   10.07%
11. Crude Petroleum Price Index, Producer Price   9.69%
12. U.S. Treasury Bonds, 1-Year Maturity   9.02%
13. U.S. Treasury Bills, 3-Month Maturity*   8.89%
13. S & P 500 Composite Index, Without Dividends*   8.89%
15. S & P Municipal Bond Yield, 15 High-Grade   8.42%
16. Disposable Personal Income, U.S. per Capita   8.28%
17. New One-Family House Price Index   8.00%
18. Inflation   7.17%
19. Gold   7.01%
20. Dow Jones Thirty Industrials, Without Dividends   6.14%
21. Savings Deposits   5.20%
22. U.S. Dollar   3.82%
23. Silver   3.35%
24. Swiss Franc   0.50%

* Note equal rate.

THE FIVE-YEAR RANKINGS:
Average Annual Return, 1981–85

1.	Dow Jones Thirty Industrials, With Dividends	15.06%
2.	Moody's Corporate Bond Yield, Baa	14.51%
3.	FHA Mortgage	14.15%
4.	Moody's Corporate Bond Average	13.66%
5.	Prime Rate	13.25%
6.	Moody's Corporate Bond Yield, Aaa	12.81%
7.	U.S. Treasury Bonds, 10-Year Maturity	12.21%
8.	U.S. Treasury Bonds, 3-Year Maturity	11.85%
9.	Lipper Growth Mutual Fund Index*	11.28%
9.	Certificates of Deposit, 6-Month Maturity*	11.28%
11.	U.S. Dollar	10.35%
12.	S & P Municipal Bond Yield, 15 High-Grade	10.31%
13.	U.S. Treasury Bonds, 1-Year Maturity	10.15%
14.	U.S. Treasury Bills, 3-Month Maturity	10.03%
15.	Dow Jones Thirty Industrials, Without Dividends	9.92%
16.	S & P 500 Composite Index, Without Dividends	9.24%
17.	Disposable Personal Income, U.S. per Capita	6.84%
18.	Inflation	5.46%
19.	Savings Deposits	5.35%
20.	New One-Family House Price Index	3.97%
21.	Crude Petroleum Price Index, Producer Price	2.17%
22.	Swiss Franc	−7.36%
23.	Gold	−12.20%
24.	Silver	−21.52%

* Note equal rate.

Chart Addendum

CONTENTS

Table A.25 / DOW JONES DIVIDEND YIELD, 1961–85
(Thirty Industrials; annual yield)

Year	Dividend* value	Yield*	Compound return on a five-year $1,000 investment	Compound rate of return
1985	62.03	4.01%	1981–85	
1984	60.63	5.00%		5.01%
1983	56.33	4.47%	. . . $1,276.94	
1982	54.14	5.17%		
1981	56.22	6.42%		
1980	54.36	5.64%	1976–80	
1979	50.98	6.08%		5.47%
1978	48.52	6.03%	. . . $1,305.32	
1977	45.84	5.51%		
1976	41.40	4.12%		
1975	37.46	4.39%	1971–75	
1974	37.72	6.12%		4.25%
1973	35.33	4.15%	. . . $1,231.52	
1972	32.27	3.16%		
1971	30.86	3.47%		
1970	31.53	3.76%	1966–70	
1969	33.90	4.24%		3.74%
1968	31.34	3.32%	. . . $1,201.60	
1967	30.19	3.33%		
1966	31.89	4.06%		
1965	28.61	2.95%	1961–65	
1964	31.24	3.57%		3.25%
1963	23.41	3.07%	. . . $1,173.62	
1962	23.30	3.57%		
1961	22.71	3.11%		

		How a $1,000 investment performed over		
5 years	10 years	15 years	20 years	25 years
1981–85 $1,276.94 (5.01%)†				
	1976–85 $1,666.82 (5.24%)			
		1971–85 $2,052.72 (4.91%)		
			1966–85 $2,466.55 (4.62%)	
				1961–85 $2,894.74 (4.34%)

*Source: Barron's National Business and Financial Weekly.
† Compound rate of return for that period.

DOW JONES THIRTY INDUSTRIALS DIVIDEND YIELD, 1961–85

This Table analyzes how well the "bluest" of blue chips create income for investors through dividends. However, it cannot be directly compared to other investments in our Tables—hypothetical or otherwise—because you cannot isolate dividends from the appreciation/depreciation in the underlying stocks. The dividend yield portrayed in this Table was basically acceptable, especially if perceived as an add-on benefit—the primary benefit being the stocks' appreciation. Note that this Table's performance never beat Inflation in any five-year interval. It also lost out to even the Savings Deposit in all time frames, except the past decade. But at least the Dow Jones Dividend Yield beat the S & P 500 Dividend Yield in all cases, proving that mature blue-chip companies do pay better dividends than smaller-sized corporations.

CHART A.25
**Dow Jones Industrials Yield Versus Inflation,
Aaa Corporate Bonds, and Savings**

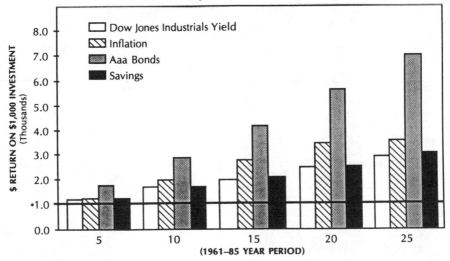

*Initial investment: $1.0 thousand.

Table A.26 / S & P COMMON STOCK YIELD, 1961–85
(500 Stocks; annual yield)

Year	Yield*	Compound return on a five-year $1,000 investment	Compound rate of return
1985	3.82%	1981–85	
1984	4.64%		4.65%
1983	4.29%	. . . $1,255.28	
1982	4.87%		
1981	5.65%		
1980	4.67%	1976–80	
1979	5.55%		4.92%
1978	5.44%	. . . $1,271.44	
1977	5.08%		
1976	3.87%		
1975	4.08%	1971–75	
1974	5.37%		3.75%
1973	3.64%	. . . $1,202.32	
1972	2.71%		
1971	2.99%		
1970	3.36%	1966–70	
1969	3.48%		3.31%
1968	2.99%	. . . $1,176.58	
1967	3.06%		
1966	3.64%		
1965	3.04%	1961–65	
1964	3.03%		3.08%
1963	3.11%	. . . $1,164.00	
1962	3.38%		
1961	2.86%		

How a $1,000 investment performed over				
5 years	10 years	15 years	20 years	25 years
1981–85 $1,255.28 (4.65%)†				
	1976–85 $1,596.02 (4.79%)			
		1971–85 $1,918.92 (4.44%)		
			1966–85 $2,257.77 (4.16%)	
				1961–85 $2,628.04 (3.94%)

*Source: Standard & Poor's Corp., *Security Price Index Record*, 1986.
† Compound rate of return for that period.

S & P 500 COMMON STOCK YIELD, 1961–85

This Table is obviously a close cousin to the Dow Jones Dividend Table. It didn't do as well, but it lost by only about .5 percent. It does reveal that many sizable companies on the stock exchanges offer yields that while not equal to Savings Deposits or Treasury Bills, are paying at least 80 percent to 60 percent of their competitors' rates, respectively. That is sometimes better than several alternatives. But the real question is whether the return of stocks through the combination of their appreciation and dividends will net the investor a fair total return.

CHART A.26
S & P 500 Stock Yield Versus Inflation, Corporate Bond Average, and Savings

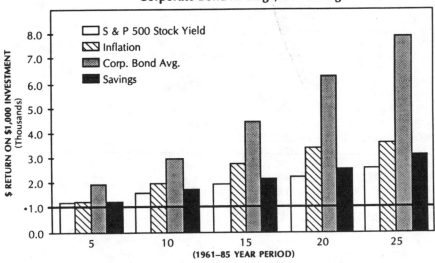

*Initial investment: $1.0 thousand.

Table A.27 / DOW-JONES THIRTY INDUSTRIALS CORRECTED FOR INFLATION, 1961-85
(year-end closing prices; without dividends)

Year	Index* value	Index growth	Compound return on a five-year $1,000 investment	Compound rate of return
1985	425.79	23.26%	1981–85	
1984	345.44	−7.69%		4.23%
1983	374.20	16.34%	. . . $1,230.02	
1982	321.65	12.85%		
1981	285.03	−17.66%		
1980	346.17	1.30%	1976–80	
1979	341.74	−6.53%		−5.89%
1978	365.61	−9.99%	. . . $738.09	
1977	406.20	−22.28%		
1976	522.66	11.43%		
1975	469.03	26.74%	1971–75	
1974	370.07	−34.73%		−6.02%
1973	567.01	−21.48%	. . . $733.07	
1972	722.09	10.93%		
1971	650.97	1.74%		
1970	639.81	−1.04%	1966–70	
1969	646.55	−19.52%		−6.80%
1968	803.40	0.07%	. . . $703.29	
1967	802.83	11.97%		
1966	717.00	−21.19%		
1965	909.76	9.01%	1961–65	
1964	834.57	13.08%		8.11%
1963	738.01	15.60%	. . . $1,477.12	
1962	638.44	−11.72%		
1961	723.18	17.42%		

		How a $1,000 investment performed over		
5 years	10 years	15 years	20 years	25 years
1981–85 $1,230.02 (4.23%)†				
	1976–85 $907.85 (−0.96%)			
		1971–85 $665.53 (−2.68%)		
			1966–85 $468.06 (−3.72%)	
				1961–85 $691.38 (−1.47%)

*Source: Calculated from Inflation and Dow Jones Tables (base year 1960).
† Compound rate of return for that period.

DOW JONES THIRTY INDUSTRIALS CORRECTED FOR INFLATION, WITHOUT DIVIDENDS

This Table was researched to find out how misleading a securities average can be, when "without dividends" and "inflation" are taken to the extreme. In a way, this analysis is unfair because no other investment was analyzed for the effects of inflation. I picked on the Dow Jones because it is so well known, and because everyone else picks on it by omitting its dividends as they follow it. I omitted the dividends too and then factored in inflation to achieve disastrous results. Instead of the Dow Jones turning $1,000 into $7,203 in a quarter century, it turned the same $1,000 into $691; it went down instead of up. I made two assumptions analyzing the same entity, the Dow Jones Thirty Industrials—and ended up with results ten times different from those I would have had with one other assumption. This Table is a testimony to the ills of inflation and the benefits of dividends when you own stock.

Table A.28 / FEDERAL INDIVIDUAL INCOME TAX RATE SCHEDULES
(1960–84)

Taxable Income	Calendar years 1960–63	Calendar year 1964	Calendar years 1965–67	Calendar year 1968	Calendar year 1969	Calendar year 1970
10,000	26.0%	23.5%	22.0%	23.7%	24.2%	22.6%
20,000	38.0%	30.5%	28.0%	30.1%	30.8%	28.7%
40,000	56.0%	50.5%	48.0%	51.6%	52.8%	49.2%
76,000	69.0%	61.0%	58.0%	62.4%	63.8%	59.5%
120,000	78.0%	68.5%	64.0%	68.8%	70.4%	65.6%
180,000	87.0%	75.0%	69.0%	74.2%	75.9%	70.7%

Taxable Income	Calendar years 1971–78	Calendar years 1979–80	Calendar year 1981	Calendar year 1982	Calendar year 1983	Calendar years 1984–
10,000	22.0%	18.0%	17.8%	16.0%	15.0%	14.0%
20,000	32.0%	28.0%	27.7%	25.0%	23.0%	22.0%
40,000	48.0%	43.0%	42.5%	39.0%	35.0%	33.0%
76,000	58.0%	54.0%	53.3%	49.0%	44.0%	42.0%
120,000	64.0%	64.0%	63.2%	50.0%	50.0%	49.0%
180,000	69.0%	68.0%	67.2%	50.0%	50.0%	50.0%

Source: Joseph A. Peman, *Federal Tax Policy* (The Brookings Institute, 1983), pp. 305–7.

FEDERAL INCOME TAX TABLES

Study this table. I doubt that many people remember that in the sixties people were paying taxes in the 87 percent bracket and the Yankees were winning a slew of World Series. Not-so-good good old days. High–tax-bracket individuals have certainly seen changes—especially considering the 1986 tax law change. But don't forget that the dollar was a lot more valuable and less inflated in the past, and that the rules on tax shelters were far less restrictive than today. Back then, there was a way to beat those high tax bills.

Table A.29 / MEASURES OF DURATION AND DEPTH OF RECESSIONS
(1960-82)

| Business Cycles | | Duration in | Constant GNP |
Peak	Trough	months	decline
April 1960	February 1961	10	−1.2
December 1969	November 1970	11	−1.0
November 1973	March 1975	16	−4.9
January 1980	July 1980	6	−2.3
July 1981	November 1982	16	−3.0

Source: F. J. Fabozzi, H. I. Greenfield, *The Handbook of Economic and Financial Measures* (Dow Jones-Irwin, 1984), pp. 170–73.

Severe recessions: 1973–1975, 1981–1982

Mild recessions: 1960–1961, 1969–1970

MEASURES OF DURATION AND DEPTH OF RECESSIONS

This Table is straight out of economics class and is meant to remind us of how bad things were and for how long. Sadly, one cannot draw a conclusion that recessions come in cycles, or that they have a commonality in length from which one could draw a sound investment strategy.

Overall, there seems to be no major trends to recessions in terms of severity or duration. That surprised me. It was also interesting to note that there have been only five recessions in twenty-five years (after adding on the time frame our source did not review). History also tells us that a recession usually lasts about one year, and we haven't had one longer than 1.3 years.

Use this chart to check out when recessions happened. Then check out what investments did either poorly or well during these time periods. You'll no doubt find a few consistent performers—good and bad. Remember to repeat this exercise the next time you feel we are heading down the financial hill. That way, you may even enjoy the next recession.

ACKNOWLEDGMENTS

You don't go from stockbroker to author without some help from your friends and relatives. And I've received my share.

I am most indebted to my wife, Barbara, who put up with my insane hours, my periods of frustration, and my initial ignorance of my now trusted IBM PC. Her understanding of my business through years of careful observation gave an added dimension to this book. I am also indebted to Pamela Painter for her exceptional creativity and editing in making this manuscript the best possible. Robie Macauley, Pam's husband, deserves credit for the insight he gave me into the publishing world through his many years as a senior editor at Houghton Mifflin.

My literary agent, Helen Rees, deserves credit for helping me go from nonauthor to author. Fred Hills, my editor at Simon and Schuster, has given his invaluable editorial judgment. The book is better for his firm guidance. Jenny Cox and Leslie Ellen were stalwart aides throughout the fine-tuning process prior to publication.

A very special thank-you to Ike Williams of Palmer and Dodge for his excellent advice pertaining to legal matters and authorship in general. John Frascotti, Ike's associate, was also of great assistance.

I appreciate now more than ever the mindset given me by my parents, Harvey and Ellen Chase, to question and research the world around me. Thank you also to Pat Forster and Bob Roe, who gave me insights into areas of Wall Street few people know. And to Nancy Forster and Helen Roe, who were supportive during the writing process.

My brother, Larry, was perhaps the most earnest of my supporters. His early enthusiasm for the manuscript often kept me going. A longtime friend, Liz Tilley, made her input in a both timely and helpful manner. Susan Burke performed critical research from start to finish and often urged me onward.

There is no way to adequately thank Cliff Lofgren for his friendship over many years and the entertainment he provided along the way. Through his keen eye for comedy, he has made my life as a stockbroker much more exciting.

The charts and indexes exist in large part because of the efforts and persistence of my assistant, Drago Rajkovic. Drago was an economics major at my alma mater, Tufts University, where he and I began our two-year search through the statistical mazes of financial libraries, computer databanks, and periodical files. Drago, now with Peat, Marwick and Mitchell, continued to help even after he had graduated and moved to New York. He will forever have my heartfelt thanks for helping me find the answers to the toughest questions a broker asks himself.

And last but not least, my dog Egbert loyally remained by my side through many long hours into the night as I pecked away at my PC. We have viewed many a sunrise together over the past few years. His companionship is much appreciated—no doubt he was a writer in his previous life.

Index

C. David Chase is a former Vice President of E. F. Hutton. He began in 1974 as a rookie broker with Merrill Lynch, where he won top national honors for opening the largest number of new accounts in a single year. In 1988 he began the Chase Investment Consulting Group, a fee-only consulting firm whose clients include individuals, corporations, and pension plans.

He released his second book, the *Chase Global Investment Almanac,* in April 1988. The almanac is a complete review of the annual returns, volatility levels, and relative rankings of the world's major investments—domestic and international stocks, bonds, real estate, commodities, currencies, and more. Its review spans over 25 years, from 1962–1988. In addition, his publishing firm, Chase Global Data & Research, publishes a monthly statistical update on over 300 investments detailing monthly, quarterly, and annual returns. The firm also supplies this investment data on diskette.

C. David Chase has appeared widely in television, radio, newspaper, and magazines. In addition to consulting and publishing, he lectures on investments and their performance as well as the strengths and weaknesses of the investment industry itself. He is thirty-eight, married, and lives in the Boston area.

For more information on the Chase Investment Consulting Group and the *Chase Global Investment Almanac* and *Monthly Update,* please write to:

Chase Investment Companies
289 Great Road
Acton, MA 01720
Telephone (508) 263-0404

Name _____

Address _____

City, State, Zip _____